Stop The Verbal Abuse

Stop The
Verbal Abuse

HOW TO END THE VERBAL ABUSE THAT CONTROLS YOU

Elizabeth Nyblade, PhD

Stop the Verbal Abuse
© 2015 Elizabeth Nyblade, PhD

ISBN-13: 9780692461839
ISBN: 0692461833

Spirit ARROW Press: Bellingham, Washington

Dedication

My patients have taught me more than I learned in graduate school or from books, seminars, and supervision. I have learned from them, and we have learned together, how people can hurt one another. I've learned that caring and persistent encouragement can heal the deepest wounds, and I have learned about my own woes and weaknesses. I owe my patients thanks for being part of my journey to understand and heal others. I hope I have a long journey still ahead of me, full of adventure and excitement, supporting others and knowing they support me.

I believe that courage, compassion, insight, and shared spiritual values can heal more than science understands, and more than the healing arts can teach. Thank you to all those I have spoken with over the years: my clients, patients, colleagues, teachers, and mentors. I thank you every day in my heart and try to be worthy of what you have shared. Please join with me in this new written journey you hold in your hands. Please mind your spirits with me. Let us support one another in the great work of healing the world that is ahead of us.

Table of Contents

CHAPTER 1

Introduction

Congratulations on taking this first step to make yourself more powerful! We're embarking on a journey of discovery. You'll discover whether verbal abuse occurs in your life and how to stop others from abusing you. You'll learn some of your own strengths and weaknesses as well as the strengths and weaknesses of your relationships. When you know the extent of the verbal abuse and become aware of your strengths, you'll learn to resist the attacks of others and keep yourself safe. You can create strong and stable bonds with others simply by controlling yourself!

By reading this book, you'll learn how power and control figure into communication and how to use power in a positive way. You'll learn to control and protect yourself and others—while you create safe relationships.

As you read, you'll see that *you are powerful now. You have power that others can't take away.* You may *give* others power over you, but no one can force you to do so. You can *decide* to keep your power or share it. This book will support and encourage you as you make your decisions.

I'm here to guide your journey. I'm a clinical psychologist who has nearly forty years of experience helping couples and families grow and become more positive. I work with couples and with singles to improve the way they interact with others. Psychotherapy also helps people deal more positively with one another. It improves the way adults treat other people, the way parents and children treat one another, and, of course, the way people treat themselves.

Gender language

When you hear the word *batterer*, do you picture a male? Some men do physically batter women, but many women strike their partners as well. Some couples fight physically until both are injured.

Men aren't the only verbal and emotional abusers. Women can also do lasting damage by verbally and emotionally attacking men. Therefore, in this book I give examples of women verbally abusing men or other women. I also give examples of parents verbally abusing their adult children and women verbally attacking their aging parents.

Same-sex relationships aren't free from problems either. Lesbians and gay men also abuse each other.

Despite this, I often call the verbal abuser *he* and the target or victim of the abuser *she*. I use so many lopsided examples because of the following:

♦ Women are more likely to see a therapist to learn new emotional skills, such as the skills this book teaches.

♦ Women are more likely to buy and read self-help books.

♦ We don't have a pronoun in English that encompasses both sexes, and it's awkward saying *he or she* or *him or her* all the time. We don't have good ways of saying *a person of either gender* in every circumstance where it applies.

♦ Parents teach girls to be peacemakers and to dislike conflict and anger, so women may tolerate unkindness and unfair criticism rather than leave the situation.

♦ Parents teach girls many communication skills that they don't teach boys; however, they don't teach girls how to defend themselves during conflict or how to resist the actions of others.

♦ Women are more likely than men to leave a marriage because they don't like their partner's behavior. Women don't leave an old relationship just to enter a new one as often as men do. Women leave to end the conflicts and disagreements even though they don't have another partner waiting in the wings.

♦ Men are less likely to want a relationship to end, but they often won't change what the woman wants them to change to keep the marriage going. If women change their own behavior, however, they can cause men to change.

As you read through this book, please don't assume I feel negatively about men or even about verbal abusers. They learned their negative verbal and emotional behavior just as they learned to speak the same language their parents speak. They didn't invent abuse. No one invented abuse.

People *learn* to abuse others, and people can learn to act differently. If you learn to recognize abuse, understand why it happens, and understand the goals of the abuser, you'll be ready to stop the attacks.

Abusers are aiming to achieve their own goals by abusing you. They have justifiable goals. They want love and affection, attention and respect, just as you do. You probably want the abuser to achieve his goals in a positive way and have a more stable relationship with you. When this happens, you both win.

Vocabulary for targets

I refer to the abuse perpetrator as the *abuser*. It's a simple, descriptive choice that doesn't label the gender of the perpetrator. But what shall I call the object of the abuse?

Mental health professionals used to call people who had experienced trauma *victims*. To call people victims means they have suffered, have been deceived or cheated, or have been sacrificed. Victims should not feel guilty about their injuries because they didn't cause them.

However, victim has connotations like *passive* or *helpless*. Providers eventually preferred to use the term *survivor* of abuse, which implies endurance and strength rather than passive acceptance of negative events.

However, victims of trauma continue to suffer—sometimes forever. Our brains are hardwired to remember fear and threat. We remember being in danger for long periods of time. In fact, our brains continue to work on avoiding or escaping or overcoming dangers, even when the dangers no longer exist. People leaving a war zone often bring the war zone with them.

I call the receiver of abuse the *target* of the abuser.

Target means:

- ◆ an object
- ◆ something you aim or fire at
- ◆ a goal
- ◆ an object of abuse, contempt, and ridicule

An object

The abuser does not see his target as a human being. The abuser doesn't see the target as an individual with a soul. The abuser sees only an object, a thing to move, command, or control. The abuser doesn't consider the feelings, needs, wishes, and rights of the target.

In other words, the abuser is not thinking "Me, Tarzan. You, Jane." The abuser is thinking "Me, Tarzan. You, grapevine," or "You, banana." The abuser thinks of you as an object, a thing. He probably thinks of you as a *desirable* object, but he doesn't believe you have rights or feelings of your own.

Something you aim or fire at

The abuser aims and fires abuse at you to damage you. Abuse is not accidental or incidental. The abuser aims and fires deliberately, intending to harm you. If the abuser succeeds in harming you, he will do it again.

A gun can hurt someone accidentally, even when you don't aim it. However, people do not aim abuse at targets accidentally, nor is the damage to the target incidental. The abuser intends the damage that occurs.

A goal

Imagine the abuser setting up a paper target on a firing range. He wants more than a small hole in the paper target. If he's a hunter, he wants to shoot deer. If he's a soldier, he wants to shoot enemies. The abuser thinks that creating damage to the target during practice will be a means to his ends.

An object of abuse, contempt, and ridicule

Archers aim at a paper target called a *butt*, like the butt of a joke. No one exalts or respects or cares for targets. Targets are cheap. You throw them away after you've used them. Abusers don't see targets as useful, so they treat them badly. Abusers *can* make someone a target, so they cheapen the target in their own eyes.

The abuser isn't a citizen of a pastoral culture; he's a hunter who obeys the law of the jungle. He thinks of the world this way:

♦   Dog eat dog
♦   Every man for himself
♦   Might makes right
♦   Survival of the fittest

In other words, the abuser is not a team player. He thinks he must protect himself and control others because no one will protect him. He believes that victims deserve to be treated badly.

Verbal abuse is a form of communication in which the abuser fights to become the top dog, fittest survivor, mightiest of all. He doesn't think he's playing doubles tennis with his partner at his side. He thinks he's playing singles tennis, and his partner is his opponent. He tries to get everything he can from his partner to make himself the last man standing.

Do you have to be more aggressive than the abuser? Do you have to outcompete and outfight him to get your needs met? I don't believe you do, but you *do* have to protect yourself from abuse and abusers.

If you are submissive to everyone you meet, you're going to attract many abusers because they're all looking for you. You won't have trouble finding a partner if you're willing to date and marry someone looking for a target. But you can't have a good relationship with him if you're willing to accept a bad relationship.

Can you be happy with someone who wants to abuse you? My answer is maybe, but I think it's too soon for you to answer that question about the person you are involved with now.

If you are already involved with someone who abuses you, I recommend you learn to end the abuse first. After that, decide whether or not to stay in the relationship. If you leave this partner, you're still going to need the skills this book teaches to be happy with your next partner.

For now, just tell yourself that "He (or she) is an abuser. He (or she) is using me as a target, and I won't accept that anymore."

Gain insight and skills here

As you read this book, you'll figure out which behaviors work and which don't work to keep you safe. You can change how you talk and behave to prevent abuse. You can defend yourself in more effective ways. Even more important, you can learn what skills it takes to strengthen yourself and your relationships. And you'll be able to learn and practice those skills slowly, step-by-step, at your own pace.

This won't be a journey that requires you to reach the end before you notice improvements in your life. Each skill you practice and use in your daily life will make a small but positive difference in how you see the world—and how the world sees you. *Your* efforts will make the difference. You won't be limited to a magical transformation at the end of the road. You'll see improvement along the way, and it will be permanent improvement. You'll transform because you'll learn new skills. No one can take that learning away.

Adults grow and change over time, and they often do so without thought or conscious choice. But adults can also grow and change deliberately. You'll need courage, persistence, and realistic optimism to change, but the process itself can be joyful. I hope our journey together won't seem like a difficult expedition to a foreign destination, but more of a joyous passage that takes you at last to your home.

If you now feel like a helpless victim of circumstances, you can begin to feel responsible, accountable, and powerful. If you now feel weak, you can begin to feel strong. You can be in control of your own destiny.

The organization of this book

Here's what you will learn as you read through this book:

In this introductory chapter, I give you a look at my philosophy, my vocabulary, and my plans to teach you how to end verbal abuse.

In Chapter 2, I warn you that it is not safe to try to train a verbal abuser who is also a batterer. The abuser may assault you if you disagree or withdraw. I don't want you harmed for following my recommendations. You need to judge whether or not you are in physical danger because of your partner. However, sometimes verbal abusers threaten to hurt you or hurt themselves only because they want to manipulate you. They are trying to frighten you, but they don't intend to do what they have threatened. I'll try to help you predict whether you should worry about the abuser following through on his threats.

In Chapter 3, I define verbal abuse and show you that it is a secret weapon. People tolerate verbal abuse from others for a variety of reasons. Often they don't like conflict and disapproval. They believe that if they give the abuser his way, they are reducing the amount of conflict in their lives. They think of relationships as good or bad, instead of recognizing that relationships can be positive or negative and also close or distant. A verbally abusive relationship is a close but negative relationship.

In Chapter 4, I give an extended example of an incident of verbal abuse. I show how one abuser threatens and puts down his target and how she reacts. I explain what makes his statements harmful and why her first responses encourage him to continue. I also show what she can do to stop the abuse. I show how she needs to think, talk, and act to end his hurtful behavior.

In Chapter 5, I show the difference between verbal abuse and disagreement—even angry disagreement. There are many kinds of abuse and some of them are very subtle, but you should learn to recognize those as well. In particular, pay attention to extreme jealousy, as this is one of the most terrifying and dangerous forms of abuse.

In Chapter 6, I address the issue of accountability. Who's to blame? What is the target's role in the abusive interaction? We'll look at the stages people usually go through when they plan to change themselves. I give you an outline of a general plan for personal change that you can apply to your own behaviors, beginning with changing your thoughts. You need to look at your self-talk and encourage yourself as you work through this issue. In fact, the biggest obstacles to changing yourself are your own beliefs because they energize your current behaviors. I list and explain beliefs that keep you from addressing verbal abuse. For example, if you believe that it is good for the abuser to be able to "vent" his anger, or if you believe the abuser has an anger problem, you'll have trouble recognizing the reality that the abuser is trying to control you with his anger and probably only has an anger problem when you're around.

Of course, you are already trying to end the verbal abuse. I know that, and you know that, but it's not working. In Chapter 7, I describe a range of tactics that don't work to defend you from verbal abuse and show you why and when they don't work.

Now that you've recognized the beliefs and behaviors that aren't working, you're ready for Chapter 8, which outlines the tactics that work to end verbal abuse.

I wish I could say ending verbal abuse only requires you to say new words to the abuser, but that's just not so. In Chapter 9, I describe the need to give some abusers a time-out to make the point that you aren't accepting abuse any more. It's no easier to give a time-out to an adult than to a child, but it's equally effective.

To predict the future accurately, you must look at the present realistically. In Chapter 10, I show you that if you aren't realistic about him, you're at risk for *wishing ahead,* or predicting the future based on what you want instead of based on the evidence you have. You will only change him by changing yourself. You may think you have only two choices. 1. You could leave the relationship now, today. 2. Or you could stay and accept his behavior, whatever it is. Many targets, though, take a third path. 3. They decide that they're going to leave, so they don't bother to change themselves. Then they don't leave because it's too much trouble. Another choice—the one I recommend—is 4. Stay and try to change your behavior before deciding whether or not to leave.

Many targets wish that there were some formula to predict whether they will be successful in retraining an abuser to treat them well. Unfortunately, there's nothing simple about prediction. In Chapter 11, I describe the variables you need to consider when you decide to leave, stay to accept the status quo, or stay to fight for a better relationship.

In Chapter 12, I summarize what you have learned and review what you must do to make your learning permanent. When your new antiabuse behaviors are automatic, you'll be a happier and healthier person.

In Appendix I, provide a series of forms and checklists that you can copy and fill out to help you make these changes. Change isn't automatic. You have to work at it, and these forms can remind you of your plans and help keep your changes in the front of your mind.

In Appendix II, I list some additional resources, including books and websites that address battering and help with escape plans.

Finally, I provide you with a brief professional biography.

How to gain the most from this book

There are many things you can do to work toward personal change. You can:

   ◆   join a support group
   ◆   start a new support group yourself
   ◆   set up regular times to talk with a friend about your progress and give each other support
   ◆   go into personal therapy
   ◆   keep a journal, and write entries that focus on changing your behavior

You're an adult. You can take information, sort it through your value system, and decide what you want to believe, and do. You can choose to agree or disagree with others. This book will help you understand your choices and put them into action.

Don't feel you must share your thoughts or feelings with your family, friends, or supporters until and unless you're ready. If you do choose to share, remember your comments may trigger feelings or memories in others, so make sure it's OK with them before you bring up these issues.

> *Time spent thinking about yourself and*
> *your needs is a time of spiritual renewal.*

This book will help you rehearse the changes you want to make. Do you want to say something new? Write the new phrase down and practice saying it out loud. Do you want to act differently? Think of possible actions to take, then choose the best one. Think about the action in the context where you want to share it. Rehearse it mentally, then try it in public.

Do you want to make a different reply to an insult that your boss often throws at you? Brainstorm some responses with a coworker, practice the best ones out loud, or in the mirror, and every time you pass the boss's door, rehearse one or two examples in your head. Then you'll be ready the next time the boss makes that comment.

Suppose the worst happens. The boss makes a sarcastic comment to you, and you say nothing, or burst into tears when that is just what you had hoped to avoid. What you say to yourself about your behavior *after* that incident could encourage you to continue learning or discourage you from thinking about it at all.

Self-praise encourages you to grow. Harsh self-criticism depresses you, punishes you, and keeps you stuck in the past. People learn best by rewards, not punishments. Yes, you need to pay close attention to your behaviors, especially those behaviors you want to change, but you learn best when you nurture yourself.

Two people flourish together when they nurture themselves and each other. They encourage each other to change and grow.

If you want to use new beliefs and new behaviors to defend yourself from verbal abuse, to make you emotionally safe with others, this book can help you, every step of the way.

Use the examples to ask yourself "Do I think that? Do I believe that? Do I do that?" Read the text to learn about the beliefs and behaviors of others, and see if those examples speak to you and your goals. Find a friend who wouldn't mind rehearsing your new behaviors with you.

Remember that you can only expect to change when you practice. Insight is just the first step, even when you have plenty of incentive to change. You need to rehearse the subroutines of your changed behaviors until they become just as automatic as the old behaviors you used that didn't succeed for you.

When do you feel safe talking to others? You feel safe when you can predict and avoid dangers. And you'll feel safe when you are confident that you can defend yourself. When you get better at self-defense, others will choose different behaviors with you. You're aiming for others to respect you and to meet your emotional needs.

Understanding verbal abuse can lead to new beliefs about yourself and others. Your old behaviors are automatic now, but you can change that by reminding yourself daily about your new beliefs. That's the way to change.

Throughout this book, I'll give you examples of adult partners talking. Try those words on for size. Do you act the same way? Does your partner say things like that? Do you get the same results I describe? If your old behaviors aren't achieving the goals you want, try new behaviors. I'm going to teach you new methods of achieving your goals.

Welcome to this psychological space, this book on verbal abuse. I admire you for your willingness to put your time and energy into learning more about yourself and others.

And I welcome you as a traveling companion. I've learned most of what I know about verbal abuse from people like you who wanted to be stronger and feel safer with others. I hope we can continue to learn together while we talk (in writing) about our lives.

Summary

In this chapter, I welcome you to join me on a journey of discovery. You'll learn to recognize and understand verbal abuse and you'll learn whether verbal abuse occurs in your life.

Both men and women verbally and emotionally abuse others. Women are especially vulnerable to abuse because they value relationships highly and seek approval from others. I'm going to call the abuser "he" and the target "she" in most of the examples, because of that. I prefer to use the term "target" for the one abused, because I think it best describes the way an abuser thinks.

The goal of this book is to give you understanding and skill in ending the verbal abuse that controls you. I'll introduce the information in the order that I think works best to help you change your beliefs and your thoughts about verbal abuse. With those changed thoughts, you'll be ready to learn the scripts and behaviors that work to end abuse.

You'll get the most from this book if you read it from beginning to end and apply the information to yourself as you read. Think about what examples and statements apply to you. Practice the words you want to say so you are ready to stop the verbal abuse.

And remember that ending the verbal abuse in your life is a step to improve your happiness and satisfaction. You deserve happier relationships. And you'll likely get happier relationships when you do your part to show others how to treat you. Keep learning with me throughout this book.

CHAPTER 2

Real Danger and Idle Threats

The verbal abuse you wish to change may not be your only problem. Are you in physical danger from a batterer?

All those who batter physically are also verbal abusers, but not all verbal abusers batter their partners physically.

All batterers begin by emotionally and verbally abusing their partners. The emotional and verbal abuse continues when the batterer is physically enforcing his demands. But verbal and emotional abusers are not necessarily batterers and may not become batterers. It is dangerous to try to train a batterer to stop battering you without the help of outside forces (like the police). However, it's probably safe to try to change someone who *only* verbally and emotionally abuses you. If you deflect the person who is verbally abusing you, will you be in physical danger? If you resist his control, might he physically abuse you? Maybe your boyfriend or husband has never struck you, but you still feel intimidated by him. You may be afraid to contradict him, or push your point because of feelings you may not have analyzed.

Ask yourself if the abuser has ever shown you his anger physically. For example, has he ever struck a wall? Broken dishes in front of you? Balled up his fists? Cleaned his gun when you disagreed with him, or when you decided something alone? Has he physically prevented you from leaving during an argument, or taken your car keys or your phone away?

You need to ask yourself whether you're with a physical batterer or just a partner who limits himself to verbal and emotional abuse. Batterers sometimes kill their targets, so you're in danger if you stay with a batterer. You need to learn more about battering and batterers and you need to make a plan to stay safe. You need to learn how to keep children and others who depend on you safe as well. You also may need to get professional help.

Are you in a battering relationship? Think about these three issues:

1. How your partner has acted toward others
2. How your partner has acted toward you
3. How your partner has threatened you and made you fear him

How your partner has acted toward others

You can probably find out if the abuser has previously been arrested for domestic violence. Sometimes you'll know the previous wife or girlfriend and you can ask her for information. Of course his previous girlfriend or wife may not be objective about him. You should always find out more when he has previously been charged or arrested for domestic violence.

Don't expect a man to tell the truth if he was violent to a previous partner. You would check the references on someone you were hiring for a job, so you should find out about someone that you might date or live with. And you should research someone that you might allow around your children.

How your partner has acted toward you

Make a list of every negative physical incident you've had with the abuser and every threat he has made to you so far. Here's a brief checklist to help you recall what he may have done. Look through it and check off the items that have occurred. A longer form is in Appendix I, Forms, to give you a more detailed look at your history.

___ He made physical contact with you, and you didn't want him to.
___ He hit you.
___ He choked you.
___ He threw you down on the floor or ground.
___ He kept you from leaving by using force.

__ He threw objects at you.
__ He used force to have sex with you.
__ He forced you to end (or not end) a pregnancy.
__ He left you somewhere dangerous.
__ He threatened to kidnap or kill the children.
__ He abused your children.
__ He punched holes in the walls.
__ He smashed or broke your property.
__ He threatened to hurt or kill a family pet.
__ He displayed weapons in a threatening way.
__ He drove unsafely on purpose while you were in the car.
__ He threatened to leave you.
__ He told you to leave.
__ He threatened to commit suicide.
__ He threatened you to make you drop the charges against him.
__ He threatened to leave town with the children.
__ He stopped you from calling for help by taking or disabling your phone.
__ He told you that you had a mental illness
__ He told others that you had a mental illness.
__ He interfered with your work or school.
__ He kept track of where you were all the time.
__ He purposely and repeatedly followed or stalked you.
__ He tried to kill himself.
__ He threatened to hurt your family or friends.
__ He threatened to hurt or kill someone you love.
__ He threatened to kill you.
__ He threatened to kill a member of your family.
__ He said he'd never let you leave him.

Now write down a detailed account of each incident of negative physical and emotional contact you have checked off and each act that frightened you. Ask yourself:

__ Does the verbal abuser have a mental health disorder like depression, Bipolar Disorder (manic-depressive illness) or schizophrenia?
__ Has the verbal abuser refused treatment for a mental health disorder?

__ Was the abuser drunk or high when the incidents occurred?

__ Has his substance abuse gotten worse or more frequent in the past year?

__ Has his physical violence gotten worse or more frequent in the past year?

__ Have his threats gotten worse or more frequent in the past year?

What have you learned by filling out this checklist and writing your detailed account? Is he abusing you more frequently now? Is he abusing you more severely now? Have you previously thought he was physically dangerous to you? Do you think so now?

Batterers get more violent as time goes on. They abuse their targets more often and more seriously. If you were never afraid for your safety with the verbal abuser, hooray! If you remember several violent incidents, you may be in trouble.

You need to think about whether you are in physical danger from your partner if he has touched you in anger, even twice. You may be keeping him from battering you more by giving him everything he wants. In that case, you are dealing with a batterer, not just a verbal abuser. If you are preventing battering by being submissive, you are in danger. Don't try to train your partner to stop calling you names when you are in danger from him.

Go to one of the good Internet sites for victims of battering and begin a safety plan (see Appendix II Bibliography). Your partner needs legal oversight and legal punishment. You cannot handle him (or her) alone. If you follow the advice in this book, you may give your abuser another excuse to batter you. It wouldn't be wise for you to provide him with that temptation.

You may be the only person who knows about the negative physical contact between you and your partner. If you aren't realistic about the past, you cannot realistically predict the future.

How your partner has threatened you and made you fear him

If your partner has never struck you, blocked you, broken your property, or threatened you physically, do you believe that he will do so in the future? Does he come close to you and loom in an intimidating fashion? It may be worth confronting him so you can tell how serious the threat is.

If someone looms over you, consider saying "If you want me to talk to you, back off right now." If he backs off, you're in less danger than you think. If he doesn't, you are a victim of battering. The other wants you to be fearful and intimidated. He doesn't plan to change that because you don't like it. It is a deliberate posture. He wants to threaten you. You are in danger. Begin reading about batterers and battering. Make a safety plan for you, your pets, and your children.

Some women feel they must be submissive, although their partner has never battered them. They believe that he *might* batter them in the future if they aren't submissive. These targets complain about the verbal abuse and wish their partners would treat them better but they won't change their own behavior on the excuse that he *might* batter them. This is much like complaining every day that you aren't getting your mail at your new address when you haven't put in a change of address card at the post office.

If you obey someone else because you fear them physically, then you are in a battering relationship. You are allowing him to control you. You are a true target of physical abuse if you obey him unwillingly because you have a reasonable fear he will harm you physically.

Your instincts should tell you if you are in physical danger from someone. If you decide that you are in physical danger if you resist his control, you should shift your focus from the verbal and emotional abuse to your danger if you remain with this batterer. Read a book about leaving a batterer. Don't follow the advice about verbal abuse in this book if you are in physical danger from the abuser. Instead, look at the bibliography. First increase your physical safety. Then work on resisting his control.

If the abuser might physically batter you, you need to be willing to withdraw (safely) from the relationship. If the abuse doesn't stop, you need to recognize that your physical safety will depend on your caution.

Someone who batters you, threatens your life or health, or uses weapons to threaten you is a criminal. Assaults and threats are criminal actions. They are criminal whether you have married the criminal or not.

Most batterers are not willing to kill their partners to get their way. Most batterers won't kill their partners for leaving them. But some will. You're in a better position than I to judge whether you are in danger. If your partner threatens your life by word or deed, take him seriously! A batterer is five times more likely to kill you when you separate from him. Leave a batterer only after careful planning.

If the abuser has threatened you, or battered you, play it safe and contact others who can explain what the local resources are for battered women. You may find that you can get emergency housing, volunteer legal advocates, restraining orders, and orders of protection, as well as legal relief from a battering relationship.

Economic dangers

Some bosses are verbally abusive, and expect their employees to put up with their behavior. Coworkers may also demand that you put up with abuse. Are you in a strong enough position at your job to confront your boss (or coworker) about his or her behavior?

Some abusers will fire you for objecting to their behavior. They'll say that you're hard to get along with. If that's your situation, try to figure out whether you are the only victim of this individual's behavior. You're in a stronger position to protect yourself and to end the abusive behavior if you can find allies. Do you have the support of others higher up in the organization? Might they support you if you confront an abuser?

You can't stop a boss from verbally abusing you if he fires you. If that's likely, you'll only have a choice of leaving or staying, not the choice of training him. Your decision will depend on many factors besides the verbal abuse.

Of course we have other financial concerns beyond our jobs. Children and teenagers depend on their parents financially. Adults may be financially dependent on relatives. Many adults feel financially dependent on their spouse or partner. Many women and men *are* better off financially if they stay in their marriages.

An abuser is likely to tell you that you will live in poverty if you leave him. He may tell you that you can't make as much money as he does. He may tell you that you will not get a dime from him for the children if you leave him. He may tell you that he will quit his job rather than pay you child support.

Some abusers do try to make good on those threats when their target leaves them. But they are likely to get a rapid reality check when they hire an attorney. The financial outcome will depend on the divorce laws in the state. If you break up with an abuser, it will not be the abuser who decides the financial arrangements, it will be the judge. The abuser may believe that he doesn't have to pay alimony or child support, but his lawyer will tell him the law, and laws rarely support men who don't want to pay for their children, or want to keep all the assets of a relationship. Even if the abuser is an attorney, that doesn't mean that he is telling you the truth about the law if he wants to keep you with him.

I have seen many women patients who were the main breadwinner in a verbally abusive relationship. Sometimes a man who brings no money into the relationship persuades his wife that the she is economically dependent on him.

Perhaps he tells her that she is a spendthrift and he needs to say no for her. Perhaps he tells her she depends on his childcare services.

For many victims of verbal violence and economic threat, the problem is not one of having money but of controlling money. Suppose the household income is $100,000 a year. Suppose the abuser controls 100 percent of the spending and is selfish about where the money goes. In that case, a much lower after-divorce income will likely feel more than adequate if the target can spend money as she chooses after she leaves the verbal abuser.

However, and this may be hard to believe, the more abusive a person is, the more dependent he or she is on his partner. He likely feels that he can't, and shouldn't have to, look after himself. Glamorous and wealthy movie stars have lots of choices of marriage partners. They feel that anyone would be lucky to marry them. Abusers, however, know in their hearts that they won't have that many choices.

Many abusers depend on their targets economically. Verbal abusers may be vicious wives who don't work outside the home. Verbal abusers may be disabled or unemployed husbands. Some verbal abusers are elderly parents or relatives who want financial support from their children. If an abuser is economically dependent on his target, he exploits and controls her with money.

An abuser may be an able-bodied man who refuses to work. He may be qualified to do high-paid work that's not available. But he still refuses to lower himself to take a lesser job. He thinks his wife ought to take any job she can, though. He may drink too much to work, but that is a choice he makes. He may complain about injustices on his jobs so much the target feels obliged to support him.

A target may be unaware of how economically dependent the abuser is because the abuser keeps telling her that no one else would love her. Most abusers are determined that the target not escape them. These abusers are at their most dangerous when the victim tries to regain power over herself.

Unhealed wounds

If your partner has never battered you and you still feel in danger, think about why you feel that way. When you were a child, did you see domestic violence at home? Were you a victim of battering in an earlier relationship? If you think of all partners or all men as dangerous batterers, you probably haven't dealt with your history of trauma. Go into therapy to learn the signs of battering and abuse. You can also learn not to mistake today's honest disagreement or today's typical anger for the dangerous rage that preceded battering earlier in your life.

It is not fair to you or your current partner to treat your partner as the cause of trauma when it comes from your past, not from him. You can't be close to your partner or positive toward him when you are anxious and afraid all the time. If your current partner isn't the cause of those feelings, you're missing a chance for a happier life. You may be having a reaction of fight-or-flight-or-freeze toward people who only *remind* you of your past trauma but aren't *causing* you trauma in the present time.

Behaviors that shade into battering

Some behaviors seem like gray areas between battering and abuse. Here are a few:

Intimidation

Someone intimidates you when he uses his looks, his tone of voice, his loudness, or his gestures to make you afraid. Maybe he doesn't threaten you by saying he's going to hurt you. Maybe he just looms over you as though he were going to grab you. Maybe he has a piercing stare that gives you the shivers. If he scares you, what are you scared he may do? If the abuser is using his size and his presence to cause fear, you should be afraid. That's not far away from hitting you.

It's time to consider again whether he is doing physical behaviors to cause you fear. Is he blocking your exit from the house when you want to leave? Is he taking the phone out of your hand if you try to call someone? Is he holding your arm in a strong grip when you are trying to walk out the door?

If you are afraid of your partner, try to figure out why you feel that way. Are you afraid because he reminds you of someone else that you had good reason to fear? Or are you afraid because he has shown you, at least once, what he can do when he is angry?

If you are afraid because of your traumatic memories, then you owe it to yourself—and to your partner—to deal with your fears. But if you've seen him engage in scary behaviors before, or you know he's done intimidating things to others, you *should* be afraid. It's time to reclassify him as a batterer and make plans to stay safe.

Abuse of children

If the abuser is verbally and emotionally abusing you, he's probably verbally and emotionally abusing your children. If you are staying because you think the children will be better off with the abuser's money, think again. You're an adult and he's verbally abusing you. You know how that feels. But the way your children feel is much worse because they see him abusing you as well.

So how does the abuser treat the children? Is he distant or absent? Does he avoid them? If the children have an active and loving father who sees them often, perhaps their stepfather won't influence them much. But if the children don't ever see their male parent, they will take their stepfather as a model for all men. The children may fantasize about their real father, but they will yearn for their stepfather's affection and support. It hurts to be told they don't count.

Is the abuser as commanding and demanding with the children as he is with you? Is he a micromanager? Does he decide what skirt lengths are proper on the girls and what sports the boys should play? Does he expect perfect grades or world-class athletic performances from the children? Does he constantly put them down?

If this is the case, the children will grow up believing that they aren't smart, aren't talented, aren't worthy, and aren't good enough. If you act lovingly to the children, they'll still see you as putting him first because you're the one who keeps him in their lives.

Does the abuser drink too much, smoke, do drugs, race off-road vehicles without a helmet on, and spend all the household money on his toys? Then the kids will think you agree with that lifestyle, no matter what you say. If you're still with him, then you have approved of him in a much more important way than approving of him verbally.

If the abuser treats you (and all women) like dirt, your sons will grow up treating you like dirt. They will also treat their own wives like dirt. They will realize that you don't protect yourself, or them, and they won't respect you. Your sons will think that kicking women around is a male privilege.

If you try to protect the children behind the back of the abuser, but not to his face, then your children won't respect you, and they won't see you as a fully loving parent.

If you allow the abuser to abuse your children, the abuser will blight their childhood. Even if you later leave the abuser, the effect on your children will be permanent. They will have lower self-esteem, higher risk of depression, and more risk of trauma and other mental health problems.

Sometimes the abuser verbally and emotionally abuses you, but he sexually or physically abuses the children. Schools or churches may discover the abuse even if the children don't report it. The children's friends may find out and tell a sympathetic adult. If you have not protected your children when you knew they were being abused, the state could remove the children from you as well as from him. If you have failed to protect your children from abuse, the state will hold you responsible just as it holds him responsible. Every state has laws against child abuse.

And you *are* responsible. You have a right to accept abuse because you're an adult. But you don't have a right to make children, even your own children, accept abuse.

Property violence

Threats shade into violence. And property violence often predicts personal violence. Abusers who punch a wall, drop a plate on the floor, or pull a phone out of the wall are trying to make you afraid of them. Breaking things is *not* evidence of an anger problem unless the abuser is breaking his own things when you are not present.

People often become angry when machines don't work the way they are supposed to. You get angry when your computer crashes before you have saved something, or when the sink doesn't drain or the toilet overflows. But I bet you don't throw something at the computer or throw the computer itself against the wall. You may tell somebody that you want to toss the computer in the toilet, but I bet you won't do it.

If the table saw stops sawing or the car quits on the way to work, few people would throw the car, or the table saw, away. You may decide to buy a new one, or you may take it to a professional to fix it. But I bet you won't hammer on the car or the table saw. Anger at objects rarely becomes violence toward objects.

If an abuser breaks your property in front of you, he's showing you that he could be attacking you and that you should be afraid of him. If the abuser demonstrates his anger physically by being violent in your presence, you can predict that he will be violent toward you in the future. He's not just angry and losing control. He's showing you that he could be hurting you just as he damaged your property.

You aren't safe with an abuser who has broken property in front of you. Make a safety plan and prepare to carry it out.

Stalking

A stalker is someone who follows you and makes you afraid. It's a subcategory of domestic violence. The abuser doesn't want you to have a private life. He figures out where you're going and shows up there himself. He hacks into your email to spy on you. He watches who you call and where you are using your cell phone. Although you have moved out of the family house and gone to a new neighborhood, the abuser begins to turn up at your new grocery store, always just turning the aisle ahead of you. Maybe he tries to speak to you and maybe he doesn't, but his constant presence is creepy enough to keep you afraid.

Stalking is threatening and intrusive. It may also be illegal. He may stalk you when you try to end a relationship. He may believe that you will come back if he is "loyal" or if he is persistent in intruding on you.

What else is he doing in your life and what else is he thinking? Maybe you have started getting hang-up calls, especially at midnight or 3:00 a.m. Is this a coincidence? Or is he checking up to see whether you're spending the night somewhere else? Maybe there's no gas in the car when you just filled it up. You open the tank and find a note that says "Don't go anywhere without me." That's creepy. You've left him, but he still sends you a red rose every Wednesday, on the anniversary of your first date. He writes you several emails a day, telling you about his day and asking about yours, although you've never responded.

Stalkers are a threat. A stalker is more likely to murder you than abusers who don't stalk. If he's following you, you shouldn't ignore him as though he's going to give up soon. Consult the prosecuting attorney and your state laws. Get a protection order if you can.

Denial of medical care

Is the medical insurance in his name? Is there any medical insurance at all? Has he ever told you that you can't get help for a medical problem? Has he ever told you there isn't enough money to treat a medical problem? Has he ever said "It's just a cold," when you had a high fever? Has he ever made fun of you when you want to go to the doctor or the Emergency Room?

Although an abuser can't *make* you avoid medical treatment, he may try to *guilt* you out of it. He may refuse to pay for treatment you need or treat you as though you were a hypochondriac. Abusers don't like you to care for yourself.

They figure that it might interfere with your caring for them. They don't want you to believe you are worth caring for.

Emotional abuse of children

If you have children with an abuser, or if you have children in the home where you are living with an abuser, he knows the kids are your weakness. He can pick on the kids unmercifully because he knows it gets to you, and maybe you think you can't stop him without leaving him.

Here are some examples:

Him: Wake up, Stan. I need you to tell mommy how mean she is. Go ahead. There she is. Tell her.

Him: Stan, you know what? Your mommy's a bitch. She's just a mean, fucking bitch. You don't love her because she's a mean fucking bitch!

Him: Stan, you've got to tell your mom that she can't leave me. You don't want her to leave your daddy do you? Tell her how much you love me and you can't get along without me. Only moms who hate their kids leave the kids' only father.

It is emotional abuse to criticize a child's parent in front of the child.

It is emotional abuse to demand that the child take sides during an adult argument.

Sometimes people think that it is better to keep a marriage together for the sake of the children. But children aren't grateful when you keep them in a home full of conflict, emotional abuse, and abandonment. The research is clear about the outcome when parents have an unhappy relationship.

♦ Children are more successful and have better mental health, when they have always lived in a two-parent home that has had a happy relationship between the parents. That's the best household for a child.

♦ Children have the next-best result when they have two divorced parents and both parents stay involved with the children. It's best if the parents are positive to one another. It's good even if they just stay civil with each other in front of the kids. It's a good outcome if the marriage is over and each parent goes his/her own way while continuing to parent the kids.

♦ Children have the worst result when they live in the middle of an unhappy marriage. A divorce improves the children's adjustment and their success in life if the parents separate *and* have less conflict. However parents who continue to contact each other often and continue to have conflict make their children miserable. In those cases the worst aspects of the bad marriage continue after the divorce.

A verbally abusive husband or boyfriend is abusing the children as well as the wife or girlfriend. Your children will have the best adjustment if they are not living in the middle of an unhappy adult relationship. Changing or ending the relationship is the best choice to meet the needs of the children.

Pet abuse

It is illegal to abuse animals. It is criminal behavior. An abuser who kicks, strikes, or starves your pets is a criminal. Your best response is to report him to the police and get a restraining order against him. He is probably abusing the pet to show you that he can treat you that way as well. He treats the pet that way to control you and to make you more submissive.

If you allow this behavior around you, your pet is not safe and neither are you. People who will abuse animals lack empathy and have poorly developed consciences. They are likely to treat you and others in their power the same way.

Idle threats

The verbal abuser often threatens the target and some targets are terrified that he may carry out the threats. But not all threats made by an abuser are credible. Sometimes he threatens to make a scene in public. Or he may threaten you with financial revenge by saying "If you leave me, I'll quit my job and you'll never see the kids again."

Divorce

Many men frighten their wives by threatening to divorce them. But abusers rarely leave their partners. Abusers are too dependent on their wives. Women who fear that their husbands will divorce them should study the divorce laws in their state and consult a lawyer in advance. During a marriage, your husband's wishes may be law, but only if you accept them as law. After a separation, the husband's wishes don't rule. The judge will decide and the judge will follow the law.

How about an abuser who says "You better divorce me!" Or "You'd better file for divorce if you're going to behave that way." The abuser *can* divorce you, without your consent, but he *can't* make you divorce him. If you don't want to divorce him, you don't have to.

Divorce doesn't happen by agreement. It takes agreement to get married but it doesn't take agreement to get divorced. One partner can file for divorce and get divorced without the consent of the other. If he wants a divorce, then he'll leave you or serve you with legal papers. He won't ask your permission to do it, and he won't ask you to do it for him. You may have legal advantages if you file for divorce, but you should consult an attorney before you decide to file. Someone who tells you to divorce him isn't serious about wanting to end the relationship.

Calling the authorities

Abusive men may make idle threats like these:

Him: I'll report you to the authorities if you leave me

Some abusers threaten to report you to the authorities for some crime, real or imaginary. They are trying to blackmail and silence their targets.

Him: If you leave me, I'll call the Immigration Service and they'll send you back to Mexico!

Him: I'll tell Child Protective Services that you aren't taking your seizure medicine and they'll take your children away!

When you hear threats like these, it's time for you to contact the Immigration Service yourself, maybe through a third party or an attorney. Find out what your status is. *Don't* take the abuser's word for what will happen if he reports something about you. He may tell you that something bad will happen, but that doesn't make it true. The authorities may come down on him, not on you.

Her: If you call Child Protective Services, they'll throw you out and have the police watch my house. And they'll help me get the money for my seizure medications!

I'll quit my job and you'll starve

Do you believe the abuser will starve himself to deprive you? That's unlikely.

Some men can work under the table and stay on the run for years to deny their ex-wives alimony or child support. While many men threaten to do this, only a tiny fraction actually do. A man with a job is not likely to quit. If he does quit his job, the judge can assign a salary figure to him and base the alimony and child support on that figure because he has voluntarily impoverished himself. In other words, the courts usually protect you against this threat.

In many states, the attorney general collects child support if a spouse gets two months behind on child support payments. That means the state chases the back child support payments so you don't have to. Even going bankrupt does not free someone of child-support debts. If someone owes you child support, you can make a claim on any assets he has, assets such as land, house, or an income tax refund, to pay the debt.

It's not always easy to collect money from someone who doesn't want to pay you. But after a divorce, few people succeed with the financial tricks they threaten. Few people try these illegal tactics, no matter what they threaten.

Plus, don't forget that you will be able to earn money that your ex will not have access to. If you can support yourself (and most women can) then you can support your children. And if you haven't worked before, you may be eligible for job training programs or scholarship programs. Do your research ahead of time and you will turn these threats into nonstarters.

I'll take the kids and you'll never see them again

Many men threaten to run away with the children, but very few ever do. If a man does go away with the children, he will probably lose all his rights to them when he returns, or law enforcement catches him. After that, the court may require him to visit with his children only with a supervisor present. Or the court may end his visitations entirely.

It's true that you often hear about ex-husbands (and ex-wives) kidnapping the children, but only a tiny number of children are snatched. To run away, a man must be able to make money under the table and leave everyone he knows. The police will watch his family until they find the children and return them to you.

The danger of the husband taking the children increases if he is from another country, especially one that doesn't recognize the mother's custody rights. If the abuser still has family there, he can flee across international borders with the children. In these cases, the story often ends badly for the mother.

Realistically, how much time does the man spend with the children now? Does he want to spend full-time forever with the children if he spends little time with them currently? If you leave him, he may want revenge, but the odds are high that he will not go this far. And children grow up. If your children know your phone number and know how to reach your relatives, it will be difficult for him to conceal the children.

If you think a man is mean enough and angry enough to snatch the kids and try to drop out of the documented world, what are you doing with him? He can damage the children much more if you stay with him than if you leave him. And he's probably doing it right now.

I'll get custody and move out of state and you'll never see the kids

Who raises the children now? Most women get custody of their children after a divorce and only 17 percent of men get primary custody. In my state, Washington, the courts keep good records about custody arrangements. The parents themselves have decided what the custody arrangement would be almost 90 percent of the time. When parents decide for themselves, 22 percent of parents choose to give the children equal time with both parents. In contested and default cases, only 5 percent of cases result in equal time for both parents.

Eighty-eight percent of cases have no risk factors like domestic violence, child abuse, and chemical dependency. Four percent of mothers and 10 percent of fathers have a risk factor. Even when a mother has three or more risk factors, only 65 percent of the fathers are likely to have full custody. When fathers have more than three risk factors, about 75 percent of mothers have full custody. Fathers are more likely to lose residential time with their children because of these risk factors.

Are there objective grounds for the abuser to take custody? Are you an alcoholic, a drug addict, severely mentally ill, or an unfit parent in some other way? If you're doing the child-rearing now, you will likely still have the majority of the time with the children after a divorce. Men rarely carry through on threats to get custody, and most don't even try. They talk big, but then they hire an attorney and get a reality check.

If you are a full-time working woman and your husband also works full time, you'd think that he might have better odds of getting custody of the children. However, the truth is that women usually work fewer hours than men and usually spend more time with the children. Women average more time caring for the children, time spent taking them to medical appointments and staying home with them when they are sick. Men often use their time with the children for play. Courts favor women for custody for these reasons. Of course courts may also favor women for custody because of sexist stereotypes.

It's true the court will likely give the husband regular and extended time with the children, perhaps much more than the stereotypical every other weekend. But it's also true that a great many fathers move out of state, or remarry someone with other children. Even when the courts give fathers visitation, a great many fathers don't follow through. And if the abuser moves away, he'll probably have to pay to transport the children to visit him at his new home.

If you leave me, I'll get the kids because you're crazy

Courts usually award custody to the *primary parent*. This means they give the most parenting time to the parent who has previously spent the most time with the child.

Have you attended counseling, for example because you were abused as a child? Have you taken medications such as antidepressants? Even so, the court probably won't worry about giving you custody of the children. The court will not let the abuser diagnose you as crazy either. One out of five women and one in ten men have had depression. A history of counseling no longer means that you look crazy to the court. Unless you have a documented history of suicide attempts or hospitalizations for mental health reasons, the court is not likely to worry about your sanity.

Have you been hospitalized for mental health reasons? Have you made known suicide attempts? If you are the primary parent of the child, you may need to show that you have sought mental health treatment in a responsible fashion and show that your mental health issues have not affected your parenting. But the court will probably require *both* of you to get a psychological evaluation if the abuser brings the issue up.

I'll kill you if you leave me

If the abuser has said this to you, even once, take it seriously. Even if he has never laid a hand on you, he is a batterer, and your life is in danger. And you should protect the children from him just as you protect yourself.

If the abuser has threatened to kill you, contact your local battered women's shelter and an attorney. Plan your escape very carefully. A batterer is most dangerous during a separation. Don't underestimate the likelihood he will try to kill you. Batterers kill their targets every day.

I'll kill myself if you leave me

If an abuser says this, many women feel so guilty that they don't think seriously about leaving. They don't want to be responsible for him killing himself even if they want to leave the relationship.

If someone threatens to kill himself/herself if you leave him, there are three possible outcomes you should consider:

1. He may be a batterer. You should be cautious and stay safe.
2. He may be depressed and suicidal.
3. He may be manipulative and in no danger of killing anyone.

He may be a batterer. You should be cautious and stay safe

A man who threatens to kill himself is a batterer whether he threatens to kill you or not. He could be willing to take you (and the children) with him when he kills himself so nobody else can have you. Contact a battered women's shelter and plan your escape with great forethought about safety.

But saying he will kill himself is usually an idle threat. Few men are willing to kill themselves because their wives leave them. They are more likely to do so, however, if they are alcoholic or involved with drugs, and if they are middle-aged or older.

He may be depressed and suicidal

A man who is depressed is sometimes willing to kill himself. If the man has sleep problems, low energy, a low sex-drive, and other symptoms of depression, ask him to go into counseling, or ask him to go to his family doctor. It's OK to agree to go with him, at least at first.

You should mention to the professional that you think he is depressed, but a competent counselor or psychologist should notice a depression in any case. The counselor should help him to get treatment for the depression. A family doctor may prescribe antidepressant medication that can help him also.

If the abuser goes into treatment, then he may learn to trust his counselor and make improvements in therapy that keep him from killing himself.

If you ask the abuser to go to counseling and he refuses, then you have done all you can for his depression. You can't save him from himself. Even if you were a qualified counselor or psychologist, you couldn't personally treat your marriage partner. In an adult intimate relationship, it's your job to be a partner, not a counselor. It's not your job to save your partner's life if he has an untreated mental health problem.

If your partner died of appendicitis because he refused to get it diagnosed or treated, would you feel that you should have operated on the appendicitis yourself? I doubt you'd think so, even if you were a surgeon. People who need medical treatment don't get it from family members. They get it by going to medical professionals. You can't make him go in for treatment, so you shouldn't feel that you're responsible if he refuses.

It is sometimes possible to put an adult into mental health treatment against his will, but these laws do not help everyone. If your partner threatens suicide, call your local community mental health center to find out what you can do. Sometimes a mental health professional can evaluate your partner to see if he is serious about killing himself. The professional can sometimes hospitalize him even if he doesn't wish to go. However, even if a professional begins to treat the abuser, you should continue with your plans. No one can prevent someone from killing himself forever. The professional's goal will be to treat the depression and prevent suicide.

If the abuser gets help for depression or other mental health problems, he is likely to improve his mood and learn to treat himself better. He probably will stop threatening to kill himself.

He may be manipulative and in no danger of killing anyone

This is the most likely case. Many women feel responsible for the abuser's behavior and feel guilty if he is unhappy. They may be more likely to stay if the abuser threatens suicide rather than homicide. The abuser has probably worked hard to make you feel this way. But just because the abuser says you are responsible for his behavior does not make it true.

No one kills himself or herself because of a single problem. Someone who is addicted to alcohol may have a hard time working or a hard time keeping a job. His wife may be separating from him. His family may want nothing further to do with him because he has burned them out with his behavior. This man may be at high risk for suicide. But the high risk is because of *all* the different problems he has. If he kills himself, it will be because of all of those problems, not just one of them.

Which of the alcoholic's problems should his wife feel responsible for? No one is addicted to alcohol because someone else drives them to it. The abuser may say you caused it, but it isn't true. If the man described above, the alcoholic with all the problems, has a hard time getting or keeping a job, the odds are that the alcohol has something to do with this, not the wife. If a man's parents or brothers and sisters, or children want nothing further to do with him, the wife cannot feel responsible for those relationships. She doesn't control them for good or for ill. She can't make him relate well to others, especially his own family, and she can't stop him from relating well to others. A wife can control whether she leaves or not, but leaving him will not be the only cause if he kills himself.

Many factors make life worth living. Every person has many ways to gain happiness and satisfaction. Here are some of those ways:

- ♦ meaningful work
- ♦ engaging hobbies
- ♦ a loving family
- ♦ a supportive adult partner

- ◆ a satisfying spiritual life
- ◆ enjoyable recreational activities
- ◆ good health
- ◆ the excitement of learning.

Someone who kills himself is declaring that he isn't happy enough to make life worth living. Or he is declaring that he has too much psychological pain to go on.

But you cannot create enough happiness for another person to end that person's psychological pain. You cannot make up for relationships the other hasn't created or kept, or for meaningful work or exciting recreation. If he only has one relationship he thinks is worth living for, that isn't your fault. You can't fill his life with meaning and you can't empty his life of meaning. Everyone is responsible for making his own life joyous and meaningful.

If the abuser has failed to create a good life for himself, and relies on the positive things you bring him, then his failure to treat you well enough so that you will stay is only one more failure. You can't stop him from killing himself, whether you leave him or not. If he values his life so little that he trashes the only thing in life that means enough to him to keep him alive, that is his fault, his responsibility, and his problem.

If you leave your partner and he kills himself, don't feel that you have failed him. He has failed himself. No one, including a counselor, can guarantee that a man who threatens to kill himself will stay alive. But a counselor can tell you, ahead of time or afterward, that it is not your job to give someone else enough meaning to keep him alive.

There are two sample statements you may want to say to a man who threatens to kill himself:

"If you're suicidal, I can't help you. You need medical care and I can't give it to you. If you're willing to go to counseling (or go see your family doctor) I'll go in with you a few times. But you need help if you're suicidal and I can't be your doctor."

"I can't stop you from killing yourself. If you do kill yourself, I'll be sad, but I won't feel responsible. It's not my job to make your life worth living. That's your job and I can't do it for you. If you are keeping yourself alive only because I'm here, then you need to treat me better so that I want to stay."

Extreme jealousy

Watch out for these major red flags. Is this the way someone behaves in your life?

♦ He checks the numbers on your cell phone to see whom you are calling.

♦ He quit a cell phone plan that didn't give him access to information about your phone.

♦ He asks about the contents of letters you get when he doesn't know the return address.

♦ He reads your letters without your permission, sometimes opening them before you get to them.

♦ He hacks into your email account, or demands that you give him the password to prove that you trust him.

♦ He demands that you give him all the details about your previous relationships, including the sexual details.

♦ He times your journey home from work to make sure you aren't seeing anyone on the way.

♦ He insists that he attend your therapy appointments, or he complains about them so much you consider ending the therapy.

♦ He asks for your medical or therapy records to prove that you trust him.

An abuser who demands that you tell him every detail of your life is pathologically jealous. Those behaviors are never justified.

If the abuser says he needs to keep careful watch on you because a previous girlfriend cheated on him, ask him to go to a therapist. He needs to learn to deal with issues like trust and he may need medication to correct a chemical imbalance.

If the abuser has mental health problems caused by others, it is not your job to be his therapist. Putting your life in his control doesn't improve his mental health. He should be seeking therapy with professionals, not demanding that you become submissive to him because of his problems.

Ask the abuser for proof that he has been cheated on before. That may not be the truth. If the abuser accuses you of cheating on him, and it's not true, don't look for a way to convince him of your fidelity because you can't. He isn't rational when he accuses you so you can't convince him rationally. Instead, ask him what you are doing that he finds suspicious. He may complain about trivia, for example you occasionally coming home late or you occasionally mention the doings of men at your workplace. If so, tell him that his behavior is offensive and that you don't see a reason to cater to it.

Her: I'm behaving the same way now as I did when we were dating. I can't make you trust me, and I can't do anything about your suspicions. If you don't believe me, then you'd better leave me. I'll never be able to convince you.

Her: I can't stop you from leaving me, and maybe you should. I'm not going to guarantee to come home on time 100 percent of the time any more than you do. If my behavior is making you crazy, then we shouldn't be together. You need a different kind of a girlfriend (or wife) than I am.

Her: If you decide to stay with me, I don't want to hear any more demands to own me. You're going to have to live with your suspicions of me. I don't want you to ask jealous questions or make jealous comments to me anymore. I'm sick of them. I don't want you around when you're accusing me and suspecting me all the time.

Summary

You can probably end the verbal abuse in your life, but sometimes it is dangerous to try. Sometimes the person you're thinking of as a verbal abuser is a batterer, someone who will attack you physically to control you. Only you can know whether your abuser is now a batterer or whether he (or she) will become a batterer if you try to escape his control.

If the abuser has touched you in anger in the past, even if he hasn't hurt you, think twice about following the advice in this book. You might trigger a violent incident with him. Rather than trying to escape his control by yourself, get outside help. Read books and talk to professionals about how to escape. Put your safety, and the safety of your children and pets, ahead of your wish to train him or her to behave. I don't want the abuser to injure you when you follow my advice.

Many abusers make threats and sometimes those threats show you the danger, for example when the abuser threatens to kill you. Treat those threats seriously and make yourself safe.

But many threats have no teeth. A partner who tells you that you should divorce him is always bluffing. If he wants to leave you he will, but he can't make you leave him. The abuser will rarely leave you. You can learn whether the abuser is likely to carry out a particular threat, and you should not be afraid to call someone's bluff to end the abuse.

CHAPTER 3

Survey of Verbal Abuse

Targets of physical abuse have pain, scars, and medical bills. They will have symptoms of trauma. But targets of verbal abuse feel equally violated and the verbal abuse may be harder to cope with emotionally. Targets of physical violence, like battered women, or abused children, often report the verbal abuse from the batterer has caused them more suffering than the physical trauma. The verbal abuse is harder to combat.

Victims of verbal abuse also feel under constant threat. Some people report that their bosses, their parents, their wives, their husbands, their friends, or their adult children verbally abuse them, and they feel controlled much of the time.

My mother taught me to say words to other children who teased me or called me names. You may remember them too:

Sticks and stones may break my bones,
But words can never harm me.

As an adult, and a psychologist, I know those words are lies. Words have more power to hurt than sticks or stones, because the brain stores memories. The brain stores words easily. If someone hurts you with words, the pain will last far longer than a bruise or a cut. Targets remember the pain long after they forget the words.

How does verbal abuse affect people?

Verbal abuse is bad for health

People who are targets of verbal abuse develop physical difficulties like headaches, stomachaches, lowered immunity, fatigue, and premature aging. Stress causes harm.

Verbal abuse is bad for personal growth

Children who are targets of verbal abuse grow up insecure, angry, and unstable. They often have difficulty in relationships, difficulty parenting their children, and difficulty finding happiness.

Verbal abuse is bad for self-esteem

You depend on your good feelings about yourself to anchor you in life, to help you judge what is real, what is true, and what is important. If you have low self-esteem, you are vulnerable to predators who want to exploit you.

Verbal abuse harms families and communities

It weakens the relationships that hold people together, and turns the most important personal bonds into chains.

It would be easier for targets of verbal abuse if they could believe the perpetrators of verbal violence were monsters. But verbal abusers look like other people. They can be loving at times. They can be good providers, responsible parents, and hard workers.

But much of the time, abusers act negatively. They try to control the target with their abuse. The abuse may be blatant. It may include name-calling, cursing, tirades and rage episodes. Or the abuse may take the form of subtle put-downs, and efforts to control the target's choices. Subtle abuse is harder for targets to recognize and call by name.

What is verbal abuse?

Verbal abuse is any verbal behavior that is negative or punishing in intent or effect on its intended target. The abuser uses words to gain and preserve control of the target.

Simply put, the goal of verbal abuse is control. Verbal abuse uses the method of punishment, rather than reward, to reach that goal.

Rick: Honey, I'd like to go to the movies tonight. Want to come?

Rick's goal is to have his way. He tells his wife what he wants, and invites her to join him. Unless he has a gun pointed at her head, which undermines her ability to make a free decision, these words are positive. He isn't using punishment to get what he wants.

Joe: You never go anywhere with me. You don't love me anymore. I'll probably have to go to the movies alone tonight, since you don't want to be seen with me.

Joe likely has the same goal as Rick. Joe likely wants his wife to go to the movies, but he puts her down and tells her what (he thinks) she feels. His invitation is indirect. This "invitation" feels more like a manipulation to his wife, who doesn't get an opportunity to accept the invitation before he has complained about her past behavior.

Note that verbal abuse is painful and soul-deadening because of the *methods* used, not necessarily because of the abuser's goal. There's nothing wrong with a husband wanting his wife to go to the movies. Joe's wife probably doesn't feel bad about the invitation, but his negative methods feel bad. When someone puts you down, sulks, pouts, curses, has a temper tantrum, or tries to force you to do things, then you're likely to have bad feelings whether you want to go to the movies or not.

In other words, the abuser may have a legitimate goal. The abuser may want love, companionship, or respect. The verbal abuse doesn't occur because Joe is a bad person or has bad goals. The verbal abuse occurs because Joe is trying to force or manipulate his wife to get his way. He is trying to punish his wife, rather than reward her to get his way. And because Joe's wife knows that Joe wants something reasonable, she may have a harder time recognizing and rejecting his negative behavior.

Abuse is a secret weapon

Abuse works best when it wounds the target, but the target doesn't recognize the weapon. Abuse is most effective when you don't recognize that a struggle for control is occurring. It may be hard for you to separate the legitimate goal of the abuser from his punitive style. Recognizing the abusive behaviors and giving yourself permission to defend against them is the most important, and difficult, decision you can make.

Does the abuser have to have negative aims to label the verbal behaviors abusive? No. Take this example:

Patrice: You'd better give the baby back to me. You've never once gotten her to stop crying. She doesn't love you like she loves me. You're never there for her, any more than you're there for me.

Bud: That hurts! Why do you always say things like that?

Patrice: Well, you know what I mean. Don't be oversensitive. You know I don't mean to hurt your feelings, but you do have a problem with our baby. If the truth hurts, it's not my fault.

You can see that Patrice is an abuser by her negative style. She implies or states these insults:

- The baby is always better off with me than you.
- The baby can tell that you're not loving, and so can I.
- You're no good at parenting now, and you never will be.
- If you can't soothe the baby today, you'll never learn.
- Your feelings aren't acceptable.
- It's your fault if I criticize you.
- My intentions are obviously good.
- Your feelings don't matter.
- You should read my mind.
- You have emotional problems that aren't my fault.

Were all these insults necessary to get what Patrice said she wanted, namely to have Bud give the baby back to her? She could just have said "Here, let me do it." Most of Patrice's comments were insulting and unnecessary. They were punishments that lowered Bud's self-esteem. Bud can't imagine that Patrice would deliberately injure him in this way, so he believes the insults are accidental, that she didn't intend to hurt him.

And Patrice supports Bud's denial, by telling him that she wouldn't willingly insult him. She tells him that she has good intentions, so he shouldn't count the effects of her actions. She tells him that he is oversensitive. She says she has told him the truth so she is not responsible for his feelings.

Abuse works best as a secret weapon. If I'm an abuser, I may be holding the knife that matches your wound, but I try to confuse you so you don't notice. Because I deny that I created the wound, you'll have a harder time defending yourself against me.

How can you tell what someone's intentions are? Frankly, you can't. Intentions are under-the-skin behavior. Intentions are thoughts that occur in the brain where other people can't access them. I'm lucky to know my own intentions. I can't know the intentions of others. Maybe I tell you that my intentions are positive, but I may be telling you a lie. I may not know what my intentions are. It is a waste of time to try to detect my true intentions.

If I call my child "turkey," and someone else comments on how negative I am, I may say "That's my pet name for him. It doesn't mean anything negative." But if my child thinks the name is negative, the name is abusive. Effects count, not intentions.

It's simple to find out if someone intends a negative effect on you, or at least doesn't care how you feel. You can ask someone not to say something, for example, to stop calling you by a pet name you don't like. If the other doesn't intend to be abusive, he or she will do as you ask.

People who care how you feel will use words in a way you like. If someone insists that he shouldn't have to change his wording and that you're oversensitive, that person doesn't care how you feel. If someone insists that you should believe him when he tells you that his intentions are innocent, then your feelings are not important to him.

In short, if someone insists on talking offensively after you tell him what you want, he intends to hurt your feelings. No matter what people say their intentions are, if they continue talk offensively after you have asked them not to, they intend for you to feel badly.

Can you benefit from your actions even without intending the results? Of course you can, and so can the abuser.

For example, suppose I pay for a purchase and the clerk accidentally gives me a ten dollar bill rather than a one dollar bill as part of my change. I may not have intended to steal as I walked into the store but I will have profited by that nine dollar mistake if I don't return the ten dollar bill. The store will take nine dollars out of the clerk's pay at the end of the day, so I have stolen from the clerk, not the store. No matter what my original intentions were, I have stolen nine dollars from the clerk. I profited from her actions whether I planned to or not.

People may have good intentions, but they usually try to get what they want. Most people try to get what they want in positive ways, but abusers, who may have the same goals, use negative means to get there.

Rewards and punishments work to change behavior even if the participants aren't aware of them. Therefore you shouldn't think of abusers as evil monsters. Their goal is not to hurt others. Abusers will act offended and righteously angry if you suggest that they aim to hurt you. Hurting others is only a method for abusers and not their goal. They are sometimes unaware that they are acting abusively to get their needs met. But even when they are aware that they are causing damage, they don't stop—your wishes and feelings don't matter to them.

An abuser may not know (consciously) that he wants to cause hurt. He only knows that he wants what he wants, for example, to take his partner to the movies. Abusers cause emotional pain in order to achieve their goals. They continue to do it because it works. But they are sometimes not aware of the fact that they are choosing punishment as their method.

This is a difficult point, and worth pursuing. Am I responsible for stealing nine dollars from the store clerk? I am if I noticed the overpayment in time to correct the mistake. Even if I didn't plan to steal from the clerk and even if I don't believe I'm a thief, I did something that was wrong. I profited from the clerk's mistake, rather than helping her correct it.

Are abusers responsible for their behavior? Yes, they are. Many targets believe the abuser only needs to find out she hurts to stop saying the damaging words. Those targets show the abuser he is causing harm. But this does not cause the abuser to stop. Telling the abuser that you hurt only tells him that he is successful. That won't make him stop. Whether he is aware of your hurt or not, he will still attack you with words because they work.

Rewards and punishments maintain behavior

I may intend to show you love, but that is likely to be a less important goal for me than having *you* show *me* love.

Remember that people have many goals. Maybe I think my goal is a carefree retirement but I spend everything I earn today. If I don't put money away for the future, you can safely assume that my retirement goal is not important to me now.

I may tell you that I want you to be happy, but if I verbally abuse you, you can assume that your happiness is not my priority. It's a less important goal to me than getting control of you, despite the hurt I may cause. Behaviors matter. You can't measure intentions and they are much less important.

If you're a victim of verbal abuse, it's important for you to know that you're not alone. Most verbal abuse happens in private, just as most physical abuse happens in private. But in private, people shout, needle, threaten, manipulate, and treat one another badly when they can get away with it. You may think you're the only one treated this way by someone you care about, but that's not so. Others may not see your abuse, and you probably don't see it occurring to others. Unfortunately, verbal abuse is all too common.

Why do targets tolerate verbal abuse?

Here's a sample of the many reasons people tolerate verbal abuse:

People don't recognize the abuse or see themselves as targets of abuse

Abuse is most effective as a secret weapon. The abuser uses all of his art and power to keep it mysterious, making it difficult to name and difficult to resist. Targets feel the pain but don't recognize the sources of their injury.

Labels like *abuser* and *abuse*, *victim* and *control*, are powerful and negative words

Most people prefer not to apply these words to themselves or their loved ones.

Targets may think that abuse is unavoidable, a natural part of life

Targets learned their behaviors and their habits of communication with others. They have seen abusive behaviors during their childhoods, on their jobs, in the media, and on the subway. Because abuse is common, people believe that abuse is natural, a necessary part of life and a necessary part of communicating with others. They don't see anything to change.

Targets may believe that they have earned the abuse

Targets believe that they must earn the right to better treatment by giving the abuser what he or she wants.

Abusers usually say the target caused the verbal abuse

Verbal abuse works particularly well for abusers when they can control the thoughts and feelings of the target. The target may believe what the abuser wants her to believe, namely, that she, herself, is at fault. The abuser tries to hurt the target and also control the target's perceptions of his behaviors.

Targets don't know what to do about it

Targets may call the behavior abuse. They may know there are alternate ways for the abuser to communicate. They may believe that they deserve better from others. Yet still, many targets don't know how to cause others to change their behavior. Targets report, "I've tried everything—confronting, ignoring, being abusive myself—nothing works." It's true that without understanding how abuse works, targets are not likely to be effective.

Targets often believe they must leave the relationship to end the abuse

People often think about resolutions or New Year's resolutions when they think about personal change. They imagine that personal change is about deciding to exercise more, lose weight, read all the classics and keep the kids down to two hours of TV a day. They are thinking of goals that they *should* be working for, or goals that they want to reach. They often give little thought to *how* they can succeed in personal change. And few people follow through on those resolutions.

Targets depend on the approval of the abuser

And here's why:

The power of approval

When you were an infant, your parents had the power of life and death over you. You were helpless and vulnerable. You could not control your own body, or your mind, in an effective way. You couldn't feed yourself, or change your clothing, or find someone to cuddle you. You were utterly dependent on your parents.

When you were an infant, you had no sense of time. You didn't know how long it would take for a parent to wake up, heat a bottle, or get off the phone. You didn't know why parents didn't respond instantly to you. Your only power came through affecting the behavior of others.

As an infant, you were powerless unless someone else cared for you. You did not even own your body. You could not separate yourself from your caretaker. You had no territories of your own, no boundaries between you and the world, no personal power or protection from the world except what your caretakers gave you.

As you grew up, you became more skilled at managing both your body and your mind. You learned to walk and to open the refrigerator door. You learned to change your clothes and run to a parent for a hug. You were more powerful now.

You also began to test your ability to say no. If your parents taught you that sometimes you had good reasons to say no and that saying no was sometimes acceptable, you emerged from childhood feeling as though you owned yourself. You learned that you had rights and you wanted others to recognize them.

But you didn't become your own person because of your increased physical skills. Your parents' permission allowed you to grow into owning yourself. Although you *could* open a refrigerator door, and get food out, *you had to have permission.* You didn't own the contents of the refrigerator. You didn't buy the food, or put it away. You couldn't decide to use the refrigerator or the food in it. You had the practical skills to get food by opening a cupboard or a can or a refrigerator, but you knew that you needed approval to do so.

Early in life, you learned that you wouldn't have your parents' approval unless you did what your parents wanted. Because of your need for approval, you still felt powerless and vulnerable. If you got into the cupboards or the refrigerator without permission, your parents would punish you. They might take the food away or yell at you. They might give you a mild punishment, or a severe one. But *you knew you were not in control of your parents.*

In some homes, parents are abusive. Some parents curse and insult their children. They beat their children with hairbrushes or belts. They burn their children with cigarettes. They send children to bed without dinner, lock them out of the house, or lock them in the closet. Parents may believe that they can do whatever they choose or that they don't need permission to punish the child or to be abusive. The state does not catch, or stop, most child abuse.

When you were older, you still felt powerless and vulnerable unless you had your parents' permission to act. Your parents controlled you with their approval or disapproval. You still didn't own yourself.

You associated the need for approval with powerlessness. When you couldn't open the refrigerator door, your parents controlled your access to food. They were responsible for feeding you, and you couldn't get what you wanted by yourself. You had to get them to do it. You thought you had to control others so they would feed you.

When you *could* open the refrigerator door, you still felt vulnerable. Just being able to do something didn't mean that you controlled your own behavior. You had learned that you must have permission and approval to act.

Many adults don't recognize that their need for approval is no longer a life-and-death matter. Adults generally don't need approval to act.

When we were children, our parents made all the decisions for us. We were dependent on their good will. If we had empowering parents, parents who gave us *enough*, we learned to feel that it was our right to have what we wanted. We learned to believe that power and control were reasonable and legitimate goals.

Disempowering parents kept us from getting to our goals. They denied us the affection, sense of belonging, sense of achievement, and sense of safety that we wanted. If we had disempowering parents, we believed that personal power was unachievable, or that others needed to give us what we wanted and we couldn't achieve it alone.

All of us had the early experience of having no real power because we had nothing to offer our parents but love. We didn't have money, we couldn't work, we couldn't offer adult comforts or conversation, and couldn't clean house. We couldn't control adults with anything other than our love. If our parents wanted to please us, we got what we wanted. If they didn't want to please us, we didn't get our way. Life was that simple.

Many adults never look beyond those early experiences. They continue to act as though the only control they have over others is through pleasing them. Those adults don't recognize their own power. They have trouble telling the difference between the ability to act and the ability to control the actions of others.

It would take another book, or a long course of personal therapy, for you to look at your history of getting and needing approval. We'll come back to the topic of approval often in this book.

Gaining power through words

Individuals always try to influence one another. Their most effective methods to influence others are words. People use words to control, to dominate, to exert power. *All* relationships involve the issue of control. When I ask you for what I want, I am trying to influence you. You may regard my words positively or negatively depending on *how* I ask, and on how you read me. If I ask nicely, you will likely see my request as an invitation, and recognize that you have a choice. You may choose to say yes or no, but it is easier to see your choices because I have acknowledged your right to choose.

On the other hand, I may say my request loudly, and demand that you do what I want. In that case, it will be harder for you to see that *you have just as much choice when I make a demand as when I issue an invitation.*

Here's what others have said about the verbal abuse in their lives:

Andrew: I feel controlled by my mother. She lives in town here, and both my sisters live so far away that they can't help me with her. My mother calls me all the time to ask when I'm coming over, and to tell me to do stuff for her. She demands even more from my wife. When I say no, she calls me names and turns on the guilt.

Janet: I can't find a babysitter who will stay with my six-year-old. He's pretty wild. He screams from the moment we leave until the baby-sitter asks us to come home. Then he gives us that angelic look. Sitters don't come back twice. They all want to hit him, and I don't allow that. I feel as though I plan our lives around his moods.

John: Nothing I do pleases my wife. I know it's tough to stay home with three kids under five. I wish she'd get help, like a babysitter part time, but she won't do it. Instead, she lays into me the minute I walk through the door. "If you were half a man, you'd tell your boss to go to hell and come home on time." Or "You old goat, all you ever think about is sex," when I haven't even hinted for weeks. I feel like

I'm walking on eggshells all the time I'm in the house. I work overtime just to stay away.

Rena: They downsized at the office, and laid off my assistant, and now I'm doing the jobs of two people. My boss couldn't find his way out of the men's room without me holding his hand. He's constantly criticizing me in front of the customers and the rest of the staff. He makes himself look good by making me look bad. He's controlling me constantly, always looking over my shoulder and disapproving.

Jerry: I think my minister is out of line when he assigns people to volunteer at the church. Our last minister wanted volunteers too, but he asked instead of demanding. This one just says that we all need to do our share of the Lord's work and he gives us work assignments. If you say you haven't time—or money, he tells you how much money to donate, too—he offers to pray for you, and apologizes to God for how weak and sinful you are. I believe in the Bible, but I can't find that anywhere in the Bible. It's starting to feel more like a cult than a religion.

Toni: I wish I could say no to my friend Alice, but she is so lonely. She gets upset when I do something with someone else. I keep thinking that I could include her with my newer friends, but she never likes them. She calls me two or three times a day to see what I'm doing. Well, when I was going through a bad period, I did the same to her, but I came out of it, and she never does. It feels like Alice makes all my decisions. I feel just awful saying that!

Suppose someone offered to pay me a million dollars to do what they wanted. You probably wouldn't think I had much of a problem. If someone offers me something positive to get an agreement, you wouldn't waste much sympathy on me. You'd think someone wanted to buy me, but most people would envy me the predicament.

When someone offers you positive choices, you can weigh the decision, and you'll always feel like a winner. When someone offers you negative choices, for example, "Do what I want or I'll call you names," you feel as though you've lost something, no matter what you choose.

This book describes three intertwined concepts: verbal abuse, approval and control. Verbal abuse and disapproval are methods people use to control others, to get their way with others. By reading this book, you'll learn to hold others accountable for their behavior. You'll also learn to be accountable for your own behavior, including such under-the-skin behavior as thoughts, feelings, and beliefs.

The two dimensions of a relationship:

I'm going to talk about some important traits, or *dimensions*, of a relationship. Let me first describe what I mean by dimensions.

Height and weight are examples of dimensions that we understand. You'd know something about a friend's appearance if you knew both her height and her weight. I've diagrammed these two dimensions along two lines.

Measuring height

Very short--Very tall

Measuring weight

Very light---------------------------------------Very heavy

If I put an *x* on each of the lines to show the measurements of one person, you'd know something about how tall and how heavy that person was.

Below, I've put the two lines into a table. Height is now vertical and weight is now on the horizontal line.

A Height and Weight Table

Tall	tall, light people	tall, heavy people
Short	short, light people	short, heavy people
	Light	Heavy

Now height and weight are on the same table and I have divided all people into two categories of height (tall and short) and two categories of weight (light and heavy.) That gives us a total of four categories. Some individuals will be low on height and high on weight (short, heavy people) while others will be high on height and low on weight (Tall, light people.) This graph categorizes people in two ways at the same time.

How do you categorize relationships? Do you think relationships have one dimension, maybe goodness and badness? Do you believe that you can measure the goodness or badness of a relationship by putting an x on a line somewhere between good and bad? Here's the diagram for this theory about relationships:

Measuring relationships
Bad---Good

Categorizing a relationship along a single line is limiting. This line suggests that a relationship that has a lot of badness doesn't have much goodness. Looking at only one dimension doesn't tell us what is good or bad about the relationship, or whether it is possible that a relationship could be high in both goodness and badness. So let's use two lines to describe a relationship, one line for intimacy and one line for positivity.

Measuring intimacy in a relationship
Very distant ---------------------------------- Very close

The intimacy measurement in a relationship is easy to understand, but hard to describe without using terms that usually describe space. I can measure the degree of intimacy I have with someone based on the number of ways our activities interact. For example, if I am married I could own and live in the same house as my husband. We could have children together. We could go to a bridge club together and so on. If he worked out of town, and we only saw each other on weekends, that would cut down on the activities and time we could share. On the other hand, if we worked in the same business that increases the possibility of time together.

At the other extreme of intimacy, I have a relationship with a woman named Jerry at the checkout counter of the grocery store where I shop. I know her name because she wears a nametag and she probably knows mine because it's written on my checks. Our areas of overlap are slight. I may see her once or twice a week when I shop. If she is on duty I may seek out her checkstand. We exchange a few pleasant words about the weather and how hard we're working. That is the extent of the relationship. I wouldn't go to her checkstand if the line were significantly longer than other lines, and I wouldn't invite her over for dinner. I don't know her that well. I have a distant, or superficial, relationship with her.

I can also look at intimacy by considering what activities we share. Do we do private activities together or only public ones? Sex is an intimate act. You wouldn't do it with just anyone. I wouldn't give large amounts of money to a stranger. I wouldn't borrow a toothbrush at work. And I won't share a hypodermic needle with anyone.

In the emotional realm, I can measure the intimacy by considering the quantity and quality of emotions I talk about with someone. In a close relationship, I will discuss my personal problems, events in my history I'm ashamed of, and my secret fantasies. In a distant relationship, if someone asks me "How are you?" I'm likely to say "Fine," no matter what is wrong with me. I don't want to share too much.

Notice I don't just share positive emotions, such as sexual fantasies or happiness with someone close. I also share negative emotions like anger, hurt feelings or distress.

Measuring positive and negative in relationships:
Very negative ------------------------------- Very positive

We can also measure the positive or negative tone of a relationship. Think of putting an X somewhere on the line above to describe how negative or positive one of your relationships is.

If I had three brothers (which I don't) then perhaps I might feel most positive about one brother. This isn't the same thing as the closeness I might feel to each of my brothers. I may have a brother who lives in the same town. We may belong to the same church and share many family activities. Another brother may live far away so I rarely see that brother or his family. But I may be angry with the brother who lives closer and I may have nothing but pleasant interactions with the brother who lives further away. Intimacy is not the same as positivity. They are two different aspects of a relationship.

Let's look at the intimacy and positivity of relationships. You can put a relationship into one of these four categories:

Positivity	Distant positive relationships	Close positive relationships
Negativity	Distant negative relationships	Close negative relationships
	Distant	Close

51

Let me give you examples of people who fall into each of these categories in my life.

Distant and positive relationships:
   My brother-in-law in New Hampshire
   My brother in San Diego
   Jerry, at the check-stand

Close and positive relationships:
   My husband
   My sister
   My best friend

Distant and negative relationships:
   Al Qaida terrorists
   My ex son-in-law
   The bureaucrat who won't give me the refund

Close and negative relationships:
   My former boss
   Family members I'm quarreling with
   My former best friend

How do you change a relationship?
How do you make a relationship closer?

+ See the person more often
+ See the person in more varied contexts: at work, socially, with family, or with other groups that share your interests
+ Invite the person to share other activities in your life or join the other in his or her activities.
+ Share information about more intimate matters, such as sex, problems, events you are embarrassed about or ashamed of.

How do you make a relationship more distant?

♦ See the person less often
♦ Limit the number of activities you participate in together
♦ Leave contact to chance rather planning contact
♦ Speak only on superficial subjects such as the weather or sports, and ignore more intimate subjects.

How do you make a relationship more negative?

♦ Insist on getting your own way when you disagree with the other
♦ Seek out opportunities to stop the other from reaching his or her goals
♦ Criticize the other, call him names, put the person down to his face, and speak badly of him to others
♦ Look for ways to see her in a negative light and see the worst in her
♦ Behave rudely and insensitively
♦ Contradict and conflict with the other

How do you make a relationship more positive?

♦ Help the other achieve her goals
♦ Praise the other, attend to him, admire him, and speak well of him to others
♦ Find ways to see her in a positive light, to see the best in her
♦ Behave graciously, respectfully, and sensitively
♦ Avoid or solve conflicts

How do people deal with negative events in a relationship?

When conflicts, misunderstandings, and fights occur, people usually deal with such problems in different ways, ways that depend on the kind of relationship.

Close and positive

The participants treat conflict as a temporary problem. They get closer by talking about and solving problems. They intend to stay positive in the future.

Close and negative

The participants treat conflict as evidence that the other is trying to hurt them or as evidence of a character flaw in the other. They stay close, but treat the problem as permanent. They protect themselves and attack the other. They cope with the negative event by engaging in attack or defense. The negative feelings continue or increase.

Distant and positive

The participants keep feelings positive by ignoring or avoiding conflicts. This creates barriers to intimacy. Each participant may be unaware of the ways that he offends the other. Or he may be unwilling or unable to solve conflicts. It's not important to solve conflicts in a superficial relationship. Participants tolerate more conflict than they would in a more intimate relationship. Participants are often more giving and considerate because of the lack of closeness.

Distant and negative

The participants stay negative by ignoring or avoiding problem-solving, so that the overall tone of the relationship stays negative. Individuals may engage in protective and punishing behaviors aimed at distancing the other rather than problem-solving. These behaviors make it hard to increase the positive tone. Negative behaviors and feelings continue. The participants hit and run, then grin and bear it. Neither participant makes the other a big part of his life.

In other words, when you try to resolve a relationship problem, make sure that your attempt works. Only successful attempts to solve conflicts are positive for the relationship. When problems aren't resolved, they lead to close and negative relationships. Those are the most intense and most distressing kinds.

Here's the bottom line. When conflict resolution is not successful, *stop trying to remain close*. Instead, stay distant to reduce negative encounters. Let a close and negative relationship become distant and negative temporarily. With luck it will then become distant and positive because there are fewer negative encounters.

The abuser in an intimate relationship insists on maintaining closeness. But he is willing to sacrifice any positive tone. When negative events occur, he fights more, criticizes more, and refuses more. However he expects to stay close to his target. The relationship becomes increasingly unpleasant for the target and she begins to think about ending the relationship.

The abuser may have seen his parents stay together for years while they raged and fought each other. He or she may believe that relationships always have a negative tone. The abuser may feel justified and righteous about his behavior because he has seen others behave this way. He feels that he must attack and complain to protect himself.

The partner who behaves negatively seeks closeness no matter what the cost to positive feelings. He seeks time, attention, and intimate contact, believing that he can punish the other into loving him more. Most batterers fall into this category as well.

Batterers begin by verbally abusing their partners in the early stages of a relationship. Many people never turn into batterers; they never go further than verbal abuse in punishing their partner. The verbal abuser believes that you must love him no matter how he treats you and you must stay with him no matter what your feelings are. He sees it as a good relationship as long as he is getting his way.

The verbal abuser doesn't care about the feelings or needs of the target. The abuser looks at the other as a tool or an object. The abuser wants to achieve his own goals. He is willing to give up positive contacts with the target to get his way more often. However, he will not give up closeness. He expects the target to tolerate his negativity without withdrawing from him.

So how do you deal with a negative partner who wants to preserve closeness? The short answer is that you deny the negative partner the closeness he wants unless you get the positive tone that you want. You'll find longer and more detailed explanations of what to do as you keep reading.

For example, if I have a happy marriage then it is a close and positive relationship. My relationship with Jerry, the woman at the checkstand, is a distant and positive relationship. If I had recently divorced, I might have a close but negative relationship with my ex-husband.

What if I have a misunderstanding with Jerry, the lady at the checkstand? I'm more likely to move to another checkstand than I am to try to solve the problem.

Jerry and I don't have a close relationship. It would be more cost-effective to cut off or cut down that relationship. I wouldn't try to solve a problem between myself and Jerry.

On the other hand, I will leap to solve any hurt or angry feelings I have about my husband. My husband and I have a close relationship, so I don't want to have hard feelings. It is cost-effective to take the time and trouble to solve problems as they come up in a marriage.

I wouldn't leave my husband for a minor misunderstanding, but I don't have a great deal invested in Jerry. I'd probably solve most problems with Jerry by simply switching checkstands.

*Getting close to someone should be rewarding. You may need
to withdraw from someone if it's no longer rewarding.*

I solve misunderstandings in a close relationship differently from the way I solve problems in a distant relationship. I have a great deal invested in a close relationship such as a marriage, so I will usually act to resolve differences. It requires energy and commitment to solve a problem between two people. You make close relationships closer by more communication, even if it is negative. If I have a fight with my husband, I feel closer to him afterward, even if we don't settle the issue. We shared more feelings and got to know each other better when we tried to resolve our differences.

But getting closer to someone is not an unmixed blessing. When I am closer to someone, he can hurt me more. Therefore, when a close relationship has a negative tone, reducing the intimacy may be the best strategy.

Verbal abuse is a form of punishment. When you are an adult, you don't have to let others punish you unless you choose. You can choose to withdraw instead. The relationship becomes more superficial, but more positive. You will lose positive intimacy, but maybe you never had it. And you will not have the hurt and confusion of negative intimacy.

Summary

Verbal abuse is any verbal behavior with a negative or punishing intent or effect on its intended target. People always try to influence one another, but people who employ verbal abuse use negative words to punish the target when they don't like something or when they want to get their own way.

Abusers use verbal punishment as a secret weapon. They don't admit that they are punishing, and they deny that they intend to hurt. Abusers confuse targets by using subtle comments in private. The abuser is likely to blame the target for the abuse by saying she is the cause of his behavior. But the abuser is responsible for his words. Abusers are aiming to get their way. When they succeed, the abuse continues.

Targets don't put up with abuse because they like it. They may think it's normal or they may think they deserve it. In most cases they don't know how to end it. Targets may leave abusive relationships, but they often don't leave until the abuse has done lasting damage to them and their children.

Targets also allow abuse to continue because they depend on the abuser's approval. They may be people-pleasers towards everyone in their lives, not just the abuser. This is especially true when the target was verbally or physically abused in childhood. Or the family and friends of the target may want the target to stay in a relationship with the abuser because they may like the abuser or they may have religious objections to divorce.

You don't need to have the approval of the abuser to end the abuse. You don't need to return the attack or become negative yourself. You can usually stop the abuse by withdrawing closeness. You don't have to become an abuser yourself to stop the abuse.

CHAPTER 4

Ted and Ivy

Take a look at this example of verbal abuse:

Ivy gets home from work late one night, and checks for anything out of place in the living room. She wants to impress her new date, Ted, who is about to pick her up so that they can drive to a political meeting together. Ivy has been looking forward to the meeting because the precinct will recognize her as the most active volunteer of the year this evening. She also looks forward to going with Ted, because she has found him charming. She is hoping that this relationship works out, as she has had a string of disappointing dates recently. This is only her third date with Ted.

To her surprise, Ted walks in the front door without knocking, goes immediately to the refrigerator, pulls out a beer, and sits on the couch, patting down the cushions.

"Hi, Ivy. Where's the remote?"

"Well, I know it's there somewhere. What are you doing? I'm almost ready to go. They'll have drinks at the meeting. Oh dear, you've already opened that beer."

"What meeting? I thought we'd spend an evening in front of the tube. I'm bushed!"

"Did you forget the precinct caucus meeting was tonight? I thought that was why you were here. Now I'm ready to go."

"I'm too tired and I don't appreciate you pushing me around. I want to spend an evening in front of the tube with you. I thought you wanted me to come over tonight!" Ted yawns and starts to channel surf. "Hey, relax. There are some good sitcoms on tonight. It could be very romantic." He leans over and pats her knee as she stands uncertainly at his side, while the music and dialogue from the TV begin.

Ivy stands frozen, trying to collect her thoughts. She doesn't know Ted very well, and she wouldn't have invited him over for a date tonight. She wants to go to the meeting. She thought that was their agreement. She makes another try.

"I'm not trying to push you around, Ted, but tonight's not a good night for me to see you. Wouldn't you like to go to the meeting? It'll be fun, and I'm getting the volunteer award."

Ted stands up, towering over her, and moving to within inches of her face. "I SAID I'M BUSHED. We're not going to that stupid meeting tonight, and you can stop bugging me about it." Ted sits down and turns up the volume on the TV. "What's in the house to eat? You knew I was coming. Why don't you fix us something? I'm looking forward to trying your cooking." Ted looks back at the TV, waving his hand at Ivy in dismissal.

Ivy flees to the kitchen, trying to decide what to do. She is afraid she can't go to the event since he is there now, and planted on her couch. If he won't go, she guesses she had better make the best of the situation and cook him dinner.

You've just read an example of verbal abuse in action. Ted used his words, his tone of voice, his loudness, and his actions to control Ivy. Ted and Ivy had different plans this evening, and Ted got his way by bullying her.

You can see that Ted and Ivy have different goals. Ted wants to stay at Ivy's home for the evening and Ivy wants to go out. There is no correct wish here. Ted and Ivy each have the right to decide what they will do. However Ted is deciding for both of them. *He does not care whether or not he has her consent.* In other words, Ted expresses a wish to control his activities this evening and also to control Ivy's actions. He does not ask for her approval, or offer other choices.

Ted did not offer any compromise, although he could have. He could have offered to go with her tonight for a short time, then leave early. He could have offered to meet her at the event later if he revived in front of the TV. While exercising his own right of self-determination, Ted successfully controlled Ivy's actions that evening as well.

Ivy's personal beliefs put her in Ted's power. She believes that she needs to be polite, no matter how he behaves, so she cannot address his rudeness. She believes that if he says she is pushing him around, she needs to prove to him that she is not pushy. She believes that if he doesn't want to go to the meeting, then she shouldn't go to the meeting. She believes that if he asks for dinner, she needs to make him dinner, because it would be impolite to turn him down. She believes that she needs to convince him that she is not a pushy broad by being compliant.

Most important of all, Ivy believes that if she is cooperative and submissive to Ted, he will repay her with cooperation and a pleasant relationship.

Do you believe someone will be more cooperative if you are submissive? That's not a good assumption. We'll keep talking about that issue throughout this book.

The message Ivy is sending Ted is: "I'm putting myself in your power. You'll have the right to control me in the future. I'm giving up hope of controlling (influencing) you, and I'm also giving you control of me."

When Ivy flees to the kitchen, submitting to Ted unwillingly, her breathing is coming in gasps and she feels as though her heart is going to pound its way out of her body. She is sweating and she has a stomach full of butterflies.

Ivy is having a physical reaction, a stress reaction, to Ted's comments and to her own actions. She knows that she isn't comfortable and she knows why.

Ivy realizes that Ted doesn't think she has a right to disagree with him. He gets angry when she does.

She realizes that Ted doesn't think that she has, or should have, independent wishes or an independent will. He thinks she should adopt his decisions for her.

She realizes that Ted is treating her as though they have been dating for much longer, while she sees him as a new and casual date.

She realizes that Ted is seeing her as a subordinate, not as his hostess or his equal.

She realizes that Ted doesn't care about earning or keeping her approval. Or perhaps he assumes that she will give him her approval no matter what he does.

Ted acted as though Ted was the only person there. Ivy will lose her identity if she tolerates much of this behavior.

When Ted thinks of Ivy, he thinks of her as though she were a part of him, just as he thinks of his arm. Ted is in charge of his arm. He tells his arm what to do. He doesn't expect his arm to have a brain of its own. Ted expects his arm to serve him. He'd like to keep the arm healthy, of course, so it can continue to do its job of serving him. But if he wears the arm out with overuse, he won't blame himself. He'll probably be angry at the arm, for not working longer or harder. It's inconvenient for him to have to cater to a weak link. He believes every part of him should be able to do the job he wants.

If Ted's arm is strong or talented, Ted doesn't attribute success to the arm. He believes that *he* has the strength and talent, because the arm is part of him. In fact, he'd be upset if people praised the arm, instead of him. And he would be irritated if he discovered that his arm needed care that he didn't want to give it.

In other words, Ted's view of Ivy is normal, appropriate, and respectful *as long as she really is a part of him.* When he defines Ivy as a part of himself, he gains all the advantages. He believes that Ivy, her behavior, and her decisions are *his territory* and come within *his boundaries.* He may believe this because his parents raised him to believe that women should serve men. Or maybe he is selfish and self-centered. He may try to exploit everyone when he first meets them. He may only continue associating with people that tolerate his behavior. Since Ted has declared that Ivy, her person, her property, and her time are his, the next move is hers.

Ivy didn't start this evening with a belief that she was part of Ted. She considered herself a separate person, with her own thoughts, feelings and beliefs. She expected to control herself. If she wants to reject Ted's definition of her as a part of him, she needs to do something different now.

As Ivy reviewed these thoughts in the kitchen, she decided that Ted's behavior would be appropriate if she really were part of him, but she's not. She sees herself as independent of him so his behaviors are abusive, an attack on her independence.

Ivy is a separate person. He can't take that away from her. But if she wants him to *treat* her like a separate person, she needs to act. She needs to define for herself where he stops and where she begins, where her boundaries are. She needs to defend them from Ted in words and actions. She needs to *show him,* not tell him, that she is a separate person making separate decisions.

Ted has acted intrusively in her house and in her psychological space without invitation or permission. He treated Ivy, her house, and her evening as though they were his, as though he owned them, and could do what he chose with those possessions.

Ted acted according to his beliefs, and Ivy cannot count on someone else to change his mind. No village wise-woman, or head of the family, or Superior Court judge will set him straight about how he should act. We don't have an easy resort to outside authorities. Ted and Ivy need to make their own decisions. No one will rescue Ivy if she chooses to go to the kitchen and start cooking dinner for Ted.

Defining and defending yourself is a job
you cannot delegate to others.

We left Ivy in the kitchen. She has some decisions to make about reconstructing, and defending her definitions of herself. As she thinks about Ted, she makes a mental list of the ways that she defines her boundaries, and the ways that Ted intruded into her physical and psychological space. This might be her list:

The way Ivy defines her rights	The way Ted behaves toward Ivy
Ivy owns her house. She believes that people should not come in without permission	Ted enters Ivy's house without knocking. He acted like an owner, not a guest.
Ivy owns her refrigerator. She may offer a guest food or drink from the refrigerator herself.	Ted takes and opens a beer from her refrigerator without permission.
Ivy owns the TV. She does not want guests to turn on the TV without permission. She does not invite guests over to watch TV.	Ted turns on the TV, and watches it without permission. He tells her to watch sitcoms with him.
Ivy owns herself. She doesn't have to do what someone else tells her to do that evening.	Ted acts as though he owns her. He tells her what she will do that evening, and tells her not to argue with him.
Ivy owns her body and others shouldn't touch her or intrude into her personal space without permission.	Ted patted Ivy without an invitation. Ted loomed over her and yelled at her to intimidate her.

You get the idea. Ted was using Ivy's house and Ivy's person as though he owned her and her property. He aimed to capture the territories that she considered hers by telling her what she could and could not do. He told her that he had the authority to dictate her choices and that he would decide where her boundaries were. In effect, he was telling her that she did not have the right to own her house, her TV, her refrigerator, or her evening without his permission.

Ted confused Ivy by his actions. She assumes that everyone is polite. She has little experience asserting herself with someone as aggressive and as disrespectful as Ted. As a result, she yielded to him, by retreating to the kitchen, as he told her to do. By doing this, she reduced herself in his eyes, and in her own. She may emerge from the evening believing that Ted has the right to behave like an owner, rather than a guest.

Even if Ivy continued to believe that she owned the house, she may not find a way to defend herself, and her house against Ted's assertion of ownership. Ivy needs experience in self-defense because Ted is a takeover artist.

What Ted wants, Ivy's company, a meal that she cooks, a quiet evening watching TV, is not actually abusive. If Ted had asked Ivy for a TV date at her house, she would usually agree. But she would not have agreed that evening. What makes Ted's actions an attack is the *methods* he used. He used verbal abuse like yelling, name-calling, sarcasm, belittling, and withdrawal from the conversation.

Ted also manipulated Ivy. He had originally agreed to go to the meeting, but he canceled that plan without notice. He kept pretending that he was entitled to an evening with her although he was backing out of his part of the deal.

Someone may have a legitimate request of you, but they may order it or demand it in an abusive way. You do not have to reject the idea of giving someone what they want to reject the behaviors they use to achieve their goals.

Everyone has a repertoire of behaviors to choose from. You can successfully defend yourself from others if you know behaviors that increase your chances of getting your way and behaviors that reduce the chances that others will attack you. When you have a larger repertoire of useful behaviors, others are less likely to succeed in taking you over.

Ivy wasn't a wimp. She didn't simply stand there, dumbstruck, by Ted's actions. She did begin to make a protest, but the protest didn't work because, without realizing it, *she was trying to influence and control Ted*. She tried to persuade him to go to the meeting with her. She told him that she wasn't trying to push him around. She was trying to get Ted to do (and think) what she wanted when she only needed to do and think for herself. She hadn't yet asserted her own position, or changed her own behaviors to prevent him from taking over.

Let's imagine a practical self-defense for Ivy.

Ivy goes into the kitchen, and takes a few deep breaths while Ted channel-surfs. She sits down at the kitchen counter and pulls out a pencil to jot notes on her telephone pad.

- ♦ *What do I want?* I want to go to the meeting with Ted.
- ♦ *Is it in my control?* Going to the meeting is in my control. Going with Ted isn't.
- ♦ *What's my second choice?* Go to the meeting alone and send Ted home.
- ♦ *Is it in my control?* Yes.
- ♦ *What price will I pay?* Likely Ted will be mad. Maybe he'll never speak to me again. Or maybe he'll figure that he can't push me around. I can't predict him.
- ♦ *Is the price too high?* No. Ted was rude, and I'm not enjoying his company. I don't want to have a relationship with him if he's going to be abusive.
- ♦ *What words shall I use?* I will...I'm going to...My plan is...Your choices are...You may...
- ♦ *What actions shall I use?* I'll turn out the lights, stay on my feet, head for the door, and speak softly.

Ivy composes sentences in her mind from the fragments she wrote on her telephone pad and she does a few more minutes of deep breathing. Then she stands, takes her purse off the hook and turns out the lights in the kitchen. She walks to the stairs, turns out the upstairs lights, and heads for the front door, stopping at the coat closet to put on her coat.

Ted stares at her and calls "Hey, what are you doing?" as she turns out the living room light. While the TV blares, Ivy responds but he can't hear. Irritably, he snaps the TV set off.

Ivy says "Thanks for turning off the TV. I've decided that I will go to the meeting alone this evening. I'm sorry we won't be spending the evening together, but I'm going on with my plans. You'll need to make other plans."

"What do you mean? I thought we had a date." Ted rises.

"Like I said, I've decided that I will go to the meeting. We had a date to go to the meeting, and I plan to go. You'll need to go now, Ted."

"Well, but I've had a hard day. Can't you understand that? Are you trying to nag..."

Ivy cuts into his side of the conversation before he can start more negative comments to her. "That's all, Ted. Don't make it worse."

Ivy now has her coat on and stands by the door, turning on the porch light. Ted rises, abandoning the half-filled beer can. He walks slowly to the door, talking the whole way. "But honey, I could go too. You don't wanna go alone. I don't mind. Really I don't."

Ivy makes no reply. As he stands uncertainly on the porch, Ivy locks the door behind him, says "Good night, Ted," and heads for her car. As she turns on her engine, he gets into his car and burns rubber out of her driveway. She sighs and relaxes in place for a few minutes longer.

As she sits in her driveway, engine running, she thinks about what just happened, using some affirmations to help her learn.

♦ *Today, I'm proud of* looking and sounding firm. Ted believed I meant what I said, and he responded when I was clear about my plans.

♦ *Today I learned* that I can handle myself well even with someone as aggressive as Ted. I also learned that Ted is a jerk. I doubt he'll call back, but if he does, we'll talk about his behavior before I make another date with him.

♦ *Next time, I'd like* to act sooner, but I can't blame myself too much. I didn't expect it.

Here's a summary of the strategy questions Ivy asked herself:

♦ What do I want?
♦ Is it in my control?
♦ What's my second choice?
♦ Is it in my control?
♦ What price will I pay?
♦ Is the price too high?
♦ How shall I act to get to my goal?
♦ What shall I say in words?
♦ What nonverbal behaviors should I use?
♦ What actions shall I take?

There's a page in Appendix I called *Analyzing a Verbal Abuse Encounter* for you to copy. Or you can write these questions on a 3 x 5 card to carry with you in your pocket or purse. When you feel overpowered or you think you haven't defended yourself well, take out the card and begin to puzzle out answers to these questions. Don't worry if you don't come to a perfect solution. We'll be talking more about each of these elements as we go along.

Ivy used three affirmations as she reviewed her behaviors in the car on the way to her meeting:

♦ Today, I'm proud of myself because...
♦ Today, I learned (these lessons about me, about others, about situations)
♦ Next time, I'd like to (improve in these ways, or make these responses instead)

Make copies of the form in Appendix I *Affirmations After an Incident* or put these three affirmations on a 3 x 5 card. Review them with the strategy questions about problem behaviors. At the end of each day, review these supportive affirmations. They will encourage you to be positive about yourself, and to learn from your experiences.

The most important concept you will learn in this book is that you cannot control others, but *you can control yourself*. If you control yourself, others cannot control you. If you control how you respond to people and events, you'll feel strong and safe in your relationships.

The truth is that power and control are important parts of *all* relationships. All relationships involve exchanges of influence. All people try to control themselves, control the other person, and control the relationship. The word control doesn't mean something bad and the people who want it are not bad people. Here's what it means:

Control:

1. to exercise restraint or direction over; dominate; command;
2. to hold in check; curb; to control a horse; to control one's emotions.
3. to test or verify (a scientific experiment) by a parallel experiment or other standard of comparison
4. to eliminate or prevent the flourishing or spread of: to control a forest fire; to control rats.

Synonyms: (1) manage, govern, rule (2) restrain, bridle, constrain.
—*Webster's Encyclopedic Unabridged Dictionary of the English Language*

Most people are ambivalent about control, and the definition above shows why. Parents bring children up to believe that people must *earn* the right to have power or control. We believe that some authority is legitimate. For example, we believe that a mother should exercise power and control over her children to keep them from eating the contents of the medicine cabinet. Parents expect to discipline children, for example to teach them good manners, though people might disagree on the specifics of what good manners are.

We believe, in other words, that parents should control their offspring. Most people, most of the time, would consider that control to be justifiable.

But, what if the mother is fifty, and the child thirty? What if the mother is trying to continue to dominate, command, exercise direction over the marriage choice, the finances, the personal decisions of a grown child who does not live with her and is financially independent, and unimpaired? People in Western society would consider most kinds of domination and control of other adults inappropriate without the consent of the adult involved.

What about domination of one marital partner by another? Is that legitimate? How about domination of one friend by another? Most would agree that a boss has a right to dominate an employee, but only on the job. Few Westerners believe a boss has the right to tell an employee what to eat, how to invest or spend money, or whom to marry. In other words, we reserve for ourselves the right to decide what kinds of control we think are appropriate.

Power is about getting what you want. Whether you want love, money, status, or eternal salvation, you feel more powerful if you believe you can achieve those goals through your own efforts. You feel disempowered, helpless, and vulnerable if you believe that you cannot accomplish your goals. You also feel helpless if you think someone else can prevent you from reaching your goals unless you can control that person.

If Jane starts sobbing at her work site when the boss asks why a report wasn't ready on time, most people would think, "Jane doesn't have enough self-control." You're supposed to be in charge of expressing your emotions, and you're supposed to have power over yourself. Self-control is a legitimate and positive form of control.

If Jane nags her husband publicly or snaps at him when he doesn't give in, most people would think that Jane is controlling. Many people consider it negative for women to control men. Men *may* be expected to control women. That is tolerated in some cultures, but not in others. It depends on the methods used to control.

Should people control others? Words like *direct, guide, instruct, manage, govern,* and *rule* have positive connotations. Words like *command, dominate, curb, control, restrain,* and *stop from flourishing* have negative connotations.

Women, especially, have a difficult time deciding how they feel about control. Many feel that it is OK to influence others, but not to control them or have power over them. Women often want to have input to important decisions, but feel uncomfortable making the decision, especially if they must contradict the wishes of others.

Parents often teach girls to believe the only feminine route to power is to please others. Parents teach girls that if they please others, others will give them the rewards they deserve. Many women feel this is nicer than trying to achieve their goals themselves. They've learned that it is pushy to aim for their own goals.

The beliefs that *I can't achieve my goals alone* and that *I can't act without your approval* are major reasons I would tolerate verbal abuse. It should be no surprise that *you* won't recognize or respect my rights if *I* don't recognize or defend them. If I see myself as powerless without you, I'll give you that message, and you'll likely take advantage of me. If I see myself as powerless without your approval, you'll withhold approval to achieve your own goals. Since you want control, you'll certainly accept it if I hand it to you.

Verbal abuse and manipulation work because they are secret weapons. They are weapons of persuasion to distract you from remembering that you still have choices about your own behavior. I can control you through words, if you let me, by offering to reward or punish you, either through words or other behaviors.

> *In a good relationship, partners try to control each other*
> *by exchanging rewards. In a bad relationship, partners try*
> *to control each other by exchanging punishments.*

Notice that I haven't said that in good relationships no one tries to control the other. That would be unrealistic.

Suppose I say "I'd like you to work for me. I can pay you a high salary." I just tried to persuade you to give me what I want by offering you money. Money is a reward, and you probably value it highly. Even if you decide to say no to me when you see the specifics of my offer, you're likely to think well of me, and of yourself. We will have a positive encounter, even if you end up refusing my offer. But remember that I was trying to get control of where you worked. You didn't think of me as controlling because I offered you a reward to give me what I wanted.

On the other hand, I could say to you "I can get you fired if you don't accept a transfer to my department. If I report you, you'll lose your job." In this case, I'm telling you that I want you to work for me, but I'm going to punish you if you don't accept my offer. The relationship will start (or continue) on a negative note. Whether you accept, or reject, the offer to work for me, you will feel negatively about me and negatively about working for me. You won't feel in control of yourself or your work situation. Notice that you still have the option of saying that you won't work for me, but I've given you notice that I will make you pay a high price for saying no.

> *I feel that I have lost control*
> *when you make me pay a high price*
> *for exercising my choices.*

In personal relationships, the most powerful reward we can offer one another is approval. The most powerful punishment is disapproval. Approval and disapproval are an ordinary medium of exchange in a conversation. "Do what I want or I'll be mad," we say to one another. "If you do what I want, I'll meet your needs too." Control plays out in a relationship through these daily exchanges. Remember, it's not *whether* people want control in a relationship that tells you if it is a good relationship. It's *how* people try to control the relationship. People are always trying to get control of others to get what they want.

This point is worth highlighting because the targets of verbal abuse are often women. Many polite people protest fervently that they don't want to control the other. On the contrary, they say, all they want is good communication. They describe this as having love and respect and talking openly about feelings. The disagreement between that view and my view is important and worth acknowledging.

If I want you to show love in a certain way, I want control. I may not try to force you into it (use negative means to get it) but I do want what I want. Many people confuse the *negative means* (force) with the *intent* to get what they want. If you want something (and everyone does), then you want control. You may not be willing to use abusive means to get it, but both the abuser and the target want control. It isn't the wish to have control that causes problems. It's the negative means, the punishment, the acts of abuse that cause the problem.

Scripts

I do not start every verbal interaction from scratch. I bring to every action a well-rehearsed set of habits I have used in the past, and continue to use because I think those are my best choices. The term *script* is an economical way of saying that. I impose order on the world by taking a role, acting a part, playing out a model that I have chosen because I think it is the best I can do. I may have seen others achieve their goals by acting this way, or I may have reached my own goals this way in the past.

Alternatively, I may have seen that others didn't achieve their goals, and I may still act like them because I have given up on achieving anything more than predictability. I act like them because at least I know what will happen. Maybe I think I can live with the results, even if they make me miserable. I may think this is the best that I can do.

To change my behavior, I have to make myself uncomfortable. I have to practice new beliefs, challenge and stop old behaviors, and start new behaviors. I feel out of control because I have trouble predicting what will happen. That makes me anxious.

To change your behaviors,
you must tolerate more anxiety.
When you change, you make
your familiar world less predictable.

Many self-help books will tell you that personal change is easy, but the changes this book suggests are not easy. In fact, they are likely to make you more anxious. I am probably challenging some of your fundamental beliefs, beliefs that support some of your oldest scripts. You'll need to struggle to learn these new beliefs and to rehearse these new behaviors.

This book will offer you ways to rehearse the changes you want to make. Do you want to think something different? Write it down, and practice saying it to yourself several times a day. Do you want to make a different reply to a jibe that your boss often throws at you? Brainstorm some responses with a coworker, practice the best ones out loud, or in the mirror, and every time you pass the boss's door, rehearse one or two examples in your head.

Suppose the boss makes a hit-and-run attack and you are, as usual, floored, and stammer something, which is what you hoped to avoid. You could punish yourself by saying "I'll never change. I just can't get it right!" "I'm too stupid, just like the boss thinks." "I deserve to be abused because I can't even get up the courage to talk back." But if you criticize yourself by making negative comments to yourself about what you did and what it means, then you will take longer to learn the new behaviors you want.

Criticizing yourself is no way to change. You are rehearsing a new way to abuse yourself when you say negative things to yourself. When you curse yourself, and treat yourself badly because you made a mistake, you are less likely to change in the future.

People learn best by rewards, not punishment. You will learn best if you nurture yourself while you learn from your behaviors.

Suppose Ted had said to Ivy: "I'm so sorry. I just don't have any energy to go to the meeting. I know I promised to go with you, but I can't do it. Would you like to go to the meeting without me? Or would you like to spend an evening here with me, watching TV?"

If Ted said that, did he offer Ivy any choices for herself that she didn't have already? She knew she could go to the meeting without him, and she could spend the evening watching TV, with or without him. When Ted pretends to offer her a choice, all he is doing is acknowledging a choice she already had. True, he controls his own behavior. He has offered her the choice of staying home *with him*. But Ivy already had the same choices about her own behavior (go to the meeting, stay home and watch TV) without his offer. When he tells her she has a choice, though, he makes it easier for her to see her choices.

When Ted says "We're staying home and watching the tube this evening," Ivy correctly reads this as a command, telling her to do what he wants, whether she consents or not. But Ted's demand did not cut down her choices. Ted pretends that he can eliminate her choices by not mentioning them. If he says she has no choice, he can make it harder for her to remember that she can go to the meeting without his consent. If Ivy remembers that she still has the right to make her own choices, then he won't be able to control her.

You cannot control others,
but you can control yourself.
If you do control yourself,
others cannot control you.

This brings us back to Ted and Ivy. If Ted says "I'm sorry, I'm just too tired to go tonight. Why don't you go alone, and we'll have the date later," he has not offered Ivy any more choices about her own behavior than she had originally. She already had the choice to go or not go to the meeting. But Ted gave her information that she didn't have previously: If she goes without him, she has his approval.

When Ivy tolerated the verbal abuse in the original example, she likely believed that she had no choice. She behaved as though she were a child again, needing the permission of a parent before acting in the way she chose. Ivy had confused her capacity to act with her need for Ted's approval before she acted. She believed that she needed his approval, when all she needed was to give herself permission to go without Ted.

Alternatively, perhaps Ivy knows she has a choice to go or not go to the meeting, but she believes the price for going will be too high. She knows the major price she will pay is Ted's disapproval, and perhaps she believes that having Ted mad at her is too high a price to pay. If so, she is still thinking about disapproval the way a child would. She still believes that if Ted disapproves, then she is powerless. It's as though she believes that she can't control her life except by pleasing Ted.

Ivy might believe that Ted's disapproval is going to be an all-powerful force in her life, just as her parents' disapproval was. This might make her too anxious to walk out of the house and go to her meeting. Perhaps she believes that she cannot afford to anger him, because she imagines him with all the power of a parent. She may not have recognized her adult right to act without the approval of others.

When Ted said "You're trying to push me around," maybe Ivy is saying to herself that Ted knows how she thinks and feels, so he must be right about her pushiness. Maybe she thinks she owes him an apology for behaving badly. If she has those thoughts, Ivy is likely to feel guilty, embarrassed, and ashamed of herself, and she is likely to be conciliatory toward Ted. Her beliefs make her feel bad, and make Ted's behavior tolerable to her.

On the other hand, Ivy could say to herself, "Ted doesn't know how I think and feel. I don't like him pretending he knows what's going on in my brain. I know myself much better than he does. Ted is trying to make me feel guilty. He is trying to get me to do what he wants by punishing me. I'm not going to buy it." With those thoughts, Ivy is more likely to feel angry, and to confront Ted about trying to push her around.

Notice that Ted's behavior didn't have to change for Ivy to feel differently. Ivy's beliefs are the most powerful influence on Ivy, not Ted's behavior. Ivy's beliefs lead to Ivy's feelings, and therefore, to Ivy's behavior. If Ivy wants to change the outcome of the interaction with Ted, she must start with her own behavior.

If you want to get better results
from your verbal interactions,
you must start by changing your own beliefs
and the scripts that come from them.

There's another mistake to avoid when you catch yourself repeating an old behavior that you hope to change. That mistake consists of excusing the behavior, or denying the problem. Remember that Ivy reviewed her actions in the second ending above. She sat in her car and talked to herself about her actions, and his. She was thinking something like this:

"What am I proud of? I looked and sounded firm. He believed I meant it, so he responded to my actions. What do I wish I had done differently? I wish I'd acted sooner, but I can't blame myself too much. It was so unexpected. What did I learn? Ted is a jerk. I doubt he'll call back, but if he does, we'll talk about what I want from him before I make another date with him."

Notice that Ivy is affirming her pride in her own actions, not in Ted's response. She could have done a good job and Ted could have reacted even more badly to it than he did, so she is paying the most attention to her own skills. She reviews first what she is proud of, and finds several behaviors to praise. And she reviews what she wishes she had done differently.

Ivy doesn't ask herself "What did I do wrong?" for a good reason. She might have done something that didn't work, but that wouldn't mean that she had done something wrong. But if it didn't work, she may want to do something differently in the future.

When Ivy considers what she wishes she had done differently, she correctly acknowledges she had earlier opportunities to defend her boundaries with Ted. But she affirms her own competence by saying, "I can't blame myself too much. It was so unexpected." When events leap out at you, it's unkind to blame yourself for your spontaneous actions. But think of the saying, *"Fool me once, shame on you. Fool me twice, shame on me!"*

Ivy also asks herself "What did I learn?" She considers the future by looking at the two most likely scenarios: On one hand, perhaps Ted won't call her again, in which case, she won't need to make further decisions about Ted. On the other hand, perhaps he will call and want to see her again. She will prepare a possible response in case he does call her. She doesn't want another onslaught of verbal abuse.

Notice that she hasn't told herself that she will refuse to see him, although she could. She has only promised herself that if he wants to continue to date her, she will talk to him about what occurred tonight before she agrees. She will set boundaries, and let him know what she will do if he ignores them.

As Ivy sat in the kitchen before she sent Ted out and went to the meeting, she affirmed her own wants, and her rights. She explored those areas where she had control, and where she didn't. She explored the consequences of going to her meeting alone. She did not have the ability, at that moment, to go to her meeting with Ted, so she crossed that off her list. She decided that the price was not too high to aim for her second choice. Then she told him what her decisions were. She rehearsed her proposed verbal and nonverbal behaviors in her mind before she tried to carry out those behaviors. Then she followed through.

Summary

This chapter provided an example of a verbally abusive interaction between a woman and her date. The abuser used his anger to intimidate and silence her. He tried to control her actions to meet his own needs.

To respond appropriately to a verbal attack, you need to focus on controlling your own behavior, not the abuser's behavior. You need to withdraw from him without engaging in argument or attacking him in return. To change your behaviors, you need to focus on the beliefs that make abuse acceptable to you. You'll need to gain awareness of your habitual scripts for responding, and change them to give yourself the support you need.

CHAPTER 5

Recognizing Verbal Abuse

B ecause it is easy to recognize one form of verbal abuse, many people believe that all verbal abuse is easy to recognize.

"You bitch! Don't say no to me! I own you body and soul. You're my slave! Get over here and lick up this mess!"

If a husband shouted that at his wife, nearly everyone would agree that was verbal abuse. If someone is loud and demanding, while cursing and calling the other person names, it fits everyone's definition of verbal abuse. But is this next quote verbal abuse? The speaker uses a normal tone of voice to his wife when they are at a friend's house for dinner.

"Oh, sweetie, you don't really want to have so much of the main dish do you? Or any of the dessert? You don't want to go off your diet, do you?"

Many would be asking "Can it be verbal abuse if he calls her sweetie?" Even if they knew those words were offensive to her, they might be thinking it was inadvertent. Maybe the husband didn't realize how embarrassing it was for him to tell her in public not to eat something she was served. And should he be telling her not to have dessert when it hasn't even appeared yet? Maybe others would think this husband must be trying to help her stay on her diet, and he was reminding her for her own good.

Many people doubt that the words they're hearing, or the actions they are experiencing can be classed as abuse. But targets know they don't like what they are hearing.

Here's how Dictionary.com defines the word:

Abuse:
Wrong or improper use; misuse: the abuse of privileges.
Harshly or coarsely insulting <u>language</u>: The officer heaped abuse on his men.
Bad or improper treatment; maltreatment: The child was subjected to cruel abuse.
A corrupt or improper practice or custom: the abuses of a totalitarian regime.
Rape or sexual assault.

Is it a wrong or improper use for a husband to tell his wife what to eat or not eat? Is it a bad or improper treatment, or maltreatment, for a husband to make comments about personal matters like diet in a public setting? Is it a corrupt or improper practice or custom for a spouse to embarrass his partner publicly? This wife hadn't even chosen the food. She was a guest in a friend's house. Those were embarrassing comments for the host and hostess as well as the wife.

The quote that begins "Oh, Sweetie" doesn't contain any harsh or coarsely insulting language. It doesn't refer to an assault, but because the comment was said publicly, the wife was mortified and livid with rage at her husband. She had asked him multiple times never to make comments about her eating habits or her diet to anyone else. She considers her diet none of anyone else's business.

This husband *intended* his wife to be embarrassed and made his comment knowingly and cruelly because he thought she could not do anything about it in public without embarrassing their hosts even further. When she brought it up to him on their way home that evening, he blithely turned the complaint aside, saying "You're oversensitive. Nobody else noticed."

Verbal abuse doesn't have to have abusive language to be abusive, not even in the dictionary. Abuse is about wrong or improper use, bad or improper treatment, corrupt or improper practice or custom. Not everyone will agree that a particular statement is abusive, but we're not talking about defining one statement. We're talking about labeling a *habit* of communication, a *usual practice* of maltreatment, an *improper practice* or *custom* of behavior.

Some people toss around the term *abuse* as though it would be abusive for someone to deny you something you want. Or maybe they think it is abusive for someone to disagree with them or be angry with them. But most victims of abuse are more likely to minimize or deny the problem. They take the blame themselves for the abusive behaviors, just as the abusers would like them to.

It's easier to see the distinction between normal behaviors and abusive behaviors when you ask yourself the question "Who benefits from this action?" For example, some men marry women who are overweight, then never lose an opportunity to call them fat or poke fun at "tub of lard over there." When asked why they do this, the men will often say that they want her to lose weight for her health or so they are more attracted to her. But people rarely lose weight when they're the subject of taunts and name-calling. Calling someone names doesn't cause weight-loss. Ridicule causes depression, lack of self-esteem, and maybe emotional eating.

On the other hand, if the woman begins a diet, rather than supporting her efforts, her husband is likely to bring home doughnuts to taunt her. He may also encourage her to eat them. He doesn't actually want her to lose weight. He was attracted to her just fine when they married. He may actually feel safer with her if she's overweight, thinking she's less likely to be attractive to other men and therefore less likely to leave him. What he wants is an excuse to humiliate her and feel powerful. He wants to feel good at her expense, even though he may be more overweight than she is. He wants her to feel bad, because it gives him a sense of control.

Abusive emotional and verbal behaviors are not trivial problems. They cause major mental health problems that last throughout the lifespan. For example, the Centers for Disease Control and Prevention (CDC) issued findings from a survey of adverse childhood experiences in 2010. They defined adverse experiences as abuse (verbal, physical, or sexual) or family dysfunction (domestic violence, divorce, or a family member who is mentally ill, imprisoned, or abusing drugs). Twenty-five percent of those surveyed reported experiencing verbal abuse as a child, and both girls and boys were targets. The CDC reported that a higher number of these adverse childhood events was associated with premature mortality, with up to twenty years of life lost because of these childhood experiences.

If targets try to ignore the abuse, it may accelerate rather than stopping. The abuser does not abuse the target for attention. He or she abuses the target for control. Attention may be only a small part of what he wants, or achieves, with the verbal abuse.

Often verbal abuse takes the form of manipulation, which means he has a hidden agenda or he is maneuvering to take control while disguising his purpose. The abuser may say that he is just expressing his feelings or venting his anger, implying that the target should tolerate abuse for the psychological good of the abuser.

I assure you that psychologists and counselors don't believe that someone who vents anger at someone else is getting psychologically healthier. We don't believe that having clients express their anger to the counselor is good for them either. We don't tolerate abuse even when someone pays us to listen. That's because verbal abuse doesn't do the abuser any good and it does the listener harm.

It is good communication for someone to explain that he is angry, but someone who says he's angry with you is not abusing you. It is abusive if he repeats it continually and uses the anger to try to control you.

When you listen to verbal abuse daily, you cannot help being affected by it. You bloom if someone compliments you day and night, and you wilt if someone constantly tells you that you are wrong, stupid, fat, immature, badly adjusted, crazy, or a bad mother. You feel badly whether you believe those statements or not. And you'll probably start to believe them if you keep hearing them.

I often use the terms *verbal abuse* and *emotional abuse* interchangeably. All verbal abuse is also emotionally abusive and most emotional abuse involves the use of words to control, punish, humiliate, embarrass, isolate, and financially control the target. Any behavior that threatens, intimidates, lowers the victim's self-esteem, or lessens the target's freedom is abusive.

Constant criticism, name-calling, and inconsistent responses are abusive behaviors designed to confuse and harass the target. Abusers may ignore, ridicule, and withdraw from the target. These and similar actions are designed to increase the control the abuser has over the target. These behaviors are also aimed at keeping the target ignorant of the abuse. Abusive behaviors blame the target for the perpetrator's problems and for the abuse itself.

Verbal abuse comes in many varieties. It's easy to recognize name-calling as abusive, but that's not the only way abusers operate. They may insult you with criticism, threaten and intimidate you when you try to act independently, and use subtle psychological manipulations.

Non-abusive statements

Just because I don't like what someone says to me, that doesn't make the words abusive. I need to consider whether the words are wrong or improper use, bad or improper treatment, corrupt or improper practice or custom, or harsh or insulting language.

A statement is not abusive just because I don't like it. These are some examples of nonabusive statements:

♦ A statement saying the other is angry with you, telling you why he is angry and explaining why he believes you are at fault is not necessarily abusive.

Many targets are so sensitized by their upbringing or by their previous experiences that they feel frightened and angry when the other person tells them honestly what he is feeling. If you have a partner who *tells* you he is angry, as opposed to *showing* you his anger, you should thank the person for doing so.

To have a good relationship with someone, you must know some things about their feelings, including their anger. You need the information to make good decisions about your own behaviors.

It may make your partner furious when you leave dishes in the drainer to dry. Maybe you've never thought about the issue and don't personally care whether the dishes get put away immediately or not. If your partner *tells* you his feelings, you may choose to put the dishes away immediately after that just because that's a hot-button issue for your partner.

But if your partner gets furious five hundred times a day, maybe he wants to control all of your behavior. You'll still want the information that he is angry, but you may decide that you don't want to change any of those behaviors. You may want him to change his habit of trying to micromanage you.

♦ A statement saying that the other doesn't agree with you and believes you are wrong is not necessarily abusive.

It is important for you to know the beliefs of your partner, whether you agree with them or not. Having someone tell you he doesn't agree doesn't make you wrong and it doesn't make him right. You should be able to hang on to your own beliefs without the other changing his views. It isn't the other's fault if you have trouble believing in yourself.

♦ A statement saying that the other wants to stop the conversation about a particular topic now and resume it later is not necessarily abusive.

It's not always possible to conclude a discussion on a topic. Sometimes one or both of you wants time to simmer down, think over the issues, do some research, or just give it a rest. Plus, life happens and one or both of you may need to go to work, go to bed, or feed the kids. Even if you feel unsettled and anxious about what's coming next, reality sometimes intrudes.

♦ A statement saying the other doesn't intend to give you what you want but intends to do what he chooses to do is not necessarily abusive.

The other person does not owe you submission to your wants and needs. Just as you don't have to give him what he wants, he doesn't have to give you what you want. You have a right to ask for anything, and you have a right to get an answer to your request. You do not have a right to expect the other person to submit to you unless you have sold him on your point of view.

♦ A statement that the other person believes that you should not be angry with him and giving his reasons for that belief is not necessarily abusive.

The other person has a right to his own opinion. He has a right to believe that his actions were correct and that you have misjudged him. He can believe that you have come to the wrong conclusion, or that you are unfair and manipulative. He has a right to tell you so—once. His beliefs are under-the-skin behavior and you are better off hearing his opinions and feelings—once—whether you believe them or not, and whether you agree with them or not.

♦ A statement acknowledging a disagreement, a conflict, an impasse, or a problem is not necessarily abusive.

The other person has a right to have an opinion about the way you are communicating, and to propose ways of solving problems between the two of you. Neither of you is the sole authority on the relationship. Each of you is the most important authority on him- or herself.

The other person can help you to understand and make allowances for his feelings and needs. You need to encourage and acknowledge the positive statements the verbal abuser makes and recognize his good proposals and agreements.

If you're going to try to change some of the ways the other communicates, remember that you want to increase the positive communications, not just decrease the negatives. Be careful not to discourage all intimate sharing.

♦ A request for what I want, even if the other doesn't like what I want, isn't necessarily abusive.

If I tell my husband I want him to be my slave, that's not an abusive statement. I do want a slave sometimes. I could use somebody to do all the jobs I don't have time to do or don't want to do. My husband is often around when I want a slave, so it seems natural to mention my wishes to him.

The reason the statement isn't abusive is that I have no means to force my wishes on him. My wishes aren't law to him (or to anyone) and he's not threatened when I ask him. He isn't worried that I could find a way to enslave him. He classifies my wishes for him to be my slave with statements like "I wish you'd get rid of those six inches of snow," and "I'd like you to toilet train our youngest tomorrow."

Kinds of verbal abuse

The goal of abuse is control. The method is negative words and behavior. What methods do abusers choose, and how can you see them coming? Here's a partial list:

Name-calling

Name-calling is easy to recognize when it is vulgar or obscene. It's mostly easy to recognize when it consists of nouns. Anyone recognizes that someone who shouts "bitch!" or "bastard!" is being abusive.

However, someone calling you a bad driver or a bad handball player is also calling you a name. Even if you agree that you have had several car accidents recently or that you're just learning to play handball, what *use* is being made of those statements?

If we're having an argument about finances and you throw in a comment about my driving, that's not intended for my information. It's intended to make me angrier and more upset. Even if a particular criticism is actually true, if the conversation is about something else, why do you bring the issue up? When someone throws in a comment about something they think I do badly or something they think I'm embarrassed or guilty about, that is an abusive use of information about me.

Repetition

Once is not enough for the abuser. He doesn't just tell you once that you are stupid. He tells you repeatedly. He doesn't just remind you once that you lost your car keys. He brings it up every time he wants to score points and get his way. His script is more like a chorus than a song. It brings up the same themes in the same ways, every time.

Repetition is the hallmark of verbal and emotional abuse. What the abuser says isn't a lone stab. It's a steady diet of put-downs that wears you down. You probably don't have the energy to respond to attacks every time. Listening to him is depressing and defeating. You would rather just tune him out and ignore him than respond. It takes less energy to nod and think about something else, until he escalates in a new direction, or hits an unexpectedly soft spot.

But you don't adjust. After hearing that you're stupid five times a day for years, you do begin to believe that you're stupid. Propaganda works by repetition. Commercials and ads work by repetition. If you hear it, eventually you buy it, at least emotionally.

Harsh and unjust criticism

Verbal abuse is often criticism that is plausible enough for the target to think it may be true.

Let's say that I admit that my driving record isn't perfect. Is there any reason for my partner to tell me so? Maybe my partner could suggest that we not share an insurance company since he may get a lower rate without me on the policy. Or maybe he proposes taking over the driving when we are together. But what legitimate goal is served by bringing up the issue for some other reason? You don't make someone a better driver by criticizing her.

A criticism is abusive, even if it is true,
when it is expressed at times or places
that hurt rather than encouraging improvement.

If someone makes a criticism once, he may be sharing information. If someone makes the same criticism repeatedly, that is abusive and aimed at controlling the target.

Name-calling shades easily into insulting criticism. Calling someone a name like *blimp* is one way to degrade someone. Criticism can mean insulting someone with sentences instead of nouns. "You're really fat. You're twenty pounds heavier than when I married you! You don't turn me on like you used to."

Maybe you agree that you're heavier than you used to be. What positive purpose does it serve to tell you so? The abuser probably insults you as punishment to make you more submissive. Abusers figure that if you have lower self-esteem, you'll give them more of what they want.

The abuser may also be insulting your looks because he wants you to feel that you have failed him and therefore that you owe him more than he owes you in the relationship. He may want you to feel that you should put more work, more money, more time, and attention into him than he should put into you. He wants you to give him his way more often because you aren't perfect.

Let's agree that you aren't perfect. You're also not eighteen years old. Do you demand that he be perfect before you praise him for anything? The abuser has a double standard in expectations. He is saying that you need to earn good treatment from him by being perfect but he doesn't need to earn good treatment from you. He thinks you just owe him the good treatment whether he has earned it or not!

He wants you to accept second-class citizenship. If you believe you should be perfect, he may convince you that your lack of perfection is the reason he treats you so badly. You may not figure out that he treats you so badly because he wants to. He doesn't think he needs to earn good treatment from you. He wants your caring and attention for free, no matter how imperfect he is.

Mind reading

Abusers like to tell the target what he or she must be thinking or feeling. They have such an air of certainty the target doubts her own feelings.

"Don't lie to me! I can tell you're mad! Get over it!"

"Stop giving me that look! You're always looking down on me, and I resent it!"

The mind reader is an abuser, and he's rarely right when he says he knows what you're thinking. The mind reader is mostly talking about his own thoughts and feelings, not those of the target.

Feel free to reject the abuser's conclusions and confront him about his behavior. Here are some examples:

"You're not an expert on my feelings."
"You can't read my mind."
"What I'm really thinking is that you're full of baloney."
"If you want to know what I think, you can ask."
Some abusers want you to read their minds, and criticize you when you can't.

"I already know that. I'm not stupid."

"How was I supposed to know that? You should have told me before."

Stereotypes
"Only a woman would think that."
"Yeah, well, if you had to work a sixty hour week like I do, you'd probably have to be hospitalized."
"She probably had to put on her face again. She'll be in the restroom for an hour."

Jibes are insults that hit and run. They don't invite conversation. They pretend that the comment is agreed by everyone. But if that were true, who would say it? Stereotypes insult whole classes of people, or demean the target for a variety of common behaviors. They have a "now you see it, now you don't" quality to them. The abuser will often deny that they are insulting, but insist that they are jokes.

Generally an abuser has two goals in throwing out a stereotype:

♦ To insult the target as part of a general class of targets.

When the abuser puts down all women, it's just another way to put down the woman who's in front of him. It's a swipe at the target, and she knows it.

♦ To get the target to jump through hoops defending herself as well as all other women.

The abuser would like you to expend your energy defending women and yourself while he continues to insult you. He wants your attention. He also wants to show you how important he is because he can make you defend yourself.

You don't need to defend women, or yourself, in this situation. We'll talk about the *abuse-defense loop* in Chapter 10 and you'll see how to handle it.

Commanding and demanding

"Set this here. No, not there, here. No, you stupid idiot, can't you do anything right? Move it over here!"

Abusers like to issue orders and put themselves in positions of command over targets. They like the role of boss. They want others to treat them as the boss, no matter what their professional status is. They like to make decisions and have others carry them out. They like others to do the work.

If the abuser wants you to do something, you have a choice to do it or not. You can hold out for an appropriate request before you respond.

"You know exactly where you want it, so you can do it yourself and get it right."

You can also apply the *expert* rule.

"If you're the expert on cooking steak, you can finish these so you get them the way you like them."

"Since you're the expert on housecleaning, I'll leave it for you so you can get it right."

Judging

Abusers like the role of judge as well as the role of boss. They are thinking:

- ♦ I will decide what is right and wrong, and you are wrong.
- ♦ I will decide who is guilty and not guilty, and you are guilty.
- ♦ I will decide questions of fact, and you will defer to my judgment.

Abusers like to take the superior role. They expect the target to be submissive and willing to acknowledge the abuser's authority.

"You shouldn't have chimed in with your stupid opinions about David's boss. What do you know about it anyway?"

"You don't discipline your kids at all! If you won't make them behave, you shouldn't have had them!"

If you'd like to respond, don't feel you have to defend yourself or your opinions. Instead, ask for the abuser to defend his, like this:

"I guess you think you're the expert on David's boss. That's interesting."

"If you're an expert on disciplining kids, please tell me what your expert credentials are."

Accusations of the truth

Abusers often accuse the target of something that is true, but they make it sound so nasty the target wants to deny it. For example, abusers may accuse the target of disagreeing.

"Don't lie to me! I know you don't want to go with me tonight!"

Actually, the target might not want to go. Her best return here is to say,

"You're right. You seem to be in a bad mood, and I don't care to spend an evening with you."

However, given the abuser's nasty tone, the target may feel confused, and say *"No, it's not that...It's just that I wish we didn't have to go...."* This response gives the abuser what he or she wants: the target's consent to accompany the abuser on this evening's event.

Many abusers will notice the target's reluctance to accompany them. They're able to correctly read the target's distress. But when your views or feelings don't suit them, the statement about your thoughts or feelings is an attempt to *change* what you think or feel.

The abuser's comments about your feelings are part of his strategy to get you to back down about something. Think twice before you deny what the abuser says about your feelings or opinions if he's right. If you think something or feel something, don't deny it, even if the abuser doesn't like it. Stick to your guns. You have a right to your feelings and opinions. Don't pretend to other feelings just because you see that the abuser disapproves.

"Just expressing my feelings"

He: I don't think even a dog would eat this. Why can't you just serve me meat without all this crap on it?

She: That's a horrible thing to say. I don't see why I should cook for you if you're going to treat me that way. You loved this the last time I served it.

He: You say you want to know my feelings. I'm just expressing my feelings. I can't help it if you're oversensitive.

No, he's not just expressing his feelings. A feeling statement sounds like this: "I feel happy (or sad)," or "I'm happy (or sad)" etc.

The man in the above example has expressed an opinion about the dog's eating habits and expressed a wish that she would serve him different food in a very negative way. She may want to hear his feelings, but as someone once said "You can call a spade a spade without calling it a fucking shovel."

When he says she's oversensitive, what he means is that he has the right to treat her any way he chooses. He also thinks he has the right to put her down even if she objects. He hasn't earned her approval, but he wants her to keep quiet, at least about her disapproval of him. He doesn't think anyone should tell him how to talk because he doesn't want to be accountable for his behavior.

But he doesn't value self-expression. He claims the right to express himself to her by telling her his opinion of the food. But he doesn't want her to express herself about his behavior. He is saying "I have rights. You don't. Keep your mouth shut unless you can say something nice about me."

If a statement begins "I feel like..." or "I feel that..." it's not a statement of feelings either. It's an opinion. It isn't a feeling if it contains a judgment of someone other than the speaker. You're only an authority on your own feelings. You're no authority on the feelings of others.

Hostile humor

Is making fun of someone funny? Many abusers think it is. Or at least they're planning to enjoy your embarrassment or humiliation when they point something out to others, or to you, that makes you sound stupid or incompetent.

Him: I can't believe you've never balanced a checkbook before. Where have you been living, Antarctica?

Him: You won't believe what Connie did this morning! She spent fifteen minutes turning the house upside down trying to find her keys, and they were in the refrigerator next to the orange juice! Ha, ha, ha. I guess she must have thought they were perishable.

Him: Give me the directions to get to your house. Don't give them to Ellen. She can't cross the street without a map. Ha, ha, ha. She gets lost in an elevator. Ha, ha, ha.

Ellen is entitled to make fun of herself, publicly or privately. If Ellen is with friends she may tell them she did something foolish or inattentive. She may joke about her "disabilities" while others laugh. A husband could also bring up a funny incident about his wife as long as no one doubts that he respects his wife and that he would have talked about the incident if he had done the foolish thing. But otherwise, laughing at someone is not funny.

It's hostile humor if the story makes someone the target of others' laughter. Stand-up comedians make their living making fun of others, like celebrities and politicians, but their targets are public figures. Comedians can be saying true things or obviously false things about their targets, and people will laugh at seeing quirks of the celebrities in new ways or hearing exaggerated claims on behalf of politicians who want to be taken seriously. But nobody likes to be the target of clumsy humor about their own foibles. It's not fun and it's not funny.

Public criticism

When we were children, our parents taught us there was a big difference between public and private. We had more rules about our behavior in public and the rules were more strictly enforced. Maybe I could come to breakfast in my pajamas, but I certainly couldn't leave the house in them. Maybe I didn't have to remember to say "please" and "thank you" every time within the family. But I'd hear about it if I weren't polite to strangers or adult friends of the family.

If a teacher wanted to criticize my homework or my test score when I was a child, she would call me up to her desk, or ask me to come in after school. Teachers knew that criticisms were private matters between us. A good teacher didn't want to embarrass or humiliate me in front of other students. On the other hand, if the teacher wanted to praise a paper of mine, she'd be glad to do it in front of everybody because she wanted to give me credit. She'd want others to see that she thought I had done well. She wanted approval of me to be public but criticism to be private.

And that's how people behave in loving and respectful relationships. They share positive things publicly and negative things privately. The same would be true in respectful friendships and business relationships.

Constant arguing

All relationships have unsolved problems. In a positive relationship, the participants agree to disagree about some issues. They may parcel out the responsibility for unresolved differences by agreeing that when it's your turn to drive the carpool to soccer, you drive the way you want to and when it's my turn, I go my own way.

In an abusive relationship, there is no resolution of differences. The abuser never agrees to disagree or agrees that we might both be right. He never lets up on the idea that the target is wrong on the issue. He never gives up on the idea that the target should be yielding to agree with him and meeting his needs.

As a result of this failure to agree, which is usually the abusers refusal to agree that the target has a right to disagree, the abuser continues to hound the target about disagreements whenever the issue comes up. The abuser criticizes, punishes, calls her names, and continually demands that she change her ways. Maybe the abuser claims it's for her own good. Maybe he claims that outside authorities take his side, authorities that trump her authority. But the bottom line is that the abuser doesn't accept the target's right to have her own opinion or do things her way.

It is interesting that in many cases the abuser is forced by events to change his own mind on the topic, or to revise his opinion to be in agreement with the target. Does he apologize and acknowledge the target's wisdom? Certainly not. Either he never brings up the issue again, or he starts in on another topic of disagreement. The fact that she already knew the facts that he is forced to acknowledge is a source of pain to him, not pride.

The abuser does not see an adult intimate relationship as a team of two. He sees it as a competition between the partners to decide who is right, who is better, who is entitled. He is not proud of the accomplishments of his partner. He sees her accomplishments as a threat to his own pride and sense of accomplishment.

Extreme jealousy

Many women are challenged by their partner's extreme jealousy. He says he's been cheated on in the past and his partner believes him and feels sorry for him. She thinks that's the reason he's so possessive and jealous. But it wasn't some past partner's behavior that caused his actions and words now. His extreme jealousy is just good old-fashioned abuse.

When a partner, especially a man, says that you're probably cheating on him, he can make that an excuse for all kinds of controlling behavior that doesn't make sense and isn't socially acceptable.

Him: I'm going through your emails because you may be looking for sex online.

Him: I'm going through your cell phone bills because I need to know who you're calling.

Him: I don't want to take you out to dinner because you'll just find somebody to flirt with.

Him: I don't want you calling your family because they'll keep your dirty secrets for you.

Him: When you turn me down for sex, I know it's because you have another lover.

The abuser in each of the above examples thinks he has an excuse for nearly any kind of controlling behavior. He believes he's just protecting himself. Many women start off sympathetic with his reasons even if they don't like his behavior.

But the abuser is working to control every aspect of his partner's life by his intrusive and vicious actions. He says he needs to find out if his target has cheated on him in the past, or is cheating on him now. He says he needs to prevent the target from cheating on him in the future. So what kinds of verbal and emotional abuse is he doing?

- ◆ *Name-calling.* He's pretty likely to be calling names like *bitch, slut,* and *whore.*
- ◆ *Repetition.* He doesn't make the accusation just once. He makes it over and over again. Even if you succeed in convincing him that he doesn't have evidence you are cheating today, he comes at you with another piece of suspicion in the next day or two.
- ◆ *Harsh and unjust criticism.* Saying you have cheated or you are cheating or you will cheat is pretty harsh and unjust if you haven't.
- ◆ *Mind reading.* "I know what you were thinking when he smiled at you. How do I know whether you know him or not?" You can respond: "Since when do you know what I'm thinking? And why would I believe you when you're really just trying to control me?"
- ◆ *Stereotyping.* He thinks any woman is getting ready to cheat on him. That's a pretty offensive way of looking at women!
- ◆ *Commanding and demanding.* So, as a result of his jealousy, you're supposed to change your life, give up your independence, avoid others, and not leave home without him? Sounds like a lot of commands and demands to me.
- ◆ *Judging.* He thinks he gets to decide when you have had enough socializing, when you are misbehaving, when he needs to take you home. You don't have any rights because he's already found you guilty.
- ◆ *Accusations of the truth.* "Don't lie to me. I know you like it when other men smile at you." Actually, you do like it, so don't deny it. You can respond: "That's true. I like it when men smile at me. You don't smile at me often enough to make me happy."
- ◆ *Expressing his feelings.* "Why are you so oversensitive? Don't you want to know when I'm mad at you" He isn't talking about his feelings if he says "I feel that you're cheating on me." It isn't a feeling unless it's a sentence like: "I feel mad" Or "I feel suspicious." Even then, if he says it once, he's expressing his feelings but if he says it over and over again, he's harassing you.

- *Hostile humor.* "Well, women are always looking for a bigger dick, right?" That isn't funny even if he thinks it is.
- *Public criticism.* "I have to keep an eye on her or she'd be dancing with every man in the room." You can respond: "Yes, I'd be dancing with every man in the room. I'd be having a much better time than I'm having sitting and listening to you harass me."
- *Constant arguing.* "Well, if you'd just do it my way, I wouldn't have to argue with you." "No, I'm doing it the way you wanted it yesterday. Today you want what you told me yesterday I shouldn't be doing."
- *The silent treatment.* You're home twenty minutes late and he doesn't even look at you or respond to your greeting. If your punctuality isn't perfect, he punishes you with pouts and sulks.
- *Refusal to have intimacy.* "Why are you always pestering me for sex? Don't you get enough from your lover?" "I told you, I'm not interested unless you lose thirty pounds."
- *Financial abuse.* "No, I won't lend you the money for the copays. That's supposed to come out of your check, not mine. If you insist on working, then the money has to go to the family, not just into your bank account."
- *Isolation.* "You already know what I think of your big family Thanksgiving dinner. There's nobody there that I want to know better. It's a waste of time. You can cook something at home."
- *You made me do it.* "I wouldn't have had to call you names if you had just done what I asked. You're always pushing my buttons, and you know what happens when you do that."
- *Spiritual abuse.* "Don't tell me what the Bible says! I'll tell you what to read and when. The man is the head of the household, and that's the end of it."
- *Denial of a personal or private life.* "I have to pick up some parts at the auto store, so get your coat on. I want you along for the ride."
- *Lack of candor and dishonesty.* "Of course I didn't tell you about that. It would have just upset you and you're upset now so I was right."
- *I'm helpless and sick so you must put me first.* "Just call in sick. Say there's sickness in the family. That's worked before, and I'm going to need you here to look after me."

Summary

The first step in ending abuse is recognizing it. This chapter defines abuse as improper communication and harsh treatment of others. Some forms of verbal abuse are easy to identify, like public name-calling and rage attacks. Other forms are more subtle. Verbal abuse is not a trivial problem. It tears at the bonds of society and causes enormous physical and emotional harm to the targets and witnesses of the abuse.

Uncomfortable exchanges are not all abusive, however. It's not abusive when someone tells you he's angry, or tells you he doesn't agree with you. Asking to postpone a conversation to another time or telling someone no is not abusive. It's positive to acknowledge a problem or a disagreement or to tell someone what you want, even if they don't like it.

Abusers aim to control targets with their communication. They call their targets names and repeat negative and annoying statements. Abusers criticize targets harshly and even if some of the criticism is accurate, the abuser uses it to lower the target's self-esteem. Some abusers make hit and run attacks with negative stereotypes of the target. Others pretend to know the target's thoughts and feelings. Abusers want targets to treat them as superior. They like the roles of boss and judge.

A central trait of abusers is selfishness. They command and demand attention. They want your goods and services without reciprocating. And they don't want to be held accountable for their behavior. Learn to recognize abuse for what it is: attempts to control you.

CHAPTER 6

Preparing Yourself to Change

I met Bill and Janna on my first day working as a psychologist in a mental health clinic. I lifted the thick file containing the record of their visits in disbelief. This couple had come in for marriage counseling weekly for the last three years! My predecessor in the agency had been giving them counseling. I would be taking over their case now.

Bill was a science teacher at the local high school, and coached baseball in the spring. Janna worked part-time at an assisted-living center and was home with their three young children the rest of the time. They made a handsome couple, but Janna didn't take her eyes off Bill, even while shaking my hand, and Bill never looked at Janna at all.

They were experienced patients, so Janna came right to the point. "Bill is the problem in our marriage," she said. "He gets mad at me and yells and I'm afraid of him. Then he gets angry when I don't want to do things with him, or make love to him. I'm always watching out when he's around, because I never know what will set him off. It's like I'm walking on eggshells all the time. That hasn't changed since we've been in therapy."

"It's true, Doc," Bill said, hanging his head. "I can't stop yelling at her. The last counselor gave up on me."

I stopped them for a moment to get some history. Has Bill ever hit her, pushed or shoved her, or kept her from leaving the room or the house during an argument? Does she feel physically intimidated by Bill? But both partners reassured me that

Bill has never hit her or kept her from leaving. He has never thrown objects in anger or punched a wall in front of her. Janna does not fear for her physical safety, only for her emotional safety.

"I've been ready to leave him before," Janna continued. "I'm only staying because he's in counseling and trying to work things out with me. Our last counselor tried hard to get him to stop the outbursts, but all Bill's promises stop right at the door here. He goes home and acts the same way as always.

"Right now, I'm trying to decide if I still love him. It's too hard living with his temper all the time and the way he attacks me. He forgets whatever he's just said but I remember. Sometimes he apologizes, but he's already done the damage. I'm tired of him losing his temper. I don't feel safe."

"I agree. It's tough to keep feeling positive when you feel like he's controlling you," I responded. "Tell me about the last time Bill had one of these outbursts."

"Actually, we had an argument just before we left to come here. He was going to come to this appointment straight from school. I had the babysitter come early so I could run some errands on the way here. But he came home instead, and insisted that I go in his car with him. He didn't want to run the errands. He yelled at me when I asked. So we just sat at home with the babysitter, then we came here in his car."

Bill sat forward on his chair. "I have a right to relax at home. You're always trying to get me to do something. I'm not going to give up my down time to be your chauffeur! We're not going to discuss that issue here, and use up our time on it. I want us to start right in about your refusal to have sex. You've been avoiding sex for years. Now you're trying to avoid talking about it!" Bill clenched his hands over the arms of his chair as he got louder. There was an angry edge to his voice.

Tears filled Janna's eyes. Both of them looked at me, but I sat quietly.

"You see, that's one of his outbursts," Janna said. "Make him stop."

"How?" I asked.

"Well, talk to him. Tell him how much it hurts me. Tell him how bad that is for us. He doesn't take anything I say seriously!"

"Hang on to that thought," I said. "I'll come back to that in a moment. I understand that you want me to stop him from yelling at you. But first, what do you each want to talk about today? The argument about running errands you just had? Or the argument about sex? You folks decide."

Bill and Janna looked at each other for a moment, before Janna turned to me. "Well, I know we have to talk about sex sometime. It might as well be now."

"Bill, I'm going to give Janna some coaching now," I said. "I'll come back to you in a minute." He nodded as I turned to Janna.

"Janna, you asked me to stop Bill from yelling at you. But I can never stop him from yelling at you as long as you reward him for doing it."

"Reward him? What do you mean?" Janna was backing up in her chair. I could see that she wasn't with me. From her point of view, I wasn't behaving properly. Any good marriage counselor should see that Bill was in the wrong here.

"You said you wanted to talk about today's argument here. He yelled at you and said that he wanted to talk about sex. Then you gave him his way. You rewarded him for yelling at you by giving him his way. What could I ever do or say that would be more powerful to Bill than getting what he wants? Bill is going to see me one hour a week, if I stay on his good side. But he's with you the rest of the week. He can afford to take a little heat from me, and ignore it, as long as you keep rewarding him by giving him his way."

"But aren't I supposed to compromise?" Janna said. "I know we have to talk about the sex eventually. It's not that important that we talk about the other argument now. I don't feel strongly about that."

"You don't feel so strongly about talking about today's argument but you do feel strongly about the way he approaches you. You didn't like what he said a few minutes ago. You called it an outburst, and you knew right at that moment that you wanted him to change. But you didn't stop him yourself. You wanted me to make him stop. If you want him to stop yelling at you, don't give him his way. If he yells at you, don't give him what he wants."

"But isn't marriage counseling supposed to change him?" Janna asked. "Our last counselor spent a lot of time talking to Bill about this. She saw Bill alone sometimes. She helped Bill see how he was acting like his father. Bill hates his father."

"It's my job to teach you both new skills," I said. "The two of you may agree that Bill is doing something wrong but that doesn't mean that you can sit out the session, Janna. If Bill is doing something wrong, the major change may need to be in your behavior. Bill knows that he shouldn't yell at you. That hasn't been a very powerful incentive for him to change. But he hasn't left you, so you have plenty of power."

"But what am I supposed to do when he yells at me? There's nothing I can do to make him stop," said Janna.

"For starters, don't give him his way," I said. "If he wants something and he yells at you when he asks, don't give it to him. Don't reward him for doing things you don't like. The time to compromise is when he's behaving the way you like."

I turned back to Bill. "Have I said anything you disagree with? Am I telling her to do anything that would take unfair advantage of you? Am I taking her side?"

Bill shook his head. "I'm with you so far. But she tries to control me too. She just stops having sex with me when she doesn't get her way."

"I'm sure you're both trying to control each other," I replied. "Everybody does. What matters is *how* people try to get their way."

Who's to blame for verbal abuse?

You know the answer to this one already. Abusers choose to be verbally abusive. Verbal abuse is not an accident. It doesn't just slip out. Abusers abuse because it works. Abusers abuse because it allows them to control others. Abusers expect to get what they want from the target after the abuse.

You'll find that many therapists are not trained, and not comfortable, dealing with anger. Many counselors prefer to pacify the abuser just as the victim does, rather than be a target of the abuser's rage. Counselors will sometimes take the quickest way to silence the abuser, by pleasing him, because that lowers the counselor's anxiety. This may mean that the counselor tries to control the target and make the target more compliant. Marriage counseling, therefore, is not always the best route to change a verbal abuser. After all, Bill and Janna had been in marriage counseling for three years without Bill changing the behavior that they both agreed was a problem.

Remember that the goals of the abuser are quite defensible. The abuser has legitimate goals. Counselors and therapists, even very well-trained and respectable professionals, often don't have good defenses against abuse. And no matter how savvy the counselor, therapy only happens one hour a week. If the target continues to submit to the abuser's control at home, the abuser will learn to look good during the counseling session. Bill knows Janna stays with him only because he goes to counseling with her, so he goes to counseling. That doesn't mean he wants to change his behaviors toward her. Abusers often behave well with the counselor present and continue to abuse the target the rest of the week. Counseling is not likely to change an abuser if the target continues to reward the abuse.

Abusers, like other human beings, want to meet their own needs and they have the same needs as others. They want love, affection, sex, loyalty, and admiration. Abusers aren't different from non-abusers in most ways. They're not even very different from targets in their life goals. If you're the target and you want the abuser to change, you, yourself, must change. You must change your own behavior in order to gain control of the interaction.

In the segment of conversation from the therapy session that began this chapter, Bill didn't have unreasonable motivations. He wanted to get right down to the subject that was most important to him. Since I had asked both of them what they wanted to talk about, Bill's suggestion was quite appropriate. If he had turned to Janna and asked her in an unthreatening way to talk about their sex life, she might have been pleased to say yes. Janna was unhappy about the methods he used to get to his goals. He used his angry tone of voice, his criticism and loudness to intimidate her. Bill got his way by bullying Janna.

Bill and Janna's marriage has deteriorated because each of them tries to control the behavior of the other with punishments. Bill and Janna have habitual patterns of negative behavior. They reenact these scripts continually even though the results make both of them unhappy.

In a couple, each person's behavior influences the other. Bill chose to snap at Janna but he could easily have acted differently. What Janna did before Bill's outburst didn't cause the outburst. He's responsible for the yelling, just as he's accountable for the rest of his behavior.

But Janna is responsible for her own behavior. She rewarded his tantrum and makes it more likely that he will do that again. The most powerful influence on Bill's behavior comes from her.

Janna is not giving Bill his way because she unconsciously wants him to treat her badly. But if she is the one rewarding him, she is the one who needs to change.

On the other hand, Janna can't hold herself accountable for all the influences on his behavior. Maybe he didn't sleep well last night and maybe someone criticized him unjustly at work. She can't fix those things. She also can't find him time to relax during the spring baseball season. She is aware of those influences on him and sometimes she allows for them. But she is the most important influence on how he treats her. If she tolerates him treating her badly because he has had a bad day, she is rewarding him for his bad behavior. She shouldn't be surprised if he continues to mistreat her if she continues to tolerate it.

When Janna starts off by saying that Bill is the problem in the marriage, she's not entirely accurate. She doesn't have to feel responsible for Bill's behavior because she doesn't cause it. But she is responsible for her own behavior, including the way she enables Bill and the messages she sends him.

Janna was willing to change her behaviors. She had a therapist who could coach her through the changes she needed to make. But not all people, and not all couples, are willing to change. Some targets feel righteous about being innocent victims and believe that only the abuser needs to change. And some abusers are so entrenched that they are unwilling to change. They will seek another target in another relationship rather than give up verbal violence toward their current target.

I see targets of verbal abuse for therapy in my office often. It is common for them to start with the belief that they have no power or control over the behavior of the abuser. It is common for them to believe that they have no power over their own behavior as well. They don't talk about choosing their actions; they talk about *having* to do what the abuser wants. Their own acceptance and agreement with the abuser causes their behavior. Targets are responsible for their own actions.

The stages of change

People learn new behaviors every day. Some learn consciously and deliberately, for example by asking a friend for advice or hiring a professional for assistance. Most people change without hiring help to do it. Many others want to change but don't know how. Two psychologists, Dr. James O. Prochaska and Dr. C. C. DiClemente, did research on the natural process of change. They studied alcoholics and others who stopped bad habits like smoking or addictions without outside help. They found that those who change a habit without help go through the same six stages of thought, belief and action.

Stage 1: Precontemplation

People in this beginning stage–*precontemplators*–haven't decided to make a permanent change in their behaviors. They don't believe that making a change would be desirable or necessary and they think it would be hard or impossible to change the behaviors.

If you're in the precontemplation stage of dealing with the verbal abuse in your life, you're not ready to take action. But you can start a list of the pros and cons of stopping the verbal abuse you're experiencing.

Do you think being a target of verbal abuse has no positive aspects? That's not true. Every situation has positive aspects. Here's *my* sample list of the positive aspects of being a target of verbal abuse:

♦ You don't have to analyze your own actions because you know you'll get more verbal abuse whatever you do. You'd have to think to change.

♦ Your life is predictable. You know what the abuser will do and say as long as you continue to say and do the same things. Changing would make your life unpredictable.

♦ You don't need energy to be a target. You can stay depressed, alcoholic, toxic from drugs, or just be a couch potato. You can stay passive while you're a target.

♦ You don't even have to please the abuser. There's no point in trying to please him if nothing pleases him. Maybe you can make him as miserable as he's making you.

Stage 2: Contemplation

People at the contemplation stage of change believe that they would be better off if they changed, but they aren't ready to take action.

If you are contemplating change, you can begin your homework. Read up on the problem and the possible solutions. Join a group, or start one, of people working on the same problem. Take notes on your self-talk, what you say to yourself when you think about the abuse. What obstacles are in your way? Make commitments to change by promising yourself to move toward your goals.

Stage 3: Preparation

In the preparation stage, you've committed yourself and you're looking forward to taking action soon. It's time to get specific with your plans. List the steps you plan to take and the ways you plan to overcome the obstacles you see. Try to anticipate what will happen so you can prepare more thoroughly.

Draw up a contract with yourself. What behaviors are you trying to change? Choose the events or conversations you are trying to respond to differently. Those should be the triggers for your new behaviors. What, specifically, do you plan to do when a trigger event occurs? How will you know you've succeeded? What's your backup plan if it doesn't go well the first time?

Stage 4: Action

You're ready to go, so go! Try *something* when a trigger event occurs. Remember to be positive to yourself, with affirmations and positive self-talk. Read supportive statements to yourself. Remind yourself that you're moving forward.

You're likely to find that you haven't anticipated everything and that things still go wrong. Or maybe everything goes as you planned and you still don't feel good about your actions or feelings. Keep taking notes and rereading them about the new situations you haven't anticipated.

Stage 5: Relapse

Many folks who are working on habit change get discouraged and fall off the track when they use old behaviors again. You know you made a brave effort and it was at least partially successful, but then you forgot to take the next step. Or you regress and do what you've told yourself you didn't want to do any more. Old thinking and old behaviors keep entering your mind and entering your speech.

Now you're noticing more and more when you're doing things that don't work. You are better at knowing what *not* to do than knowing what to do next. Your thoughts may be filled with doubt and self-criticism. You wonder if you've taken on too big a task, or if you're able to succeed at this. You feel more like a failure than you did before.

The relapse stage is the most critical stage in the process of change. Having a relapse doesn't mean you've failed. It's just another stage in your process of working toward a permanent change in your thinking and your behavior. A relapse is an *opportunity* to learn something new, to add a new strategy you hadn't anticipated or to design a new process to work on something you hadn't thought of before. If you are using new behaviors, the abuser will as well. You can't necessarily anticipate everything that will come up.

How you treat yourself when you relapse predicts how successful you will be. Don't criticize yourself, tell yourself that you'll never learn, or that you don't deserve happiness. If you do, you'll make the road to change hard or impossible. You need to support yourself when you make mistakes and remind yourself that nobody's perfect. Persistence causes success. You're not running a sprint; you're running a marathon.

Remind yourself that you haven't relapsed about everything. You've learned new behaviors and your learning hasn't gone away. You'll have plenty of other chances to do it the way you want to. Remind yourself that you're only responsible for what you do and say, not for what the abuser does and says.

Stage 6: Maintenance

In this stage, you've made it. The new behaviors are just as natural to you and just as automatic as your old ones were. You don't have to think about them anymore. In a sense, you've arrived back at the precontemplation stage, because you have a set of behaviors that feel natural and normal and you're satisfied with the way they're working for you.

Not everyone proceeds through this model of change in the same way or over the same time period. Some people who want to change may remain at the contemplation stage for their whole lives. Others may think about changing for many years, believing they don't need to change and don't want to change. Then an event occurs that motivates them.

For example, one smoker who hadn't thought about changing watched her father, who also smoked, die of lung cancer. If the smoker decides to give up smoking, she may call up her doctor, fill a prescription for a nicotine replacement chewing gum and throw all her cigarettes in the toilet in one day. However, a week and half later, she'll be in nicotine withdrawal. She has gained weight, felt restless and couldn't stop thinking about her cravings. She may go back to the precontemplation stage. She starts smoking again and tells herself that she'd rather give up her last few years of life than have a poor quality of life now.

In a sense, that person is an example of someone who rushed into change before she was ready. You could predict that she would fail this time. She didn't know how long the withdrawal period from nicotine was. She hadn't prepared herself mentally for the sensations and feelings she would have during withdrawal. And she didn't get the support of others for distracting and nurturing herself through withdrawal.

Other individuals thinking about change may spend years in each stage. They think about the horrors that await them if they try to change and minimize the benefits of changing. They think about changing as though it were mountain climbing and they think that starting will be like climbing Mt. Everest.

You can make change so hard on yourself that you can't succeed. To succeed you need to persist and you need to make the change easy (enough) on yourself.

Changing your response to verbal abuse is much like dieting. At first the changes need to be conscious and deliberate. Over time, those new behaviors can become automatic reactions that you don't need to think about any more.

How you treat yourself matters. When you are learning a different way of responding to verbal abuse, you need to praise yourself for trying to change. If you make a response you regret, the faster you move on to a more effective way of behaving, the better off you will be. If you're trying to count your successes, don't just count your time doing the new behaviors. Instead, count how fast you return to the new behaviors after you relapse.

Beliefs and scripts

Beliefs are basic to your feelings. Most people believe that an event triggers the emotions that follow, which would look like this:

The Activating event leads to the emotional Consequence

or

$$A \rightarrow C$$

However a psychologist named Dr. Albert Ellis explained that emotions don't work that way. Ellis said that between the Activating event (A) and the emotional Consequence (C) there are thoughts, or Beliefs (B) that control the feelings.

The Activating event leads to Beliefs that lead to the emotional Consequence

or

$$A \rightarrow B \rightarrow C$$

Suppose you are having a conversation with your partner about your children and he says "Don't try to discipline the children when I'm around. You're a pushover, so you'd better let me do the discipline!"

If you feel depressed after this statement, maybe you think that what your partner said (the Activating event) has led to your emotions (the emotional Consequence).

But not everyone who heard her partner make that critical statement about her parenting would feel depressed by it. Let's look at the possibilities.

- ♦ She thinks (B): *He's right. I'm a terrible parent.* So she feels depressed (C)
- ♦ She thinks (B): *He doesn't know what he's talking about.* So she feels angry (C).
- ♦ She thinks (B): What does he mean? None of the kids are in trouble. So she is puzzled (C).
- ♦ She thinks (B): I can't believe he made that stupid statement. So she is amused (C).

In each of those examples, he has said exactly the same thing to her. But depending on her thoughts and beliefs (B), she has different feelings that lead to different reactions to his statement.

Beliefs and thoughts lead to habitual patterns of responding. Beliefs control both our feelings and our behaviors. You can hear yourself saying these little sentences ("He's right. I'm a terrible parent" or "He doesn't know what he's talking about") if you listen carefully. That constant monologue going through your mind is what psychologists call self-talk.

Your self-talk serves the useful purpose of guiding your actions. You may not be aware of your self-talk now, but by labeling it and listening for it you can increase your awareness.

The first step in changing your behavior is changing your self-talk.

Habitual self-talk runs through our minds constantly. It leads to patterns called scripts that guide our actions. We rely on habits to guide our behavior because starting every new action or conversation from scratch would lead to chaos.

Remember how difficult it was to tie your shoes when you first learned in elementary school? A five-year old may need to concentrate for the better part of a half-hour on tying his shoe, doing nothing but trying to accomplish this goal.

Practice makes actions more rapid and skilled. Adults can tie their shoes while carrying on a conversation or studying a map. They don't use their full attention or think of each action separately. When an adult wants to tie his shoes, the script takes over and he doesn't need to think about it further.

Our behavior scripts operate in the same fashion. We learned small pieces of these actions in childhood, probably by concentrating on the problem and trying to achieve the best solution. We came up with choices that seemed to work in certain situations. We only have to think about what we are doing now when something unexpected happens, or when we have to teach the process to someone else. Without scripts, our conversations and actions would be chaotic. We would be paralyzed, unpredictable to ourselves and others.

On the other hand, if you've ever tried to break an old habit, you know how hard that can be. Maybe the hardest thing about changing an old habit is noticing that you need the new behavior *right now*. The abuser says something and you'd like to make a new response. But you've already made the old response before you realized it.

You first need to call attention to the behavior habit (the script) in your mind. Then you need to stop yourself from doing the old behavior while you simultaneously try to substitute a much less familiar response. Scripts are efficient, but if they don't work, you need to change them. You want your scripts to be both efficient and effective in achieving your goals.

Empowering yourself to change:

Here's a template for action that can work for you. Think of sending an ARROW toward your target: Let's walk through that template for action.

A   AFFIRM your new beliefs about verbal abuse. *Affirm* your rights and be *accountable* for your results.

R   RESOLVE to move ahead with change. Decide what you will do and plan the steps to take.

R   REHEARSE the new behaviors.

O   OPERATE just as you did in the rehearsal. Put your plans into action.

W   *WITNESS* the changes you made. Pay attention to what you did and praise yourself for doing it. "WOW! I made the change. I'm on my way!"

Affirm your rights.

Begin by noticing the abuse and naming it to yourself. Label it: "That was verbal abuse." Remind yourself that the abuser chooses his behavior.

You may want to start an abuse log, a daily list of things the other says and does that you classify as abuse. There's no need to keep the list a secret if you don't want to. Post the list on the refrigerator if you think that might be helpful. It's likely to get the attention of the abuser. If the abuser asks what you're doing, feel free to tell him the truth. You can say something like this:

> *I'm starting to keep track of the way you treat me. I'm writing down the things you say that I don't like because I'm deciding what to do about them.*

You'll find a sample Abuse Log form in Appendix A. Keeping an abuse log will help you pay attention to what the abuser does and says so you can plan how to respond.

Notice how often things happen that go on the log. Is it daily? More often? Is it in many different situations? How are you responding now?

Keep track of your feelings after the abuse because they are an important outcome. Also notice whether the abuser is getting what he wants because of the abuse. Are you giving him approval? Does he get what he wants because he acts that way?

Resolve to change your responses.

Make specific plans for how you will respond to some of the incidents on your abuse log. You are aiming to keep the abuse from paying off. Figure out the best response you can make. Then guess what the abuser is likely to say next, and figure out a response to that. Don't be satisfied with writing down one possibility.

Rehearse the script you plan to use

Begin to say your new responses out loud to yourself. Every time you review an attack from the abuser, ask yourself what you wish you had said. Then say that sentence or two out loud, maybe to a mirror or maybe to a supportive friend or counselor. It's your rehearsals out loud and in advance that will help you to be prepared when those next attacks occur.

Operate now

You're never going to be perfectly ready. You won't be perfectly comfortable with your new behaviors at first so you don't have to wait until you feel relaxed before you start operations. Your goal is to begin so you can learn from your mistakes. You can't anticipate everything, so your goal is to learn what happens next.

Wow! Be a good witness and praise your own efforts

Keep track of what happened by taking notes as soon as you can. First tell yourself how important it was that you tried, and maybe how difficult it was for you. Remind yourself that you're going to learn new skills so your actions don't have to be perfect, or have a perfect outcome. You're aiming for a *permanent* change in your behaviors.

Beliefs Can Be Obstacles to Change

The beliefs and instructions I list and explain below aren't accurate. They don't represent good predictions of the future. If you share these beliefs, you need to change them to end the verbal abuse in your life. For example, do you believe that when you're angry you must show the anger to be healthy? Or that it's good to express your anger?

> Frank: What time is dinner?
> Rosie: It'll be about an hour. I just got home.
> Frank: Well, forget it then. I can't stand to wait that long. If you gave a damn about me you'd make a bigger effort. You know I'm putting in long hours this week. I don't know why I thought you cared about me. I'm going to get a hamburger, and I'll be home when I'm home. (He slams the door as he leaves.)

Frank and Rosie have been married a long time. She isn't thinking that he is a jerk and that she doesn't have to tolerate his tantrum. Frank has Rosie trained, so she thinks "He must have had a bad day at work. He can't yell at anybody there, but it's good for him to be able to express his anger. Even though it hurts my feelings, I should just let it wash off me. I'll let him yell because it's the least I can do for him when he's had a bad day. I wouldn't want him to have a heart attack from keeping his feelings bottled up."

Frank certainly wants Rosie to think this way. It's convenient for him to be able to treat her any way he wants, without her resenting it or asking for a change in his behavior. Frank tells Rosie that it's bad for him to bottle up his anger, and that she should be a willing target. He tells her he needs to vent.

This line of reasoning assumes an underlying psychological theory that I have called the hydraulic theory of anger. Let's look at it:

The hydraulic theory of anger

Negative events in your life cause anger to build up in your body like steam in a kettle. You get rid of the anger by yelling or acting it out. If you fail to express it, it continues to build up. Pent-up anger can cause a psychological explosion, like blowing the lid off a boiling kettle. This can lead to heart attacks, strokes, or other long-term health problems. Therefore it's a good idea to express your anger and show others how you feel.

Most people have this view of anger, but they have never reviewed why they think so or what evidence they have to support the theory. Certainly, abusers believe this and will try to convince you it's true.

But the hydraulic theory of anger is not accurate. It does not describe how anger works. The truth is that events don't cause anger. Thoughts cause anger but we have control of our thoughts.

Anger is an emotion that includes uncomfortable physical changes, the changes that occur with the fight-flight-freeze reaction. These include increased blood pressure, muscle tension, headache, and stomach upset. Showing your anger, or shouting the anger is more likely to *increase* the fight-or-flight feelings than to decrease them. Yelling at someone is less likely to improve your mood than cooperative actions are.

It is true that yelling at someone may feel good for a time, but only if you praise yourself for acting correctly. It is the *belief* and the *self-talk* that makes expressing anger feel good. Frank may tell himself that she deserved it. Telling himself that he was correct makes him feel good. It wasn't yelling at her that felt good.

Perhaps he expects that he *should* yell at someone, or that he has a right to yell, or that yelling *should* make him feel good. Perhaps he congratulates himself on "being a man" or "standing up to that so-and-so."

But it is the praise he gives himself about showing anger that makes him feel good, not showing anger by itself. If he praises himself for cooperating, for holding his temper, for finding a win-win solution, he'll feel just as good.

Showing anger becomes an addiction, much like a drug addiction. There is a short-term rush, and long-term negative fallout. There are many positive ways to deal with angry feelings, but having a temper tantrum is one of the worst things for mental health. Abusers may *want* to show their anger to you, but it doesn't help them, no matter what they say. It's only a method to control you.

Remember that people choose their actions. In the example of Frank and Rosie above, if Frank were feeling too hungry to wait an hour for dinner, there are some other, and better, responses he could have made:

Frank: I don't think I'll last an hour. If I hang around here, I'll probably start yelling at somebody. I'm going to get a hamburger and try to pull myself together. I'll be back when I'm human again.

Frank: Have you started cooking anything yet? Why don't we just go get a hamburger? It sounds as if your day went like mine, and we both need a break.

Frank: I won't last an hour. What can I eat now? I want to go soak in the tub while I snack. You could come tell me about your day if you want to risk my lousy mood.

Frank: How about if I take over in here and cook dinner? I'd like something fast and I know just what I want.

In each of these examples, Frank still has the same problem of a lousy day and a bad mood. But in these examples, he is telling about his mood, not showing it. He is taking responsibility for his mood, not blaming it on her. He is trying to make his mood go away, with or without her. Having a bad day doesn't cause

Frank to verbally abuse Rosie. It doesn't make him feel better and it makes her feel worse.

The abuser says awful things because he believes them.

Do you think the abuser believes the things he is saying? He probably doesn't. He says them because he is getting rewarded for saying them. He's not telling the truth; he's giving a commercial for his point of view.

When you get information from a source, you always need to determine whether the source is biased. That bias will influence what information the source gives you and how the source presents it. Most of us are conscious of looking for bias when we're reading a newspaper or listening to a news broadcast. We're less aware of doing it when we're talking to friends and family.

If your own family doctor told you that Glamour Potion kills bad breath germs on contact, you might believe it right away. But if you saw a TV commercial for Glamour Potion starring someone in a white coat who said "Nine out of ten doctors recommend Glamour Potion" you'd probably ignore it, at least consciously. Yet people who would be embarrassed to believe a television commercial believe the most outrageous statements their husbands or wives say.

Perry and Janet are having a fight because he intends to join a competitive bowling league that will take Perry on many out-of-town trips. Last year, when he was in a less competitive league, Perry bowled four nights a week, leaving Janet without a car in the evenings, and alone with two preschoolers after her full day of work. He admits the new bowling league will take him away from home even more. At the climax of the fight, he says:

Perry: Do you know what you are, Janet? You're selfish! You only think about your own needs. You don't put yourself in my place and think how hard I've worked all week! I need to relax more. I need the change of pace. You're so wrapped up in yourself that you can't see what you're doing to our relationship!

Janet is a sophisticated, well-educated woman. Yet when her husband tells her "You're selfish," she makes two assumptions: (1) if he says it, he must mean it, and (2) if he says it, it must be true. Let's analyze those assumptions in turn.

If the abuser says it, he must mean it

It is to Perry's advantage to say "you're selfish." He expects Janet to reward him for this verbal abuse by giving him his way. He wants her to agree not to make any more critical comments about his absences in return for him not calling her selfish again. If abusing Janet gives Perry what he wants, he will keep doing it.

In other words, Perry has a bias when he says "You're selfish." He's not saying it because he means it. It's his tactic to gain control. He wants her approval of his bowling schedule. Perry is willing to make his wife unhappy to get his way. Calling her names is part of his strategy to control her. He wants to get on with the business of meeting his own needs and nobody else's.

If the abuser says it, it must be true.

Janet reaches a second, more devastating conclusion when her husband tells her "You're selfish." She assumes the statement must be true. Here are the assumptions she uses to reach that conclusion:

No one would say such an unkind thing unless it were true.

Do people tell lies in order to gain an advantage? Yes, they do. People sometimes stretch the truth or tell a lie in order to get something they want. Therefore, you shouldn't believe that something must be true because you hear it, or because it appears on TV.

He wouldn't lie to me. He loves me.

OK, he loves you. But wouldn't he forget facts conveniently, stretch the truth, and pass on incorrect information to get his way? Do you think your husband puts your needs and wishes ahead of his own? Don't people who love each other still try to get their own way?

He's an authority on this. He knows better than I do.

If your husband is an accountant, he does know more about financial management than a nonprofessional. But that doesn't mean he will provide you with truthful information about the status of the checking account if he wants something. Professionals know many different ways to accomplish goals and you're going to hear the way *he* wants to get it done. Unless you are buying the services of a professional, you're dealing with an interested party, not a neutral, unbiased one.

And by the way, the abuser may be an expert on money or cars or marketing but he will never be a greater expert on *you* than you are. He's definitely a biased source when it comes to information about you.

This criticism must be true because I've heard it before.

Unfortunately, many adults had critical parents. If your mother or father told you that you were selfish, you may be easy to convince that anything you want is a selfish desire. But if we look closely at Janet's case, clearly selfishness is not a good description.

Let's define *selfishness* as putting your own needs first. And let's say that Perry is correct that she is putting her own needs first when she wants him to stay home more. Whose needs is he putting first? Hers? Clearly, he is acting selfishly also. If he truly valued selflessness, he would be asking her what she wanted him to do, and then doing it, rather than putting his needs first.

The fact that Perry calls Janet selfish makes the abusive nature of his message clear. Perry doesn't value selfless behavior in the abstract. He values selfless behavior from Janet because it benefits him. He's happy to abuse her, to make her feel bad, and call her names because it benefits him. The name-calling doesn't occur because he *believes* she is selfish, and it doesn't occur because she *is* selfish. He is not an informed, unbiased, neutral observer of Janet. She can safely conclude that he calls her selfish because he wants to get his way and get her into his control.

He is abusing me for attention.

Pete's wife, Cookie, is a flirt. When he goes out with her in public, she hardly speaks to him. But she's on the arm of every other man in the room. She whispers in male ears, makes suggestive comments, tells dirty jokes, touches male arms, and pats male fannies.

When Pete's friend, James, raised his eyebrows at Cookie's behavior, Pete responded "She's doing it to get my attention. She wants to make me jealous. She'll stop when she figures out I'm not going to give her extra attention."

Pete's logic is faultless. If Cookie is flirting to get his attention, then she will stop if he ignores the behavior. However, Pete has been married to Cookie for eight years now, and each year her flirting increases. If ignoring it were going to work to lessen her flirting, ignoring should have worked by now.

Pete's assumption is wrong. Cookie is not flirting to get attention from Pete. She's flirting to get attention from other men, and she gets it. Since he never objects to her behavior, there's no cost to her at all; ignoring it won't make it go away.

Always look for the goal of the behavior. Ignoring someone calling you names won't work to stop the behavior. The odds are good the person calling you names does so because he likes to. He thinks calling you names helps him reach his goals. His goal may be to make you feel bad, for example, or to make you angry or sad. If there are no negative consequences to the abuser, then the name-calling is likely to continue.

The abuser is probably giving himself a reward. He probably feels good about calling you names maybe because he wanted revenge, or because he thinks it will make you more submissive. Ignoring the abuse won't stop the abuse if the abuser is rewarding himself. The abuser is talking to himself just as you are. He may be telling himself that he's doing the right thing. The abuser may have gotten his way from you already so this abuse is just an investment in keeping you down in the future. Many verbal abusers only need an audience, not a particular response to keep going.

Believing I can't do it is an obstacle to change

When someone tells me "You can't do that!" they are often mistaken. They often mean "You shouldn't do that" or "I won't like it if you do that," or even "I will punish you if you do that." But I *can* do it if I have the physical ability to do it.

Some people may confuse you by telling you that you cannot do what it takes to get what you want. But this doesn't remove your choices and your ability to act. If you can physically do something, you can do it without the other's permission.

Others may confuse you by telling you that you want their approval more than you want to reach your goal. But their beliefs do not take away your choices or your ability to act. If your true goal is to get what you want and you can get what you want by yourself, it is within your power to achieve your goal.

Others truly control only their own behavior. They don't control your behavior, no matter what they say. They control their approval of you, but it's your choice if their approval controls your behavior. You're the one who has to decide whether the cost of their disapproval is anything you need to pay attention to.

When you are in a relationship with someone, you can do as you choose, do the things that are in your own power to accomplish. Or you can do what the other wants you to do. That is a choice between acting with the other's approval or acting without the other's approval. It's not really a matter of whether you can or cannot do something.

Believing I shouldn't get angry is an obstacle to change

Parents often bring their children up to believe that getting angry is wrong and bad. Even though the parents may get angry frequently, some parents punish children for showing anger, and especially for showing anger at the parents. Many parents call this learning to show respect for them.

When a parent demands that a child not show anger, the parent can't help a child understand anger and learn to manage it. It's unrealistic to pretend that only adults should be allowed to experience anger. Children need to practice getting angry and handling themselves appropriately when they are angry. Trying to suppress anger in children does more harm than good.

Emotions are not good or bad. They are not evidence of vice or of virtue. Emotions are normal, human, physical reactions to life. They are signals to the brain from the body. People need to pay attention to their emotions and use that information to make good decisions about their behavior.

I need to notice my anger and encourage myself to be aware of it. My anger is a valuable alarm signal ringing in my brain. If I deny that I'm angry, I'll be more likely to ignore my anger until the situation is more difficult to change.

Anger is an under-the-skin emotion, but you have direct contact with your own anger. You know what your body feels like and what you are telling yourself. You probably use the word *anger* to describe your feelings at some moments every day.

It is *never* an advantage to tell yourself that you aren't angry. It is *always* to your advantage to know how you feel. Knowing your emotions lets you choose your words and actions wisely.

But knowing about your emotions doesn't mean that you must share that information with others. You can choose to tell others you are angry. You can show your anger to others. You can hide your anger from others.

You should correct others' behaviors on many occasions without anger. If I'm introduced to somebody as "Beth" and they respond by calling me "Bess," I'll point out the error pleasantly. I assume they don't want to call me an incorrect nickname and I've never used the nickname "Bess." I can correct people who are misspelling my name and I can correct people who are repeating my address wrongly. I don't have to treat them as though they were incompetent or malicious. Correcting children and other adults is an ordinary matter. It can be a pleasant part of the business of life.

I try to repel attempts to control me just as automatically, whether I'm angry or not. That's part of protecting myself. I value and support my anger. But I can and should correct others who ignore my wishes even when I am not angry.

If I think it's *wrong* to be angry or to show anger, I'll make it harder to be aware of my own angry feelings. Nobody likes to feel that she's doing something wrong.

Some people get angry too often, or express anger too much for their own health. This doesn't mean that they should ignore or suppress their angry feelings. And it doesn't mean that they are wrong to have the feelings in the first place.

Angry feelings, like all feelings, come from thoughts. An abuser who raises his voice, gets red in the face, and clenches his fist when his wife refuses to do what he wants is not immoral for being angry. And he isn't angry because his wife has said no to him. His self-talk makes him angry. He's probably saying sentences like these to himself:

♦ She has no right to say no to me.
♦ If she were a good wife, she'd do what I want.
♦ She should put my needs first.
♦ I'm entitled to her services whether she likes it or not.

It's this self-talk that makes him angry, not her telling him no. If he were saying some of these next statements to himself instead, he wouldn't be feeling so intensely negative.

♦ She doesn't agree with me, but she has a right to disagree.
♦ I haven't convinced her yet, but I'll work on her again later.
♦ It's better if I sometimes give in for the good of the marriage.
♦ I'd rather have her happy than get my way this time.

In other words, the abuser is creating his own anger by his self-talk. He'd be better off if he didn't ignore his anger or try to hold it in. He probably wouldn't succeed at that for long anyway. His best choice to stop getting angry is to change his self-talk.

If someone gets angry and feels like he/she has a head of steam, he doesn't need to take the lid off and express the anger, to use the old analogy. He needs to take the pot off the burner by examining his self-talk and correcting it.

Targets often have the opposite problem. They aren't aware of their anger soon enough. Since they may believe that it's bad and unfeminine and wrong to get angry, they may deny their feelings when they're only irritated and continue denying feelings as their feelings increase in intensity. Like an abuser, they may only notice their feelings when they are enraged.

The healthiest choice, for both abuser and target, is noticing angry feelings immediately. If you know you're irritated, you can review the situation or the problem and decide calmly how to reduce the angry feelings. If you wait until the anger has increased to rage, both the situation and the feeling will be more difficult to deal with.

So abusers and targets are both dealing badly with anger. The abuser is probably building up inappropriate anger with mistaken self-talk and mistaken beliefs. Then he's turning his rage on the target because it's a weapon he can use to conquer her. He's very aware of his anger, but he pumps it up internally as though he were feeding a fire to launch at her.

Meanwhile the target also has inappropriate self-talk. She could be saying to herself

- ♦ I shouldn't get angry with my husband.
- ♦ Women shouldn't get angry.
- ♦ He's entitled to his feelings, so I guess I have to put up with his words.
- ♦ He's treating me badly but I deserve it.

If the target reviews her self-talk, she may tell herself more accurate statements like these:

- ♦ I'm angry with my husband, and I have a right to my feelings.
- ♦ Anger is a human emotion, not a male emotion. It's OK for me to get angry.

- ♦ He's entitled to his feelings, but he's not entitled to treat me badly because of them.
- ♦ I deserve better treatment, so I need to protect myself from him.

My low self-esteem is an obstacle to change

I have both positive and negative feelings about myself. My set of beliefs about myself is called self-esteem.

We learned how to treat ourselves by seeing how others treated us. Usually our parents have the biggest influence on what we feel and believe about ourselves. Your parents taught you to judge yourself and your achievements, and maybe you learned that you had to earn the right to feel good.

If you believe you're valuable and have many personal resources, you will have high self-esteem. If you think that you're poor in resources, or dependent on others, you will have low self-esteem. If you think that others control you or that you are helpless without others, you'll also have low self-esteem.

The judgments of the members of your family about you, who you are, what your talents or skills or flaws are, are not necessarily accurate. You were a growing and changing being when you were a child. Also, parents really don't know everything. They often can't be good judges of how valuable or talented their children are. It's true that some parents see nothing but good in their children, but also true that some parents see nothing but bad.

Harsh criticism and other verbal abuse directed toward you as a child prepares you to believe that you don't deserve good treatment as an adult. You may feel that because you are not perfect, others have a right to treat you badly.

You may also feel that it's OK for someone to criticize you, even harshly, if you agree with them that you have a fault. But that's not a rational or useful belief.

Everyone learns better from rewards, not from punishments.
Even you!

If you have a problem that you'd like to correct, someone who constantly points it out to you in negative ways is stopping you from correcting the problem, not helping you to improve. Punishment is not good for you. If you're trying to change something about yourself, focus on rewarding yourself for efforts to change and demand that others be encouraging or keep their mouths shut!

My idealization of the abuser is an obstacle to change

While I'm devaluing myself, I may be pretending that my partner has positive characteristics simply because he is my partner. It's as though I've got a suit of clothes that I label "boyfriend" or "husband" and I'm thinking of the characteristics of the suit, not the man.

For example, I may feel that I need to consult my husband on all decisions about running my business because I want to have good communication with him. But maybe my particular husband has never run a business, can't manage a checkbook without constant overdrafts, and works alone because he doesn't get along well with people in authority. In this situation, consulting with my husband is asking for trouble, because his comments won't be useful to me and may cause problems between us. Not all husbands have all virtues.

You may know more than your partner about fixing cars or taking the temperature of a two-year-old. It is absurd for you to pretend that family members have all the skills you wish them to. Letting others criticize your decisions because they have the role of husband or boyfriend is unrealistic and inappropriate. My partner won't pick up knowledge of car repair because I assume he has it. Not all men know what men are *supposed* to know.

My fear of vulnerability is an obstacle to change.

What causes people to feel safe emotionally? Emotional safety is not much different than physical safety. You learn what your parents teach you.

Parents provide the protection for their children. They give their newborns toys with rounded corners and large parts. They make sure that the newborn always has a caretaker within crying distance. Parents look ahead for dangers in the environment. They remove the dangers, or they remove the child. When the child begins to crawl and walk, parents plug up the electrical outlets and lock the medicine cabinet.

At a later point, parents teach their children about safety because the child must learn to protect himself. They may not lock the medicine cabinet any more, but they've taught the child about poisoning, and the child tries to make himself safe. Because parents can't follow their children everywhere now, parents can no longer protect their teenagers from all dangers. Parents try to *teach* teenagers about the dangers of taking drugs and drinking alcohol, especially when driving a car. But teenagers may decide to take risks anyway.

In other words, our first vision of safety is of someone else making us safe by removing the hazards in our path. We often define a loving or caring relationship by just that quality of feeling safe. We expect that someone who loves and cares for us will protect us from hurt.

Basic safety is about taking the dangers out of our environment. More advanced safety involves studying ways to avoid future dangers or to keep the dangers from hurting us even if they are in our path.

We feel emotionally safe when we can predict and avoid the dangers in our environment. We feel emotionally vulnerable when we can't predict or can't avoid those dangers. As adults we depend on our skills and competence to avoid danger. Hopefully we can protect ourselves without avoiding all people and all environments.

If you decide that it is someone else's job to protect you from hurt, you will have few intimate relationships and they are not likely to be satisfying. Others cannot do as good a job of protecting you as you can. And if the only way you can protect yourself is to leave a relationship, then you'll likely have more bad relationships because others can't learn from experience how to treat you.

On the one hand, if you give up on safety and simply numb yourself when things go wrong, then you'll endure enormous hurts without recognizing them. If you try to keep yourself from feeling pain, you won't fix conditions that hurt you and you won't leave circumstances that injure you. It's time to review the Serenity Prayer.

God, grant me the serenity to accept the things I cannot change,
The courage to change the things I can,
And wisdom to know the difference.

It's important to feel the pain that tells you what is going on. It's important to use that pain as motivation to improve your situation. That's when you need the courage to change. It's important to feel pain when you are hurt so you work to avoid situations that are painful.

You need the wisdom to know the difference between situations that will be painful in the future (because they have been painful in the past) and circumstances that have good prospects for emotional safety.

Believing the abuser has an anger problem is an obstacle to change.

It's true that some of the men who are verbal abusers are very angry men. They were abused in childhood and now they're returning the favor to the world. When crossed, they will bulldoze everything in their path to try to get what they want. They have an attitude of entitlement, believing the rules others obey don't apply to them. They believe that others should serve them and they won't nurture others in return for the services they want.

But that's not true of all verbal abusers. If the major problem with someone is an anger problem, the person will have trouble at work as well as at home. The person will have trouble getting along with his parents as well as his adult partner, friends, and buddies as well as children. Men (or women) with anger problems have trouble working for others because they get angry with authorities, not just with their wives or husbands. People with anger problems have a restricted social circle because they don't get along well with others.

However, victims of child abuse usually learn to handle their anger in most situations. They only abuse when they think they can get away with it. Most abusers only abuse their adult intimate partner and their children. They are abusive where they see weakness. They have learned, over time, to treat coworkers, social friends, and bosses much better than they treat the people they see as beneath them.

Look at the social worlds of the abuser. If he continues to relate to his parents and doesn't bully them, then he has control of whether or not he is a bully. If he doesn't get fired because he has a temper tantrum when his boss yells at him, then he has learned to hold his temper when he wants to. He could equally be holding his temper when he is with his wife. If he can hold his temper when he wishes—and nearly everyone can—he doesn't have an anger problem.

Believing the abuser loses control of himself is an obstacle to change

The same reasoning applies to the idea that the abuser flies into a rage and loses control of himself when he verbally abuses you. I hear men say this to me all the time, and women often believe that this is what happens.

If I'm interviewing a batterer who has just told me that he lost control of himself when he hit his wife, my next question is "Why didn't you kill her?" The batterer is usually shocked and responds that he would never do that, now or later.

I respond "Then you were in control. You kept yourself from killing her and you believe that you can continue to control yourself that way in the future."

A verbal abuser who says "I lost control. I didn't know what I was saying. It won't happen again" is contradicting himself. If you lose control and aren't responsible for your actions, than you can't guarantee that it won't happen again.

People are responsible for their actions both legally and in the judgment of others even if they are drunk or drugged. There are many people who drink too much or take drugs irresponsibly and claim that they're not responsible for what they do after that. That is believable if they give up alcohol and drugs after one episode of battering or abuse. If they don't give up drinking or drugging after damaging someone else while they were under the influence, it is clear that they allow themselves to do damage, that they don't care if they damage other people. They are responsible for taking the alcohol or drugs in the first place.

Believing I'm going to leave the abuser soon is an obstacle to change

Many women say that it is too much trouble or that it would be too painful to learn to change their own behaviors. They don't want to feel those painful feelings and they say they are going to solve the problem by leaving the relationship. They don't want to fix him when they're going to be leaving him.

These women believe that there are only two choices: the choice to stay with the abuser, abuse and all, or the choice to leave the abuser and leave the abuse behind. But the world doesn't work this way.

Women who say they are going to leave this relationship in the future often don't have a plan for doing so. It's not that they are saving money, looking for an apartment, finishing school, or waiting for the last child to leave home. They're usually waiting for the abuser to do something awful. They're waiting for him to do something they can't justify to themselves the way they usually justify whatever he does. They are waiting for the abuser to do something that will be the final straw for them.

In other words, women who say they are going to leave are often looking for some action by the abuser that will allow them to feel OK about leaving. Since they haven't defined what they're waiting for, they may stay for years or even a lifetime. They're not about to leave (without working out the logistics) and they're not working on the logistics so they can leave in the future. But they're also not working on making the relationship better.

The truth is, you have three real choices here. You can (1) leave a bad relationship or (2) stay there just as it is, abuse and all. But it is also possible (3) to change yourself, with or without leaving the relationship.

If you change yourself, you may still want to leave the relationship because you don't like or love the person you're with. You may leave the abuser because you have too many bad memories of the way he's treated you over the years, or because you think you'd be happier alone even if he has shown improvements. Nothing about changing yourself and ending the abuse makes you stay in the relationship. In fact, you'll have more leverage to change the abuser if you decide you're willing to leave. Changing yourself doesn't mean you can't leave the abuser.

Indeed, changing yourself is probably something you need to do for your happiness whether you leave this partner or not. If you have a habit of accepting abuse from others, what's going to keep you from choosing another partner who abuses you? How will you know the difference between abusers and non-abusers if you don't learn what abuse is and how to respond to it without encouraging it?

I've seen women who leave an aggressive, verbally abusive partner and then pick a new partner who simply walks out of the house or doesn't speak to her for a week when he doesn't like something she said. That isn't verbal abuse, but it is emotional abuse. She could have foreseen that problem at the beginning of the relationship if she had begun to make the changes in herself that I am talking about here.

I've also seen partners go from being the target in a verbally abusive relationship to being the abuser in their next relationship. Those targets didn't become abusers because they were evil but because they only knew two ways to relate. They had decided never to be a target again, so they ended up taking the part of the abuser. It didn't make them any happier, so I don't consider that a good choice to make.

Sadly, many women who leave one verbally abusive or battering relationship quickly find themselves in another verbally abusive or battering relationship.

That's because they haven't changed themselves. They didn't learn how to spot problems in advance or how to fix minor instances of abuse on the fly. They also didn't learn how to judge whether a relationship was currently abusive or would become abusive in the future.

You don't leave abuse behind when you leave a relationship; you only leave one abusive partner. If you have to have a continuing relationship with that partner, because of children in common, for example, then maybe it's better to learn good responses now. Then you can set a good example for the kids who will still have to deal with their father.

Believing you will leave me if I change is an obstacle to change

Realistically, the abuser might leave you if you stop giving him everything he wants. If you are afraid the relationship will be over if you seriously challenge the abuser, it's time to look closely at that belief.

Children who are being abused by their parents sometimes complain about the abuse, but most don't, because they have a much more important worry. As part of the abuse, most abusive parents threaten to leave the child, kick the child out, leave the child in a parking lot, or send the child to a foster home. Those parents have probably left the child multiple times already; the child is never sure that the relationship will continue. As a result, children who have been abused often grow up with a life-long fear of abandonment. They have always believed that there is something worse than being abused. They think it is worse to be abandoned.

And abandonment *is* worse for a child. Children don't know whether or not the foster parents will also abuse them. Children don't know that their favorite biological relative will likely raise them if they are taken away from their parents. Children don't know that the State will work hard to give them a better life. Children only know that if they lose their parents, even abusive parents, their world will disappear. This goes much deeper than the fear of disapproval. The fear of abandonment is closer to the fear of mortal injury, pain, and death.

The fear of abandonment is a serious, long-term, paralyzing fear that appears in the gut, not just in the intellect and the brain. It's often an irrational fear, but that doesn't make it less frightening.

Has the abuser ever done anything that makes it likely that he would leave, other than saying so? Has he stayed away overnight? Has he left you (separated from you) for periods of time before? Has he spoken to an attorney or filed for divorce?

If you're in a relationship where the abuser is constantly threatening to leave, look at the evidence. Look at his behavior, not his words. Even if you know the abuser has affairs all over town, he probably doesn't want to leave you. After all, what other woman would tolerate as much as you do?

Men who are abusive may kid themselves that any woman would want them, but it is a lot of trouble to woo and win a woman. The abuser probably has many undesirable traits that are apparent to anyone. And he's not looking for just any woman. He's looking for someone who will put up with him! When you compare what he puts into the relationship with what you do, is he really so desirable?

If the abuser leaves you, you won't have to feel guilty about abandoning him. If the abuser leaves you, you're likely to get sympathy and support from your friends. You can live a peaceful life, with all the personal support you can earn.

It is *not* better to be abused than abandoned when you are an adult. It is better to be free and to choose positive relationships. It's better to reject relationships that make you unhappy most of the time. The abuser is not likely to abandon you, but if he does, you'll find many advantages in your new life.

Believing I'll have less conflict if I ignore minor abuse is an obstacle to change

Every time I go into the grocery store, I am reminded of the persistence that allows children to get their way. Mom runs into the store to get a half-gallon of milk, a dozen eggs, and a roast chicken. She's rushing and doesn't have time to do a full shopping trip. But her preschooler wants to look around and he wants a candy bar. She doesn't want him to have a candy bar just before dinner so she says no.

The child starts wailing at the top of his voice. Maybe this grocery shopper smacks the kid, but more likely she yells at him to shut up. The kid keeps wailing anyway. Everybody in the aisles turns to look at her, so she gives him a candy bar to keep him quiet. Has she saved herself from a future scene in the grocery store with her child?

Of course not. When you reward kids for crying loudly in public by giving them what they want, they learn to cry the next time. Pacifying someone by

STOP THE VERBAL ABUSE

treating them well when they're behaving badly simply increases the amount of bad treatment you'll get. The child may stop crying at this minute because of the candy bar, but you're setting up a situation in which the child will cry for twice as long next time to get the candy bar. Pacifying abusers by giving them what they want just sets you up for problems the next time.

Many targets feel they're in just such a situation when the abuser makes a scene in public. She'd like to keep him quiet because she's embarrassed and she doesn't want anyone to think that she is at fault. But you can't stop abusers from making fools of themselves in public. It won't be your fault if he does. Just step aside and let him. If he starts screaming at you in public, feel free to address everyone else in the room with questions.

"Can you believe that he really acts like this?"
"See what I have to deal with all the time?"
"Would you want a man around who acts like this?"

You're not responsible for his behavior and you're not responsible for keeping it secret. Let him shame himself and see if anybody else in the room will come to your defense.

All verbal abuse is emotional abuse and most emotional abuse involves the use of words to control, punish, humiliate, embarrass, isolate, and financially control the target. Any behavior that threatens, intimidates, lowers the victim's self-esteem, or reduces the victim's freedom is abusive.

If you want to change your own behaviors so you can stop verbal abuse in your life, look over the list of beliefs above. Consider whether you secretly believe them yourself. If you do, it's time to look more realistically at the world, and at the behavior of the abuser. It's time to hold him, and yourself, accountable.

Summary

People are responsible for their own behaviors. An abuser is responsible for what he says and does to a target. She can't cause his behavior and she can't stop it. He chooses his words and actions. But the target is responsible for her behaviors. She's not to blame for what he does, but if her actions increase the chances that he will attack her, she shouldn't be surprised if he decides to do it again. It's not what the target does *before* the abuse that makes a difference in the abuser's behavior, even though he tells her it is. It's what she does *after* the abuse that causes him to feel successful or unsuccessful in reaching his goals.

Along the road to change, you need to increase your awareness of your self-talk, the short sentences that you use to guide your beliefs and behaviors. Your self-talk controls your feelings and determines your behavior. Your beliefs and reactions to events, not the events themselves, determine your feelings.

Your beliefs, thoughts, and feelings are collected into scripts, habitual ways of reacting and feeling that we aren't aware of unless we pay attention. To change those scripts requires active and deliberate choice. That may make us anxious because we are making our lives less predictable. It is longer and harder to change a habit than to start a new one from scratch.

Aim an ARROW at your goal. You need to Affirm your new beliefs, Resolve to move ahead, Rehearse your new behaviors, Operate by putting the plans into action and Witness, or celebrate your changes.

Some beliefs result in ineffective defenses against the abuse. Here are some rational beliefs to counter them:

- Most abusers don't have anger problems. They choose their behaviors. Expressing anger isn't good for them any more than it's good for you.
- Abusers don't lose control of their behavior. They decide what they want to do and say.
- The abuser doesn't believe everything he says about you and he definitely isn't telling the truth when he attacks you. He abuses for control, so ignoring him rewards the abuse.
- Your low self-esteem is an obstacle to change and may cause you to be unrealistically positive about the abuser.

Do you plan to leave the abuser? If so, you should learn everything possible about verbal abuse. Maybe you're only planning to leave because you think that's easier than changing or staying, but you'll find that it will always be useful to understand and defend yourself against verbal abuse.

CHAPTER 7

Ineffective Verbal Self-Defense

Nan found the message on her answering machine as she walked in the door for a quick lunch: "Hi, honey. Guess what? We can't pour today, so I have the afternoon off. He won't pay us for it, the jerk. I'm on my way home. Call in sick, or something, and we'll go fishing together. See you soon!"

Nan stood by the phone with her stomach in knots. Her husband, Peter, was a charming, carefree rascal, who always had another joke or prank up his sleeve. He worked for a concrete contractor (sometimes) and was unemployed (often) because he could only work when the weather was just right. Although he had other construction skills like hanging dry-wall and welding, he never wanted to pursue other work. He preferred to play between jobs.

Nan had thought this was a marvelous lifestyle when she first married him. She felt like she was on an eternal honeymoon, because she could spend all day as a housewife, and play with Peter full-time when he was free. But after their son, Jimmy's, birth, Nan realized that playtime had ended. Peter's income wasn't sufficient to save so they could buy a house. In fact, they were barely scraping by.

Nan had a head for figures, and Peter cheerfully admitted he didn't, so she took over the family finances. Nan was shocked to see how little money Peter was bringing in. Although he was proud of earning sixteen dollars an hour, far more than she ever hoped to make, he wasn't working enough days to have more than half-time employment. Nan went back to work as a bookkeeper for a real estate office. She earned eleven dollars an hour, and Peter constantly reminded her that his work was more valuable.

Moreover, Peter didn't like her working again. She wasn't free to leave at a moment's notice to see an air show or go to high school basketball championships. He acted as though she could drop everything to play as he did.

While Nan mused about the problems of life with Peter, he walked through the door. Nan bulldozed into her reply to him:

"Oh, Peter, I got your message but I just can't go with you this afternoon. It's near the end of the month, and we have the quarterly figures to get ready. Besides, if I'm going to take an afternoon off, I want to take Jimmy out of day care and spend the time with him too. We don't see enough of him as it is. I just can't go with you, Peter. My boss is noticing how often I'm absent, and with Jimmy sick all last week...I just can't go."

An ominous silence fell. Nan's heart pounded wildly and her jaw muscles tightened. Peter looked down at the floor and Nan wished she could sink through it. "I'm so sorry," she said.

When Peter did speak, it was the voice of a little boy. "Nan, how can you do this to me? How can you attack me all the time when I love you so much? You don't care about me at all, do you? You don't want to be with me. You'd rather be with your boss, or Jimmy, or anybody but me. I don't ask much of you. But how can you call this a marriage when you won't spend any time with me? We never do anything fun anymore. And I'm still in love with you! It's not fair!"

"I still love you, Peter. Of course I do! It's just that...I don't want to lose my job! Oh, Peter, don't be upset with me. I'll go, if it means that much to you. Peter, stop looking like that! I'm sorry I hurt your feelings. I didn't mean to attack you. Look at me, Peter."

When the argument was over, they kissed and made up. Peter went to pack the fishing gear in the car, but Nan still sat in the kitchen. She didn't think she was going to digest her lunch and she knew she was grinding her teeth. She wished she could give Peter her dental bills, but she knew she would be paying them.

She wasn't going to enjoy the afternoon. She was doing it out of duty. Peter would spend a happy evening playing with Jimmy after the fishing but she would have to go in to work, alone, to finish her month's figures for the staff meeting tomorrow. So why did she always feel like the bad guy?

Nan and Peter, in the example above, have a difference of opinion. Who has the right to decide for Nan? Nan believes that she has the right to decide whether or not she will go fishing with Peter. Peter doesn't agree. Peter believes that when he is free, or when he invites Nan, then Nan should always say yes to an invitation to play. He believes that he has the right to determine if Nan's reasons for saying no are good enough. If Nan does not convince Peter that she has good reasons not to go, then Nan should go with Peter. Peter believes that Nan's time belongs to him. Peter sees any attempt on Nan's part to control her time as an attack. He sees Nan as his personal property. Are her attempts to act independently really attacks?

Let's define an attack as an attempt to control others. Let's define defense as an attempt to keep others from controlling you. Does Peter have a right to decide what Nan will do that afternoon? Does Peter have a right to decide whether Nan has a good enough reason to say no when he demands her company?

When Peter accuses Nan of attacking him, Nan is horrified, since she didn't intend to be aggressive. What she has tried to do is defend her own boundaries.

An attack is an attempt by one person to gain control of another person's psychological or physical space. A defense is an attempt to repel such an attack.

Remember the difference between aggressive, assertive, and passive behaviors?

♦   Aggressive actions attack others.
♦   Assertive actions defend against attack.
♦   Passive actions are ineffective defenses. A failure to act is passive and allows aggressive actions to succeed.

Self-defense is a valid concept in law and in common sense. If someone attacks you, you are justified in defending yourself.

So was Nan attacking Peter? In Peter's eyes, yes, because Peter had decided that Nan's use of time should be in his control. In Nan's eyes, there was no attack. Nan had not tried to influence Peter's decision about going fishing. Nan had only tried to exert control (and failed to do so) over her own person.

Nan needed to decide that her use of her time should be in her own control. She needed to resist Peter's invitations. She needs to ask *herself* whether she had attacked Peter. He may say that she didn't have the right to choose but that doesn't make it true. Nan tacitly agreed with Peter when she was apologetic. She tacitly agreed that if Peter didn't give her permission to say no, she must go fishing with him.

This chapter will describe defense tactics that don't work to deter the abuser. I'm not saying that they shouldn't work, just that they don't. These tactics don't address the reason the abuser is attacking. They spring from beliefs that lower your effectiveness so they don't stop verbal attacks.

Don't ignore the attack

When you do nothing, you aren't defending yourself. Think about raising children for examples. All children misbehave. They aren't born with an innate knowledge of right and wrong. The parents' job is to teach children how to behave. But punishing children harshly when they misbehave teaches them to behave the same way toward others and toward themselves. Spanking, emotional abandonment, name-calling and threats of future punishments all distract children from learning to behave. The parent's goal should be to teach children, not to punish them. Punishment doesn't teach as well as rewards.

Ignoring the attack causes you to feel weak and helpless. The abuser knows the attack was effective because it didn't cost him anything. The abuser's tactics are mainly punishments. He's punishing you to get control and he thinks if you aren't in his control then you must be controlling him.

The abuser sees relationships in a black-and-white way. He sees a top dog, who gets all the rewards and an underdog who works for the top dog. So he's going to be the top dog. If you do nothing, his behavior continues because it's paying off.

Don't beg or plead with the abuser

Don't expect the abuser to stop the abuse because he realizes that you are unhappy. The abuser is behaving the way he does to cause your negative feelings. It doesn't help you and it probably hurts you to tell the abuser that he is disturbing you.

But you don't need permission from the abuser to do something or stop doing something that is in your own control. If the abuser tells you that you must or must not do something, don't let the abuser con you into believing that you need his permission. If it's in your own control, exercise your self-control and do what you choose.

It is easier to get
forgiveness than permission!

Don't attack the abuser

What's the best way to respond to an attack? In the movies, characters respond by attacking back, applying more force, using bigger weapons. The media says the shootout at the OK Corral is the correct model for self-defense.

In real life, it's not that simple. A Pyrrhic victory means that both parties are so badly injured that nobody wins. If I attack you when you attack me, and you retaliate, as you are likely to do, I'm likely to be injured in the fray. It doesn't heal my pain to know that you are bleeding. My goal is not to destroy you, but to defend myself.

If someone attacks you and you respond when you usually don't, you may surprise the abuser and he may be more cautious in the future. The abuser can learn that he can't attack you without cost. On the other hand, if you snap back, you may begin an intense verbal fight that will leave you emotionally drained. You may still feel like the loser at the end of it.

If there is a fight, *you aren't to blame for it.* You're responsible for everything you say and do, but you're not responsible for what the abuser says and does. Even so, try to avoid that unpleasant contact in the future. You can't always avoid a fight, but attacking the other person raises the odds that you'll have a fight.

Don't forget that you can't always know what the abuser will call an attack. When someone says you have attacked him, it may not be true. When someone acts as though you have attacked him, you might have done nothing offensive. An attack is an attempt to control the other. When I tell you what to do, call you names, or insult you, I am attempting to control you. If I respond to your attempt to control me by an attempt to control you, you may take that as an excuse to step up your attacks on me. If you are determined to control me, my attack on you is very recognizable. You'll muster more of your attack forces immediately.

Besides, if I attack back, I may set us up for a long-running contest to discover who can attack better. The goal in stopping verbal abuse is not to win an abusive exchange by hurting the other more than he hurts you. Your goal is to end hurtful exchanges so you don't have to deal with them another time. If I attack back, you may consider my behavior a challenge. You may decide to work harder at being negative to me to get me to stop punishing you.

One goal of self-defense is to teach the abuser that his attack behavior has a cost. However, punishing the other for an attack should be your last choice. You'd only attack to remove yourself from a difficult or dangerous situation. If you find yourself continually using attack behavior, something is wrong.

Your goal is not to become a better abuser. That's the way to create an ugly relationship. Don't call the abuser names, scream or yell, or threaten punishments you wouldn't carry out.

Don't hide his behavior from others

If the abuser attacks you in public, you're going to have to respond to him in public. The others present are witnesses and potential allies. Most people are going to feel negatively about his attacks on you. They're not going to think he's charming and appropriate. They're going to think he's a bully and you shouldn't take it. If your friends don't support you, you need a new bunch of friends.

Don't participate in an attack-defense-loop

This heading probably confuses you. Isn't this whole book about self-defense? I mean that if the abuser accuses you of doing something he doesn't like, don't respond by telling him "No, that isn't true," or "That isn't what happened." The abuser already knows it isn't true. He wants you to jump through hoops to defend yourself. He has gotten what he wants if you defend yourself by responding in those ways.

Consider this exchange:

He: Why is dinner late again?

She: I got off work late. The boss made me do another draft of that thing he's working on.

He: Yeah, right. Easy for you to say when I can't check up on you.

The problem with the conversation above is that the late dinner is only the *surface* issue. The subtext is his criticism of her for not having dinner ready at *his* convenience. He's willing to pretend he disbelieves her reason to criticize her again. If he accepted her defense that would imply that it is OK for her to have other priorities in her life besides him. So he renews his attack from another direction.

I call this pattern the *attack-defense loop*. Responding to a criticism with a verbal defense of your actions often prolongs the verbal battle.

But doesn't a good defense stop an attack? The short answer to this question is no, although most people don't realize this. Targets believe that if they defend themselves well, the other will stop the attack. They are baffled and despondent when they work up the courage to defend themselves and find they have entered a prolonged battle. They feel more like a loser than when they said nothing. Why is this so?

Remember the psychology of the abuser. The abuser wants to control you. He wants to get his way, or at least to punish you if you don't give in. Nan, the target in the example at the beginning of this chapter, had a good reason not to go fishing with Peter. Her reason didn't insult Peter. She didn't complain about Peter's behavior. Nan was asserting her right to control her time. Peter didn't disagree that Nan would need to lie to miss work. He knew that to keep her paycheck, she would have to arrange to do her work some other time. Nan made a good response that she thought Peter would accept. She expected Peter to withdraw the request graciously and continue to be pleasant toward her.

But Nan thought it was only a good defense if she got Peter's approval. Since he continued to disapprove of her, she gave in. The abuser wants to keep up the attack because he wants to control you, no matter what your defense is.

We already knew that Peter wasn't going to accept Nan's reason for not going. Peter didn't want to consider Nan's point of view. He wanted a companion and Nan's needs didn't matter to him.

That defines the attack-defense loop. The abuser has a history of attacking her and the target decides to stick up for herself. After she has worked up her courage, she responds to the next attack with a spirited defense of her point of view. She explains why she is right about the subject. Then the abuser launches a second and third attack against her. Her defense has only prolonged the attack rather than cutting it short.

In other words, a good defense may not lessen the attacks. Many targets conclude that there's no sense in defending themselves. That makes it worse. The target comes to believe the attacks will pass faster if she pretends to agree or says nothing.

The abuser is trying to control the target. He has more experience attacking than the target does. The attacker has fewer scruples about what he says to the target. The abuser has years of practice defining the needs, thoughts, feelings, and boundaries of other people. He punishes others for fun and profit. Abusers like the rewards that come from getting their way.

Peter wants Nan to go fishing but that is not abusive. Intentions, even intentions to control, are not abusive. However, Peter intends for Nan to go no matter what she wants. His pressure makes his actions abusive. When Nan politely declines the invitation, Peter proclaims that Nan is abusing him, that she doesn't love him anymore. Abusers often complain that the target is abusive or controlling. They say this because sometimes these statements convince targets to back off.

The abuser gets rewards from the target even if she responds defensively to the attack. The abuser set the subject for the conversation and the target acknowledged and responded to his subject. The abuser asks the target to jump through hoops. He pretends the target must convince the abuser of the target's point of view for the abuser to accept it. However the abuser will rarely agree with the target's point of view, no matter how well reasoned. Abusers enjoy making nasty comments and they enjoy the target's discomfort.

In addition, many abusers enjoy the repartee with the target. They consider the conversation an enjoyable contest or game in which they are trying to outwit the target. Since the talk is about faults of the target, abusers don't have as much of a personal stake as the target does. The conversation can present an intellectual challenge to the abuser. But targets find the conversation personally involving and emotionally upsetting.

Don't speak to an abuser who is drunk or high

Do I need to say this? Don't waste your time speaking to someone who is high or drunk because they will not learn anything. Avoid the person as much as possible and protect any children in the house.

If the abuser gets drunk or high regularly, you should first learn more by getting well-informed or professional help about the problem. You need to attend Al Anon, or Nar-Anon, or a self-help group for relatives of alcoholics or drug addicts. You can also go to a professional substance abuse counselor yourself to learn how to handle the abuser. Let the abuser know that you're going for help. That will make the point that you do believe he has an addiction. You aren't just saying he has an addiction to be abusive. You'll learn real skills at those meetings or in those counseling sessions: the skills to defend yourself and disengage from his substance abuse.

Don't worry about the question of whether or not the abuser is really an alcoholic because the abuser is going to deny it whether it is true or false. In any case, you don't need to make a diagnosis of alcoholism. You only have to decide whether you enjoy his company when he is drunk or high, and whether he is safe with you or the children.

If the abuser denies that he is drunk, hand him a glass bottle with a lid and ask him to pee in the cup. Then take the cup to the Emergency Room or a lab that does this work to see if he is over the legal limit.

If you love someone who is an alcoholic or drug addict, consider whether you love him enough to save his life. If he drives away drunk, you could save him and others on the road if you call the police and give them his car license number and his destination. If police arrest the abuser for a Driving While Intoxicated offense, let the state decide what to do with him. It may be the best phone call you ever make.

Don't deny the truth

Abusers sometimes accuse their targets of thinking or feeling something that is true, but they make the accusation sound so horrible that you are tempted to deny it. Don't give in to the temptation. Look at these two examples.

He: Don't just stand there with your mouth hanging open! You don't trust me, do you? You think I'm lying to you!

She: You're right, I don't trust you. And you wouldn't trust me either if I came home drunk in the middle of the night with my clothes hanging half off. I'm sleeping in the study. We can talk in the morning.

Or this:

He: I thought you'd love me forever, but you couldn't even keep up the pretense! You're out running around with other men every time my back is turned.

She: I'm not going to pretend I love you right now. Why should I love you when you treat me like that? I'm going to sleep on the couch. Don't bother me any more tonight.

Don't reassure the abuser about your positive feelings

Many abusers hurl accusations that you don't love them just to attack you. They're not feeling insecure; they just want you to jump through hoops. You shouldn't do it.

He: And you stopped loving me a long time ago!
She: You've been screaming at me for half an hour. I don't even like you right now.

Or this example:

He: If you loved me, you'd say yes!
She: Then if you loved me you'd say yes to me. Does that mean you don't love me, since you're not saying yes to me? You're trying to bully me now. You're not showing your love for me by giving in, why should I show my love for you by giving in?

It's your job in relationships to express your positive feelings to others as often as possible, whether they are adults or children. But timing is everything. Don't get into the habit of reassuring the abuser about your positive feelings when he behaves hatefully. Saying good things to him is a reward, and you shouldn't be rewarding him when he's abusing you.

Also, some abusers get negative about themselves to guilt you or trick you into saying something good about them. It's a real temptation to reassure them about your feelings at that moment, but if you reward them for being negative about themselves, you're paying them to say it again. Don't reward either adults or children for making negative comments about themselves. That's a bad habit in them you don't want to encourage.

Don't use a bomb threat

Targets placate and appease the abuser until they become enraged. Then the target may threaten the abuser with a bomb.

I use the term *bomb* to mean a threat of serious punishment used to stop the other's behavior. When you threaten to end the relationship, that's essentially a bomb threat. Using a big threat like that should theoretically stop aggression because you're saying that you can retaliate massively. A bomb threat tells the other that you are willing to leave.

"If you do that, I'll divorce you."
"If you do that, I'm moving out."
"If my boss does that again, I'll quit the job."

However, because a bomb is so destructive, nations don't use it except for *intolerable* aggression. That is also true of people. If she says "I'll divorce you if you don't take the garbage out now," you can be sure that if she leaves him, it wasn't just the garbage that caused the trouble.

If you constantly threaten to leave the abuser, but never do, the abuser won't believe you. When the target actually carries out her threat, for example by moving out of the house, seeing a lawyer or quitting the job, the abuser is incredulous. The target of the attacks hasn't laid the groundwork for the abuser to see the cause-and-effect relationship between his behavior and the target leaving him.

I often see this happen in marriages that go past the point of no return. She has been threatening to leave him for years, but she doesn't go. Those threats have no influence on him and he continues to abuse her. When she finally moves out, he is shocked. "Of course I knew she wanted me to change, but I didn't think she was serious!"

When she has threatened to end the relationship often, he doesn't pay attention to the threats and his abuse stays the same until she leaves. He doesn't believe she means what she says. He doesn't believe that it is *his* behavior that is the problem. The abuser believes the target has random outbreaks of nastiness. He's telling himself she must have premenstrual syndrome or she must be in a bad mood. He doesn't associate his negative behavior with the target's wish to leave the relationship.

When you threaten someone with a divorce, you aren't defending yourself. You are training the abuser to ignore you. In the aftermath of a bomb threat, the target doesn't trust the abuser to change and she's right. The abuser won't make serious changes because the target hasn't changed.

Threatening to leave doesn't change the other because it doesn't change you. It doesn't convince the abuser that you are going to leave him or that he should change his behavior to keep you. He sees the threat as a natural disaster like a hurricane. He thinks he may be able to predict a hurricane but he can't avoid it. He knows the hurricane isn't his fault. He expects that when the hurricane (the threat to leave him) is past, you will subside. He expects you will put up with anything again when the relationship returns to normal.

The abuser will do or say anything to get you back for a while. He thinks of your threat as random, because you have been random. He couldn't predict whether you would ignore his attack, try to placate him, or threaten him with a bomb. When you want someone to learn, you must act consistently. Unless you respond consistently to all or most instances of the behavior you don't like, the abuser isn't going to learn or change.

Don't abuse him by withdrawing

This book is planned to help people in relationships stop a verbal or emotional abuser from continuing with abuse. You haven't ended the abuse if you become an abuser yourself. It's possible to abuse someone by withdrawing from them just as it is possible to abuse someone by approaching them and calling them names.

It is abusive to withdraw from someone as a punishment when you don't get your way. Suppose you and your partner are having a pleasant exchange of opinions on a topic. Your partner doesn't agree with you and doesn't agree to do what you want. It's OK to postpone the conversation by mutual consent. But it is not OK to withdraw from the conversation and the relationship to punish the other for having a different opinion.

Here's an example of an *abusive* withdrawal from the conversation:

"You know I won't accept that schedule. I'm leaving until you give me what I want."

The following example is an *acceptable* withdrawal from the conversation:

"I've run out of time. I've got to go to work. Let's talk about this again. I hope we can think of a solution."

This is also an acceptable way to handle it:

"I'm fried. How about talking about this again, maybe on Tuesday night? In the meantime, I'm going to turn on a movie and forget it."

Don't just leave the conversation when the discussion is positive. Instead postpone it, propose a truce, or suggest another time to talk. Acknowledge that the situation isn't resolved yet, but let him know that you're feeling OK about it.

Don't leave a conversation because the other person is angry unless the other is abusing you. It's OK for you to be angry or angry with the other person. It's OK for the other person to be angry or angry with you. It's not OK for you to treat the other badly or for the other to treat you badly.

Here's an *appropriate* expression of anger:

"We aren't getting anywhere! Why can't we resolve this? I hate it when these arguments just drag on forever and we don't agree. And I can't think of a way out!"

The preceding example shows anger and frustration, but the speaker isn't blaming the partner.

The following quote also shows an *appropriate* expression of anger:

"I hate it when my parents come between us like this. Why can't they stay out of our lives? You'd think a thousand miles was far enough away for us to move, but no! They have to come here to interfere and get more attention! I wish I knew what to do about it!"

That example shows anger and blame, but the speaker isn't blaming the partner.

This quote shows *inappropriate* expression of anger:

"You stupid idiot! You know I'm right! Act like a wife, not like a baby!"

That example shows anger, blame and name-calling, all directed at the partner.

This quote also shows *inappropriate* expression of anger:

"Well, what do you expect? You're supposed to get along with my parents! It's not like they treat me so great either, but I suck it up! Stop being a princess! Call them up and make nice! They live a thousand miles away, for God's sake! You don't get to avoid my parents because they're lonely and crabby. You're pretty crabby yourself!"

The preceding example shows anger, blame directed at the partner, and other abuses like name-calling, mind reading, commands, and demands.

It's inappropriate to leave a conversation because you hate conflict and want to avoid it. You may not like conflict, but if you're an adult and you want to talk to other adults, it's your job to learn ways of dealing with conflict constructively. You don't have to like conflict, but if you avoid it all the time, you won't get your way much and that will be your own fault. If you get knots in your stomach or a headache when you think about disagreeing with your significant other, it's time for you to learn to cope with that.

This quote shows an *inappropriate* avoidance of discussion:

"Wait! Stop! I don't need to hear this! I know you're going to get mad like you did the last time. I can't stand it when you get mad! You've got an anger problem! I'm leaving and you should get into therapy!"

He may have gotten mad the last time but if he can talk without abusing you, you need to discuss the matter. You want him to talk to you about your differences without treating you badly, not avoid all discussions because he sometimes gets angry.

This quote shows an *inappropriate* avoidance of discussion:

"Stop! I know you want to change the schedule but I don't! Things are going just fine now and there's no reason to talk about it. I'm leaving if you bring that up again."

The speaker may think things are going fine but the speaker's partner doesn't. Avoiding a discussion when you're getting your way and your partner isn't doesn't make the process of resolving differences any easier. What if the partner unilaterally changed the schedule and began following a schedule he liked without your permission or agreement? If you can just refuse to discuss something, so can he.

This quote shows an *appropriate* avoidance of discussion:

"Look, we've been over this six times! If you don't have anything new to add to the discussion, I'm not willing to put any more time into it. We have an agreement to do it this way, and I've done my part. You're just trying to get out of your part of the bargain! I'm not willing to listen to you tell me over and over again that you're not happy with your part of the bargain now that I've given you what you wanted. Do you have anything else to say about it? If not, I won't discuss it with you. And if you keep trying to get me to listen to you again, I'll leave the room."

Demanding to discuss something repeatedly is verbal abuse if the person bringing the issue up brings nothing new to the table. Don't berate your partner. If you say it once, it's a legitimate expression of feelings or wants. If you say it over and over, it's an attempt to punish him into giving up.

This quote shows an *appropriate* avoidance of discussion:

"You know we don't agree about my mother. Why do you care whether we agree about her anyway? I don't impose her on you and I don't complain about her to you. I don't need to hear your opinion about her over and over again when I'm not asking you to like her or do anything with her. It's my business what I do with my time when I'm not with you anyway. And if you're going to keep harping on her now, I'm out of here."

Some partners won't agree to disagree about issues that don't interfere with the relationship. Conflict is unnecessary when you don't need to have an agreement. You shouldn't need to defend your mother every time your partner wants to badmouth her. And you don't need to listen while your partner attacks any of your opinions he/she disagrees with. Most disagreements between two people don't need to be resolved by coming to an agreement about them. You can agree to disagree.

If he's giving you the silent treatment, don't approach him

You'll be upset and nervous if the other says nothing to you for days or weeks. In fact, you'll feel abandoned. But trying to tempt him or guilt him into talking gives him the wrong message. You're telling him that *his* company and attention are invaluable and that you cannot do without them. If he is a verbal abuser and he cuts you off with the silent treatment, consider yourself lucky and go on with your life silently.

However, if he chooses not to speak to you, don't continue doing your usual chores for him. Don't bother cooking him dinner. Don't bother wishing him good night. Don't bother doing any personal services for him, like doing his laundry or putting gas in his truck. If he can't interact with you like an adult even when he's mad at you, you don't need to do whatever duties would usually fall to you.

This means, also, that you shouldn't bother telling him where or when you are going when you go out, or when you'll be back. You shouldn't bother to make plans with him for the future, or include him in your plans. And you shouldn't hang around him. Make plans with outside friends and family and avoid him in person as much as he is avoiding talking to you.

Abusers who give you the silent treatment figure that when they are done with their pout, you will be ready to resume the relationship. They think you'll be grateful for a resumption of pleasantries and you'll be eager to forget the time while he wasn't speaking to you. If it's been a short pout, maybe that's your best choice. But if it's been days since he spoke, you don't have to resume communication just because he wants to.

When the abuser is ready to talk to you again, feel free to say "I'm not ready to talk to you yet. You'll just have to wait until *I'm* ready now!" Set yourself a date or a deadline before you include him in your life again. If he cut you out of his life for 24 hours maybe you want to cut him out of your life for an additional 24 hours. Or maybe you want to exclude him for 48 hours once he's ready to resume.

You can't make him interact pleasantly with you, so you shouldn't try. But he can't make you interact pleasantly with him, either. If giving him tit-for-tat seems childish to you, remember that sulking and cutting you off is a very childish attempt to get his way. It's like kids who say "I'm going to hold my breath until I turn blue."

Giving him a time-out from you will bother him a great deal more if you are ordinarily positive and loving. And that's a good reason to be positive and loving to your partner.

Getting the abuser into therapy may not be your best solution.

In an ideal world, you would demand that your partner go to therapy, but this isn't the ideal world so you should consider this issue carefully. Not all therapy is created equal. You can't find a counselor in the phone book and send your partner to her or him with the confidence that this counselor will be helpful, either to your partner or to you. Here's why.

Most counselors, therapists, psychologists, psychiatrists and social workers have *no* training that is helpful in teaching verbal and emotional abusers how and why to stop their behavior. Most verbal and emotional abusers don't try their tricks in public, so they frequently won't show their abusive side to a counselor.

Nearly all counselors, of whatever stripe, are only comfortable working with people who volunteer to get counseling. People who want to make personal changes are motivated to continue counseling because they are personally uncomfortable with how their world is working. But verbal and emotional abusers *like* the results of their behavior. They like the submissiveness in their partners and the control the abuse grants them, so they are usually not motivated to change. Therefore the abuser's goals will be on a collision course with the counselor's experience and training.

If an abuser chooses to go into individual therapy with a good counselor and chooses to share information and work on his abusiveness, the abuser will probably change. But that calls for a lot of choosing. People getting individual therapy work on what *they* choose to work on. They only persist if they see benefits for themselves.

If the abuser sees a counselor to please his partner, he's going to talk about what bothers him. That's not likely to include his behavior toward his partner. It's far more likely he will see the therapist once or twice then tell his partner the therapy isn't doing him any good, so he's going to quit. Sending an abuser to individual therapy doesn't usually eliminate the abuse.

In an ideal world, marriage counseling would train people out of verbal and emotional abuse, but often it is not helpful. Not every individual counselor is good at marriage counseling and many of them don't realize it is not their strength.

If the target has a therapist who is willing to see the couple, that may not be a good solution either. The therapist may not be able, or willing, to make a good alliance with the abuser. If the therapist is clearly aligned with the target, the abuser will recognize that the partner and therapist are ganging up on him and he will refuse to continue.

Most counselors are very nice people and they are often poor at confronting strong personalities and verbally aggressive clients. They may prefer to tell the target to get a divorce because the counselor can't manage the abuser. The counselor may bandage the relationship and end the therapy rather than struggle with the abuser herself.

Some therapists (like Bill and Janna's previous counselor) will confront the abuser and instruct him to stop the abuse. She may think that her authority will stop the abusive behavior but that's not likely. When the therapist plays the heavy, abusers don't change. Remember that Bill continued the therapy with the previous counselor because Janna said that was what was keeping her in the relationship. He wasn't motivated to change himself, only to keep Janna, and one hour a week seemed a small price for him to pay. It's the target who has to learn skills to manage the abuser successfully.

Some targets decide that anger management classes or counseling for anger management will help, but they are usually wrong. Abusers may have bad tempers, but if they are not verbally and emotionally abusing their bosses or coworkers, the problem is not the anger. Abusers don't abuse their bosses because their bosses would fire them. Abusers abuse their partners because the abuse makes them the boss and their partners don't fire them.

An abuser's angry words and emotional abuse don't come from the abuser's anger. Abusers abuse others because they can. They abuse others because they want control. They continue the abuse because targets allow them to gain and keep control. An anger management class can be good personal therapy for abusers. It teaches them how to relax and how to notice triggers for their anger. But it often doesn't motivate abusers to stop the abuse.

Domestic abuse therapy, or domestic violence therapy, *is* a good treatment for verbal and emotional abusers. Most domestic violence offenders are court-ordered into treatment; the offenders don't wish to be there. The therapists in those classes often have special training to work with perpetrators of abuse. Counselors who treat perpetrators are skilled at working with the control issues that are the basis of verbal and emotional abuse, just as they are the basis of domestic violence.

If you can exert pressure on the abuser to go to treatment, a domestic abuse group would be the most suitable treatment and the most likely to result in significant change in his verbal and emotional abuse.

Summary

In this chapter, I've listed some defenses that don't work and I've described why:

- Ignoring an attack rewards it because the abuser has the company and attention of the target and his own good feelings about being on top.

- Begging and pleading won't help because the abuser wants the rewards he's getting. Hearing that he is hurting you just tells him how successful he is.

- If the attack comes in public, responding to him in public works best. You'll find allies if you do.

- Don't defend yourself by responding to the subject the abuser brought up. That's just jumping through his hoops.

- If he accuses you of something that's true, feel free to admit it.

- Don't approach an abuser who is giving you the silent treatment. Instead, stop actively participating in the relationship. Give him your own silent treatment after he wants to resume the relationship.

- Attacking the abuser doesn't change the pattern. You want to stop the abuse, not get better at attacking the abuser.

- You can't delegate your job of stopping the abuser to a therapist or anyone else. You're the one who needs to change.

- If the abuser is drunk or high, postpone any conversation until later.

- Don't tell the abuser you love him if he's just treated you badly. And don't tell him you love him if he's pitying himself and angling for praise. Don't reward people for acting badly.

- Don't threaten to leave the relationship unless you plan to do it in the next week. Anything else trains him to pay no attention to your threats.

- Abuse is an ineffective defense against abuse. It may distract the abuser, but it won't lower the level of abuse.

If you're responding to the abuse in these ineffective ways, keep reading to learn what to do instead. Stay focused on the issue of rewards and punishments. You're going to learn how to reward the abuser and how to withdraw those rewards to train him.

CHAPTER 8

Effective Verbal Self-Defense

In this section, we'll be talking in more detail about what *does* work to end abuse. You'll learn the beliefs and the responses to change the conversation.

Don't think about the problem, think about the solution.

When you worry about a conversation with an abuser and go over all the ways it has gone wrong, you are thinking about the problem. That causes depression and paralysis. That's the exact set of circumstances you want to avoid:

"He said this, so I felt bad. Another time he said this and I felt bad again".

"He could say this, and I would feel bad, or he could say this, and I would feel worse"

No! No! No! Stop thinking this way. Don't think only about the verbal attacks he made and your bad feelings, or the verbal attacks he *could* make and more of your bad feelings. That's a way of hurting yourself further by repeating his punishment of you.

When you only think about the verbal abuse to repeat what happened and re-experience your feelings, it feels bad so you put the thoughts away and try to avoid or deny them. Nobody likes punishment. Rehearsing these negative thoughts freezes you into immobility and depression, or it increases your negative emotions, such as sadness, anger, and embarrassment. There's no good purpose for that.

But you need to think enough about the past to plan your future. You also need to think about possible results from your responses.

You need to convert your thoughts into an action plan. Every time you remember a past episode or worry about a future one, follow up the thought with a plan for what you will do in the future. Here are some thinking patterns to rehearse:

"He said this and I felt bad. Next time he says that, I plan to respond with _____, or _____."

"Next time, I could say _____. Or I could say_____ and do _____."

In other words, do not pile up examples of what he has said and done in the past. As soon as you think of *one* example of what he said or did, acknowledge your emotional reaction. Then consider what you *could* say or do in the future to make a difference. Don't stop thinking about the future when you think of one possible response. Keep thinking about that example until you come up with several useful responses to use.

You are trying to *learn* these helpful reactions, so you may want to write out your possible responses, and to reread them during the day. You want to feel competent and powerful and you'll feel that way when you think about your choices in advance. Your goal is to recall and use the responses that you compose when you are thinking about the past. And plan to do it again when you think about the future:

Never go on thinking of a second example of what the abuser *could* do until you've picked out some responses that you wish to use for the first example you thought of. Piling up examples of bad things he says causes paralysis and avoidance. Convert your thoughts from "he said this and I felt bad" to "he said this and I plan to respond in this way when he does it again."

You *should* think about what the abuser said in the past and you *should* recognize your emotions. Keep going. When you're planning to change, plan your responses. Your emotional reaction when you expect a confrontation can put you at a disadvantage. It's better to *acknowledge* unpleasant emotions and then plan to avoid the negative possibilities. Calmly anticipate what the abuser thinks and what the abuser may do.

When you can predict a certain statement, you can plan your response to it. As you plan your response, you can rehearse and remember your plan. As you rehearse, you can refine and improve your skills. Your calm rehearsals at low-stress times will give you a sense of your power.

In other words, don't use your time and energy thinking about what the abuser did, does or will do (the problem). Spend your time planning your own statements in response and review your own alternatives (the solution.) Create your plan and rehearse it!

When I'm coaching a target on how to respond to abuse, I will often give an example of an effective response. Then I ask "What will he say then?" Usually the target can give two or three different examples of attacks the abuser commonly uses. Then I give another sample response to the abuser's typical statements. But often when I ask "What will he say then?" the target will say "I have no idea. I've never said anything like that before."

You don't want to memorize effective statements that I or your therapist make up. But you do want to learn new beliefs and new behaviors. Your statements will be more effective than mine because you will be using your own words. When you find responses that are comfortable for you, they are likely to stick in your mind. Aim to keep control of yourself, not to take control of the abuser.

Address the process of the discussion

Stop addressing the content of the conversation, and start addressing the process. For example,

"Dick, this conversation has gotten ugly because of your name-calling. I'm not going to keep talking to you now unless you stop calling me names."

Name the behavior you don't like, the behavior you think is abusive.

"Dick, I'm tired of you yelling at me."

Don't let the abuser change the subject to your faults or to the subject he previously introduced. You just continue to talk about your subject, namely his negative communication. Insist that you two discuss your agenda item next.

"Dick, you're not helping matters by calling me names. If you won't agree to some rules about your language, this conversation is over."

Hold the abuser accountable for his behavior:

He wants to discuss your faults and be abusive. Don't continue along those lines. Hold him accountable for what he just did. Blame the abuser for the actions or words he just used.

"If you want to talk to me, stop calling me names. Maybe I did something you didn't like, but I didn't make you call me names. You're to blame for what you said, not me."

"I can't stop you from calling me names, but you can't make me talk to you if you continue. I don't let the kids treat me that way, and I've stopped letting you treat me that way either. If you call me a name, that's the end of the conversation."

For the abuser to learn, he has to hear what specific behavior of his (yelling, calling names) you want to end. And you need to specify that he is accountable for that behavior, not you. You can't make him talk the way you like, but he can't make you hang around to hear it.

"If I controlled your behavior, you wouldn't be talking that way. It's a bunch of garbage to say it's my fault. You have plenty of choices of what to say when you're mad at me. You don't have to call me names."

"You don't call your boss names when you're mad at him, so I know you're not losing it with me either. You're responsible for your own behavior, and you *decide* what to say every time. And I can decide whether to listen or not."

You're going to remain in your own control and you're going to do what you *can* do without his permission or approval. The abuser needs to know that when he verbally abuses you, you withdraw from him rather than continuing the abusive conversation.

Most targets are not trying to achieve a hard-won victory in a verbal abuse battle. They're not looking for the skills to do a better job of verbal abuse than the abuser. They're looking for ways to end the battle, not win it. If my response to a pattern of verbal abuse (my defense of myself) results in prolonging the battle, I need to exit. If I allow the abuser to continue while I am an audience and participant, I may be tempted to retreat and ignore his comments.

The goal of the abuser is control of the target. The goal of the target should be self-control and avoiding further abuse. You must keep his attack from increasing his control over you. If he doesn't get control of you, he's less likely to abuse you in the future. So stay in control of yourself and point that out to him. You take away his victory by keeping yourself in your own control.

A verbal defense that denies what the abuser is saying is not likely to succeed. Look at these examples:

Abuser: You're ugly and your mamma dresses you funny.
Target: Does not! You dress funnier than I do!
Abuser: Weirdo! Weirdo!

Abuser: Can't you even make change, for God's sake? If this is what you got back from the clerk, he cheated you again. I don't kill myself earning it for you to give it away!
Target: Count it again, you jerk! You never even passed algebra!
Abuser: Oh yeah, you bitch! I suppose that's the reason I bring home twice what you do! It goes to show how worthless your two extra years in school are!

If I didn't label these little scripts and tell you who the abuser is, you'd have trouble seeing any difference between the abuser and the target. Many people defend themselves only by attacking the other person.

The abuser is more likely to continue the battle if you attack him. But even a spirited self-defense that addresses the issues raised by the abuser can make it more likely that an attack will continue instead of stop. Look at these examples instead:

Attacker: You're ugly and your mamma dresses you funny.
Target: I see you don't want any favors from me.
Attacker: What?
Target: If you want anything from me anytime soon, you'd better watch your mouth.

Above, the target tells the abuser she can take away rewards the abuser wants in the future.

> Attacker: Can't you even make change, for God's sake? If this is what you got back from the clerk, he cheated you again. I don't kill myself earning it for you to give it away!
>
> Target: Do you want something? It was hard to tell in the middle of all that anger.
>
> Attacker: Of course I want something! I want to know what happened to the rest of the change!
>
> Target: I'll give you the receipt to go with the change if you ask for it nicely. And I'll even answer that question about the change if you ask nicely.

Here the target ignores the abuse, and gets the abuser to focus on his goal ("Do you want something?") That makes the conversation more pleasant.

The target doesn't deny the charges of the abuser in either of the examples above. She doesn't accuse the abuser of other sins. Instead, the target reminds the abuser that she has the power to give or deny rewards the abuser wants. She links her willingness to give him rewards to the way the abuser treats her.

Remember this formula for your words: name, blame, explain.

Don't defend yourself; ask the abuser to defend his attack.

> Abuser: You're ugly and your mamma dresses you funny.
>
> Target: What makes you think you can call me names?

> Abuser: Can't you even make change, for God's sake! If this is what you got back from the clerk, he cheated you again. I don't kill myself earning it for you to give it away!
>
> Target: I know you're upset, but that's no excuse for taking it out on me. Maybe some people take it, but I don't anymore.

Consider using one of the following strategies to end an attack with the least cost:

- Remind the abuser of rewards in your control. Point out that the abuser can't get them without your consent.

As we'll see in the next section, the biggest reward you have to offer the abuser is your own time, attention, and approval.

- Comment negatively on the abuser's behavior, and refocus on what the abuser wants. Or talk about what you want out of the conversation.

Comment on the tone of the conversation. Don't talk about the subject the abuser brings up. Instead of saying anything about the clothes you bought, or the money you spent, give your opinion about the abuser's emotions or the way the conversation is going.

Remind the abuser of rewards in your control

Point out that the abuser can't get them without your consent.

"Were you hoping I was going to pay attention to you this evening after you said all that? I don't plan to have anything to do with you."

"Did you think I was going to cook you dinner and spend a nice evening with you? Not after what you just said."

"So you call me names instead of doing what I want? I don't need your permission. I'm packing the kids up and I'll see you when we get back."

In other words, don't plan on getting the abuser's approval or services for a while. Find other ways to run your life. If you're doing all the work and he's content with that, what do you need him for? If your company and attention aren't worth anything to him, then you've discovered that he is not willing to contribute anything positive to your life.

Comment negatively on the abuser's behavior, and refocus on his goals.

"So, you're willing to call me names to get your way about the workbench. What's your long-range goal? Did you think that if you call me names in the short-term, I'd stay with you in the long-term?"

"You think that yelling at me is going to help you get your way? I can't stop you from buying that workbench, but you can't stop me from buying what I want either. If we can't agree about how to spend our money, then I'm going to have my check deposited into a separate account. Then I'll make my own decisions about how to spend it. You don't have my approval to spend that money, and if you do spend it that way, you're not going to like the results."

"You're acting like I can't add. If you got your way over my objections yesterday, and you get your way over my objections today, do you think I want to be married to you tomorrow? You're not giving me any reasons to want you around in the future. If I can't get along with you, we don't have a future as a couple."

Comment on the process of the conversation

"This is a really unpleasant conversation. I'm not hanging around to hear any more."

"If you want a response from me, you can start by apologizing for what you just said. After that I'll consider answering your question."

"That's bad manners. I'm not OK with what you said. Start over and don't include all that yelling and nasty language. Or I'm going on with my day without you."

"I'm keeping track now, and at the third curse word, I'm leaving this conversation. That's one."

Don't threaten the abuser with actions you won't carry out. If you're willing to stay and hear more abuse, don't say that you'll leave. If you aren't willing to deposit your check in a separate account, don't say you will.

What the target is saying in each of the examples above is that she is willing to act without the abuser's approval. You're not demanding that he change his ways. You're telling him what you will do if he doesn't change his ways. You're describing consequences that are in your control (leaving the conversation, depositing your check in a separate account).

You're not demanding that he change, which would be laughable. You're telling him that you've changed and you're no longer dependent on his approval. You have control of yourself and you're keeping it. You can act in ways he won't like but can't prevent.

Remember not to increase negative intimacy

Old-fashioned parents depended heavily on punishment, often physical punishment, to teach a child what the parent believed was good behavior. Verbal abuse is a natural extension of that way of raising a child. Old-fashioned parents believed that children were naturally evil. They thought that parents must beat the devil out of them, literally, to teach them good behavior.

In that theory of child rearing, if you begin beating children when they are young, they fear doing wrong. They become moral adults who follow the right path. And some of these children did emerge with high moral standards, but a great many considered the beatings abuse and wanted nothing more to do with their parents when they grew up. Other children raised in homes with that philosophy grow up violent, angry, and very troubled. Raising children with harsh punishment leaves them angry, not moral.

Modern parents give a young child a time-out rather than a beating. A time-out, as psychologists define it, is not a punishment. It is a time away from the rewards naturally occurring in the child's environment. Those rewards include the freedom to choose activities, the ability to move around, and the positive attention of the parent. A time-out takes the rewards away from the child but isn't a punishment.

A time-out makes a relationship temporarily more distant. A beating is a punishment, but it can increase closeness.

Rena has a friend, Patsy, who is often verbally abusive to her. Patsy breaks promises to Rena. For example, she won't show up for lunch when she has arranged that with Rena. When Rena complains that she was waiting for Patsy, Patsy tries to blame Rena. Patsy will say that Rena got the time wrong, or ask what kind of friend would try to make her feel guilty. Rena usually says nothing after Patsy dismisses her feelings, and she usually lets Patsy change the subject.

After Rena began to work on defending herself, she came up with a new script. She is willing to drop the relationship if this does not work.

Rena: Patsy, we had a date for lunch yesterday, and I waited in the restaurant for a half hour for you. I was very upset when you didn't come.

Patsy: Oh, come on! It's your fault. The date wasn't until next week. I don't appreciate you bringing it up.

Rena: Now I'm upset about two things. I'm still upset about you not keeping our lunch appointment. And I'm upset about the way you just put me down. I don't like you treating me that way.

Patsy: I don't know why you're making such a big deal about it anyway.

Rena: I don't like you treating me that way, so I'm going to solve the problem myself. I'm not going to make any more dates with you for the future. If you want to do something with me, we can decide when we're already together and do something right then. And I don't want to hear any more of your put-downs. If you don't agree with me, I guess I don't want you for a close friend any more.

When you're an adult, no one can punish you with words unless you decide to listen to the words. As a child, Rena had to stand (or sit) still for whatever punishment her parents gave her but as an adult she does not have to accept verbal punishments from her friends.

If Patsy wants a close friendship with Rena, she can get that by working out the misunderstandings and settling the disputes that arise between them. But Rena doesn't want to be as close as Patsy does. Being close to Patsy hurts. Rena doesn't want to continue the relationship with her. If Rena wanted a closer relationship with Patsy, Rena could try to explain herself or try to agree with Patsy about how Patsy will behave.

Rena wants something different out of the relationship than Patsy does. Rena wants a positive relationship more than she wants a close one. Therefore she is willing to withdraw until she gets to a safer distance from Patsy.

Here are some responses Rena could use if she has decided to distance Patsy without any discussion.

Rena: Hi Patsy, it's me.

Patsy: Oh, wonderful! If you're home already, we can leave now.

Rena: Wait a minute, Patsy. I just got your message asking me to go along. You're asking at the last minute and I have other plans. Thanks for thinking of me. I hope you have a good time.

Patsy: Uh…other plans?

Rena: Sure enough. Nice to hear from you. Bye.

Rena has withdrawn from Patsy, providing a polite but vague response. Rena does not offer to share with Patsy what Rena's afternoon plans are. Rena has defended herself simply by declaring her right to privacy, and she has exited a potentially explosive conversation cheerfully and rapidly. As a result, the friendship between Rena and Patsy will become more superficial and more distant. But the relationship will be more positive. Rena limits how close she gets to Patsy so she can feel more positive about Patsy.

Rena doesn't have to talk with Patsy about Rena's afternoon activities. Patsy cannot force Rena to say what her plans are. And Patsy cannot force Rena to stay on the phone if Rena chooses to hang up.

The abuser counts on the target's willingness to stay close to him, no matter how negative the relationship gets. But unless the target stays close to the abuser, the abuser cannot punish her. The abuser can't attack you verbally if you are far away or paying no attention to the abuser.

Targets often desperately want closeness to the abuser. They try to solve disagreements by talking out the problems. But the more they approach the abuser, the more verbal punishment the abuser gives them. To get a more positive relationship with an abuser, you need to withdraw from him. You need to withdraw closeness, just as parents give their children timeouts.

Abusers want closeness to the target, and verbal abuse gives it to them. When the target leaves the abusive conversation, she creates a more distant but more positive relationship. Her withdrawal denies the abuser the rewards of closeness, including her attention and her presence as an audience.

Joe, I'm leaving this discussion. I hate it when you interrupt and criticize me when I'm trying to talk about our finances. I'm going to Sue's house, or maybe Toni's if Sue's not home. I'll be home by 10:30, but I'm done talking to you for the night. We can talk about this again tomorrow, after work, if you agree to mind your manners while we talk. If we can't agree about the finances, then I'll make up my own mind about what I need to do. Then I'll do that, whatever it is, whether you agree or not.

Consider the tactics that the target used in that example. That is a script that you can use under many different circumstances. Here's the outline:

> "I'm leaving this discussion."
> "I hate it when you (interrupt and criticize me when I'm trying to talk) So I won't keep talking to you."
> "I'm going _____ (where)"
> "I'll be home by _____ (time)"
> "But I still won't talk about this. I'm done talking to you for _____ (period of time)."
> "We can talk about this again _____ (when) but only if you agree not to (make abusive comments)."
> "If we can't agree then I'll make up my own mind about what I need to do. I'll do that, whatever it is, whether you agree or not."

You don't need to control others to get your way if what you want is in your own power. In that case, the worst that will occur is the abuser will disapprove of you. That need not be costly because you don't have to listen to the abuser's comments. You can act without the abuser's permission.

Change the subject

You have not completed your response to verbal abuse until you have changed the subject. You don't want the abuser to continue to harass you about whatever was on his mind. If you make a good response, one that stops the abuse, he's still going to try to address the same subject. He picked the subject, so it's probably negative about you. Change the tone of the conversation by picking a new subject for the conversation.

The abuser is not going to change the subject because he was using that subject to be abusive. You don't want a debate about your response. If you want to continue the conversation and not take a time-out, keep talking on a subject of your choice.

"No, I'm not going to do that for you after the way you just demanded it. And there's no sense continuing to talk about it. What *did* happen at the shop today?"

"No, I won't. I'd love to hear what happened to your boss after Jim turned him in yesterday."

It takes two speakers to consent to the subject of a conversation. If the abuser wants to discuss your faults, you can respond on another subject, for example the subject of the abuser's bad verbal behavior.

If the abuser says "We're going to talk about this now, dammit!" that is still only a *proposal*. The abuser can act as though the subject of the conversation is in his control, but that is a bluff. He can't single-handedly carry on a conversation or force you to respond to his choice of subject.

If the abuser makes offensive comments, you have a choice of responses. If you stay on the subject that he brings up (for example, your faults) you're liable to encourage him to attack you further. Consider changing the subject of the conversation to one of these:

♦ The goals of the conversation
♦ The rewards and punishments in your relationship
♦ His bad conversational manners.

With these strategies, you are more likely to avoid another verbal attack.

Refuse topics of conversation you don't like

Conversation, like sex, should occur only with consent. If the abuser brings up something you don't want to talk about, like your faults, feel free to bring up a topic of your own:

"Sounds like you're trying to pick a fight! What's the matter, bad day?"

"I'm not going to keep repeating myself. My past sex life isn't up for discussion. Do you want to talk about our current sex life? Or lack of it?"

"You're drunk and I'm not speaking to you until you're sober. If you keep taunting me, I'm going to a motel for the night. So simmer down or I'm out of here."

Refuse complaint, accept protest

If the abuser wants to tell you how wrong you were in the past (complaint) feel free to redirect him to current and future decisions (protest).

"I don't want to hear about that. That was two years ago. If you're thinking about your mother's next visit, feel free to propose a different solution for that."

"I can't change the past and I don't feel guilty about it. What exactly did you want me to do about it now?"

"You've done lots of stuff I didn't like. Why are you bringing that up now? If you want me really mad at you, keep going."

If the abuser wants to problem-solve, feel free to say yes, if the time is convenient. But set your rules for the conversation (your boundaries) ahead of time.

"Sure we can talk about the budget, but I have conditions. You'll make a proposal of what you want and I'll make a proposal of what I want. The minute you call me names or start yelling at me, I leave the conversation and I keep doing the checkbook exactly as I please."

"I'm glad you mentioned your mother's visit. Let's talk about it, but only if you don't interrupt me or tell me how it's going to be. You can propose a solution, but so can I. And I expect you to be respectful to me, or I'm out of the conversation."

Rapid takeover

Nobody reacts as fast as someone who has planned how to react. If the abuser demands an answer *now,* that doesn't make it urgent. You don't need to accept his deadlines or work to his time schedule.

"You may want an answer now, but I don't have one yet. You'll have to wait until I've thought about it."

"Just because you're in a hurry doesn't mean I have to be. I don't have to decide that until next month, and I probably won't."

If I can reasonably foresee what you will think or feel or do, I can prepare for it. I can rehearse what I plan to say in response to you. That leaves me ready to defend myself, because I'll have better aim. I need to *use* my weapons to be familiar with their range. When I avoid thinking about the future, I leave myself at the mercy of others who may not mean well toward me.

Watch your boundaries

Stay alert! Look for skirmishes at the edges of your territory. They warn you about possible future invasions. Checking and surveying others' behavior is a daily task that you cannot assign to anyone else.

Expect the abuser to be persistent. He figures you're going to give up if he repeats himself. A single act of good self-defense is a good beginning but you must follow up with persistent monitoring, and consistent responses to abuse.

Reward small steps

If you try to control the other with punishments, you create a bad relationship. If you try to control the other with rewards, you create a good relationship.

Don't spare the positive comments, attention and encouragement when the abuser behaves more pleasantly. You can't wait until he has perfect behavior before you notice and praise his efforts. The abuser won't continue new behaviors unless they work. The abuser has to achieve his goals with the new (nonabusive) behavior to keep the behavior in his repertoire. If he wants your attention and he asks for it in a positive way, let him know that you noticed and that you appreciate it.

The abuser needs to notice that you are no longer in his control when he verbally abuses you. In turn, you need to notice when he compliments you or gives you what you want. You have to be positive to him if you want him to behave a certain way. If he thinks you don't notice or that it makes no real difference to you, why should he continue doing it? It's unfamiliar to him and he never thought he should have to do it to get what he wants. You have to show him it matters.

Don't wait until he's behaving perfectly. Praise small steps along the way. Persuasion works better than force to cause change.

Be consistent in your responses

Figure out what kind of verbal attacks you want to tackle first then plan your responses. When the abuser attacks you you'll need to give your planned response over and over without fail.

Why won't the abuser learn the first time? You've undoubtedly made good responses to the abuser's attacks many times in the past. But if you haven't been consistent in responding, he can afford to outwait you. He doesn't think you've changed until you've stopped giving him ineffective responses. He just thinks you've become more random so he won't always get his way. He thinks that if he persists (and he specializes in persisting) then you'll give in and come back into his control.

To end his behavior you have to prove that he is wrong in this thinking. You have to make a permanent change in yourself to make a permanent change in him. You won't teach him that he has permanently lost control of you unless you are permanently in control of yourself.

You're more effective if you respond rapidly

The faster you can make an effective response, the easier it will be for the abuser to learn. If your response always comes the next day, he'll have trouble seeing the connection between his behavior and your response. You want him to know that when he does *this*, you do *that*, and he does not get his way. You want him to think ahead *before* he does the abusive behavior, not just get mad at you because you are disobeying him.

I'm not saying that one ineffective response or one delay in responding is going to ruin two months of effective behavior on your part. I *am* saying that you need to make your responses as automatic and as rapid as you can. You need to practice being effective to achieve the results you want. He isn't going to change if you are incredibly effective once. He's not going to change immediately just so you don't have to change.

Rehearse your responses in advance

Nan (from Chapter 9) made a mistake in not rehearsing her responses before Peter came home. She expected that Peter would not accept her going back to work. She knew he would protest when she turned him down.

Nan knew that she was going to have a difficult conversation with Peter. She had many physical symptoms of emotional stress, symptoms such as stomach jitteriness and tightness in the jaw. Nan was afraid that she would go along with Peter, so she moved quickly to get the conversation over with. She expected a bad reaction from Peter (which was realistic), but she did not plan responses that would get her out of going fishing yet keep as much of his approval as possible.

Nan's responses resulted in Peter's disapproval, and her own emotional upset. She didn't manage to extract herself gracefully from going with him. She didn't plan ahead, and rehearse her strategies, taking into account what he would probably say.

Many people, especially many women, have a strong emotional reaction when they believe that they are about to encounter conflict, so they neglect to plan how to reduce or avoid the conflict. They recognize that they will be uncomfortable during the conversation, but they try to overcome their fear by giving a rapid response. They haven't planned or rehearsed, they just wished things would go their way. No matter how often their wishes are disappointed, many targets continue to *wish ahead* instead of making a more realistic prediction. It's as though they're saying, "When I fall asleep at night, it's an enchanted sleep. All the property markers and surveys disappear. I don't need to figure out what others will say or do. They are unpredictable."

This naiveté is damaging. If someone has behaved in a certain way in the past, you should expect that he or she will do so again, unless you have a concrete reason to predict a change in behavior.

Remember that behavior is most easily predicted from knowing history and from knowing incentives, not from knowing what someone *should* do. If someone has been angry with you in the past when you said no, you should anticipate that she'll be angry when you say no this time. If you can predict a danger, then you can rehearse a way to cope with the danger.

Give up the all-or-nothing thinking

Some targets believe that the abuser must change overnight, or their own efforts aren't working. They believe that only a radical difference in the abuser's behavior, from one day to the next, will mean that they should continue working on it. In effect, they say "I'm only giving this a day or two to work. It's too much trouble to change what *I* need to change, so I need to see results right away. If not, I'll go back to ignoring the verbal abuse."

If you are impatient, the abuser only needs to outwait you. The abuser believes that you will shortly come back into his control. The abuser thinks that normal for a target is staying in his control.

Belief that abusers will change overnight is really all-or-nothing thinking. Do you think that *any* verbal abuse is as bad as a lot of verbal abuse? If the abuser improves a little, do you feel that it's not good enough, so it's OK for you to fall back into your old behavior patterns?

Changing the abuser may take a while, not because the abuser won't change overnight, but because *you* won't change overnight. Your old scripts tell you to ignore verbal abuse, or to cry or scream at the abuser, and then give him his way. You'll need to be uncomfortably aware of everything you say and do when dealing with the abuser for a long time while you are learning to respond rapidly, consistently, and effectively.

You're not going to perfect your new habits overnight, and he is not going to be changing his behavior on purpose, or because he needs to, overnight. He's still got habits and scripts that he has to overcome, and he doesn't have your motivation for changing. Hopefully the abuser wants to be with you, even if you change. He's got to go through an uncomfortable period too, and he won't like it.

A specific example: extreme jealousy

Here are some examples of effective defenses to deal with extreme jealousy.

◆ Copy the form *Your Jealous Comments* from Appendix I. Date the form and put it on the refrigerator with a magnet.

Respond every time he says or does something based on his jealousy. Break off the conversation, go to the refrigerator, and fill out a line or two to document what he just said and did. Put an entry on the list every time he says something that is jealous and offensive.

◆ Reframe his message every time he gives it. Tell him that you think he says you may cheat because he's insecure. Or say "you don't think you're good enough for me," or the equivalent.

He won't like those comments. If he says "You don't know what I'm thinking" or "You don't know what you're talking about" respond with "You think you know my mind better than I do. Why shouldn't I know your mind better than you do?" After that, every time he makes a jealous comment, give him a broken-record version of your conclusion about him: "You're feeling insecure again today, huh?" or "It sounds like you're thinking you're not good enough for me again."

Talking about what's going on in his head is punishing and generally offensive. I don't recommend it for milder provocations but the ramifications of a man's extreme jealousy are dangerous. Withdrawing rewards and waiting for him to give up jealous behaviors may not work fast enough.

♦ Have a serious talk with him when he isn't angry at that moment.

Tell him that you want to have a talk about his jealousy. If he dodges you or tries to avoid it, say "I can't make you talk to me, but you can't make me do stuff either. If you want to take your chances on what I'll do next, then we don't have to talk about it. I'll do just what I want, without your permission." And then follow through by doing as you please, no matter what he wants, for a while.

Here is the basic outline of your script for the serious talk:

"I've been keeping track of all your jealous comments to me. You've probably noticed them on the refrigerator too. In the last week, you've said: (*give him some samples*). Those are really offensive comments and whenever you say them, I don't want to be around you. You're making (the relationship *or* living with you) so unpleasant that sometimes I don't want to be with you."

"I can't prove that I haven't cheated on you and I can't prove that I won't cheat on you in the future. But you couldn't possibly *make* me stay faithful to you because I'm an adult and a citizen and I have rights. All you're doing with your jealous comments is driving me away. You aren't preventing me from cheating. You're just driving me away."

"Since you can't guarantee that I won't cheat on you, I don't know why you're with me. You must be living an unhappy life, always thinking I'm cheating. And you're making me unhappy too."

"So do you want me to stay with you? Do you really want me to stay in this relationship with you, even though I might be cheating on you? You might be happier just living by yourself. You know you'd suspect your next girlfriend like you're suspecting me. I can't change your thoughts and feelings. I think you're always going to be suspicious of me and anyone else you have a relationship with."

Assuming he says yes, he wants you to stay, have him repeat this statement: "Yes, I do want to be in a relationship with you. I know you can never prove to me that you're not cheating." Or have him repeat some other wording that says he wants the relationship despite his possessive and jealous feelings.

"In that case, if you want a relationship with me, I'll stay for now, but I have a condition. If you want me in this relationship, I don't want you ever to say anything about me cheating on you, or finding other lovers, or spending time with other men."

"I want you to agree that if you discover that I'm cheating on you, you will leave me immediately and end the relationship. If you don't find evidence I'm cheating, you can think whatever you want, but don't make nasty comments to me or try to get me to tell you I'm still faithful. *You'll* have to reassure yourself. Don't try to get me to do it for you."

"If you want to leave me, go ahead and do it. But if you want to stay, shut up about me maybe cheating. I can't change the way you think and I don't want you beating me up verbally all the time about stuff that isn't true. Either you want the relationship with all your worries about me, or you leave me. You can't control me into being faithful to you."

If you believe he's suffering too, as opposed to just making you suffer, ask him to go to counseling to deal with his history of trauma. He probably had a very traumatic past with his parents and that caused him to be dependent on women.

He should go to counseling alone and work on his issues, whatever they are. Don't try to tell the therapist what he should do or try to manage his therapy from a distance. Just be sure he picks an experienced trauma counselor.

If he says that he can't control his feelings of jealousy, tell him he doesn't need to control them. He only has to control his mouth.

Tell the abuser that he only has to stop himself from making jealous comments, no matter how he's feeling. Remind him that he is thinking before he speaks or he'd be saying random syllables or just grunting. When he is talking, he is in control of what he says.

Point out to him that you aren't in control of his mouth and you aren't in control of his actions. If you had control of his actions, he'd be acting differently, and you'd like it a lot better.

Summary

In this chapter, I've laid out the principles for effective responses to verbal abuse. Here's an outline of those rules:

♦ Think about better responses to the next attack, not how you felt after the last one.
♦ Talk about the tone of the conversation, not about his criticisms of you.
♦ Remember this mnemonic for responses: name, blame, explain
♦ Don't defend yourself. Ask the abuser to defend his attack.
♦ Don't approach him when he's attacking. Withdraw from him physically and emotionally.

Good responses can follow this outline:

I'm leaving this discussion.
I hate it when you (name the abusive behavior) so I won't keep talking to you.
I'm going _____ (where)
I'll be home by _____ (time)
But I still won't talk about this. I'm done talking to you for _____ (period of time).
We can talk about this again _____ (when) but only if you agree not to (make abusive comments).
If we can't agree, I'll decide what to do by myself and I'll do that, whatever it is, whether you agree or not.

Other useful tactics:

♦ Change the subject after you have made your response.
♦ Respond rapidly and consistently. He'll learn faster and more easily if you do.

- Always stay alert and aware of the way he treats you. Don't let bad behaviors pile up.
- Reward the abuser's small steps to better behavior.
- Rehearse your responses in advance
- Be patient. You'll both need time to change.
- Be especially careful and consistent with men who are jealous. Jealousy is pathological and difficult to change.

CHAPTER 9
Taking a Time-out

Many victims of verbal and emotional abuse feel they cannot stop their partners from trashing them and they say they have tried everything. However, if you understand that the verbal abuser wants closeness to you, then you can train the abuser to lessen his negative behaviors. In this chapter, we'll deal mostly with training him by using negative reinforcement.

Behaviorism 101:

If you give someone a *reward* after he does something you like, he's more likely to do it again. That works with, pigeons, rats, monkeys, children and adults.

If you give someone a *punishment* after he does something you don't like, he's less likely to do it again. That works with the whole animal kingdom as well.

If someone behaves in a certain way because he expects a reward, but the reward doesn't occur, the person is likely to behave that way less often. When you take away an expected reward, you are giving someone a *negative reinforcement.*

Giving a child a time-out is a way of decreasing a child's negative behavior, but it is not a punishment as I have defined it above, and as psychologists commonly use the term. Spanking is a punishment, but a time-out is not.

A time-out is *negative reinforcement*. Time-outs for preschool children and grounding for teenagers are examples of negative reinforcement. The company and approval of a parent are rewards for a preschooler. Hanging out with friends or playing video games are rewards for teens. You can withdraw the visits and the videogames to increase wanted behavior such as doing homework. You are lessening the attention and approval of the parent when you give a child a time-out. You are lessening activities of a teen when you ground him by forbidding him to use anything electronic for a week.

To make a time-out effective, you shouldn't talk to a child while the child is in his room or a chair for a time-out. Many parents say to me that time-outs don't work with their children. That usually means the parent can't bear to lose the child's attention and approval when the child is in his room or in the chair, so she isn't really giving the child a time-out. These parents continue to talk to the child, argue with the child, or beg and plead with the child while the child is in time-out.

If you have a child in time-out, don't speak to the child, hug the child, hold the child in the chair, or otherwise pay attention to the child. Those behaviors make time-outs ineffective. You have to cut the child off from adult company and approval for the time-out to be effective.

When adults tell a child to take a time-out, the adult is in charge. The adult orders the child to go to the chair or go to her room, and that withdraws the child from adult company. An adult can order a child to take a time-out, and enforce it, at least when the child is physically smaller than the adult. That type of time-out is only effective with young children but if you use time-out effectively, you shouldn't need to keep using it to get obedience.

When you give an adult a time-out, you should succeed in the same way as you would with a time-out for a child. As an adult, you can tell another adult to take a time-out, but you can't enforce it. You can't, and shouldn't, physically move an adult someplace else. Don't demand that the abuser leave. You can't control him. Therefore, you need to take yourself away from the abuser to give him a time-out.

If you and the verbal abuser don't live together, feel free to tell him to leave your house. Or hang up the phone or delete the text or the email to cut yourself off from the abuser. Of course, an abuser may wait to abuse you until a time when you can't easily escape him. If you're driving with a verbal abuser think ahead because you may need to make a quick exit. Try driving your own car and meeting in public places where he can't easily trap you.

You don't need permission from the abuser to give him a time-out. You can deny the abuser the pleasures of your company, your attention, and your approval. If you are not in the presence of the abuser, you're not paying attention to him and you're not approving of his behavior. Therefore, an adult time-out is an effective response to verbal or emotional abuse.

Changing behavior using rewards

When you're trying to change a child's behavior, rewards are a powerful way to do it. A child will do more of the wanted behavior if you give him rewards for it. But the best choice is to taper off tangible rewards like food or money and substitute your own attention and approval. So if you pay a child twenty dollars for each A on his report card, he'll stop getting good grades when the payments stop—unless he finds other rewards from getting good grades.

When you're trying to change adult behavior, attention and approval should be your main rewards to increase the behaviors you want. When you reward some behaviors you like with praise, *you* become associated with the rewards and the other adult wants to spend more time and be more positive to you in return.

However, rewards only work to increase behavior that an adult has already done, so the other must do the behavior before you can reward it. You can promise rewards in the future for doing certain behaviors because adults have good memories. If an adult believes you will reward the behavior, and your attention and approval is worth something to him, he's likely to work for the reward even if it isn't tangible or immediate.

Changing behavior using punishments

In theory, to stop someone from verbally abusing you, all you have to do is punish him whenever he does it. Why doesn't that work?

With animals, children, and adults, punishment is not a good long-term approach to changing behaviors. People associate rewards with the person giving the rewards and they associate punishments with the person giving the punishments. Therefore, when the author of the punishments is not there, the child or adult doesn't see any reason to stop doing what he wants.

You can force a child to do as you want because you're bigger than the child and you can temporarily control the child physically. But that only works temporarily. The child needs a reason to obey other than the punishment. Parents who punish physically and harshly raise angry children who believe that might makes right. Those children expect to punish others to get what they want.

When you often use physical punishments like spanking, you can't control the child when he is in middle school or high school. That's because he learns how to avoid you and therefore he can avoid the punishments. Also, when children get bigger, it's more difficult, and more dangerous, to punish them physically because they can strike back physically. Children who were well-behaved only to avoid punishment become badly behaved teens and adults. They end up angry and violent because their parents punished them with anger and violence.

Those angry people are the verbal and emotional abusers we've been analyzing. Those are the ones trying to punish you into loving them more. They don't think they should have to convince you to do what they want. No one convinced them to behave themselves and they don't see the point in convincing others. Their parents forced them and they think they can force you into loving them by punishing you.

For all these reasons, punishing the abuser back isn't a first choice. You'll just get a rotten relationship. It's possible for two verbal abusers to get into a relationship and increase each other's bad habits. I've seen it happen.

That's why your goal with the abuser is not to accept the verbal and emotional punishments the abuser wants to dish out, nor is it to do a better job of punishing him in return. Punishing him back makes you an abuser also.

Changing behavior using negative reinforcement

Your best approach to reduce behaviors you don't like is to use negative reinforcement. That's why a consistent and rapid use of time-out works better than physical punishment in children. Verbal and emotional abuse of children by yelling and withdrawing doesn't work well in the long term. A time-out is not as harsh as physical punishment and it is much more effective, immediately and later.

Suppose you take your attention and approval away from a preschool child, or take away specific rewards a teenager already has. That child will decrease the behaviors you don't like and won't react with the fear and anger that physical punishments cause. You also don't have to be present all the time for the consequence to be effective. You can take the video game system or the car keys with you. Use negative reinforcement to decrease behaviors effectively.

What the target of abuse gains by giving the abuser a time-out

When a target of abuse withdraws from the abuser with a time-out, she gives herself time to regroup and nurture herself. She can go about her business without interference from the perpetrator of the abuse. She puts more distance into a bad relationship, hoping to make it more positive.

If the target stays to listen and react to the perpetrator's negative words and deeds, that will make the relationship worse for the target. If the target leaves, she is no longer an *audience* to the perpetrator's words and deeds, or a source of rewards to the perpetrator.

What the abuser gains from getting a time-out

The perpetrator should gain a learning experience, although he won't like it. The perpetrator is not facing reality. He doesn't have a *right* to the target's company or a *right* to communication with the target. Those are privileges. The perpetrator does not have a *right* to act any way he chooses and expect the target to tolerate bad behavior. If he behaves badly, the target can walk out, either for a short time, or, if the abuse continues, forever.

The perpetrator needs to learn that verbal and emotional abuse is a temporary measure only. You need to teach him that he cannot continue to get his way by punishing you with emotional and verbal abuse. You must stop staying close to him and providing him with rewards such as your attention and your approval. If he can choose to behave badly, you can choose to take your approval and your company away from him. You don't have to tolerate abuse, because you are no longer a child.

You should take an adult time-out when you've tried all the verbal responses you know but the other person has not stopped emotionally or verbally abusing you.

The goal of the abuser is to control you by punishing you for doing something he doesn't like or to control you by punishing you for not doing something he likes. The target should have these goals:

♦ First, stay in control of yourself, no matter what the abuser does.
♦ Second, show the abuser that he is endangering the relationship when he punishes you.
♦ Third, take your company, attention and approval away so the abuser learns to communicate more positively.

Let's look at each of these goals in turn, and give some sample methods to get there.

Stay in control of yourself, no matter what the abuser does

The major reward that an emotional and verbal abuser seeks is control of you. If you give him control of you, you have rewarded his verbal abuse and he'll abuse you more often. Your response to the abuser should make him realize that he hasn't controlled you and that he'd better try something different the next time.

Him: How dare you keep paying for the kids to have music lessons? I've told you we can't afford it, and I'm not going to let you drive me into poverty frittering away my money!

Her: Are you ready to write a budget that limits your spending money and not just mine and the kids?

Him: No, dammit! I've told you I won't even discuss it. You're the spendthrift, not me.

Her: I'm spending as usual until you're ready to work on a budget for both of us. Getting nasty with me isn't going to make me more cooperative about it.

In other words, tell him that he doesn't control you and that if he wants to discuss the issue with you, he has to be willing to put his own spending habits on the table.

In the example above, she has *told* him that she is not in his control. She has *shown* him that she is not in his control by refusing to give him what he wants despite his abuse. And she has *offered him a solution*, a possible agreement that may meet both his needs and hers.

Just saying "No! You can't treat me that way!" won't be effective. Show him another way to meet his needs without abusing you. Probably his family of origin used verbal abuse rather than pleasant discussion to come to agreements when they disagreed.

You need to know more than he does about how to reach agreements if you want to salvage the relationship. It's not fair, but who said life was fair?

If you curb your spending because of his nasty comments, you have rewarded the way he treated you, and rewarded the verbal abuse. Giving someone his way when he is abusive encourages him to have bad communication habits.

Good parents sometimes give their children treats. But good parents don't give their children treats when the children are screaming their heads off in the grocery store. That just pays the children to scream the next time they're in a grocery store.

You should think about both the immediate and the lasting consequences of rewarding your children's behavior. And you need to think about the immediate and lasting effects of rewards on the abuser's behavior as well. Your partner can make nasty comments about your spending habits and you can make nasty comments back about his spending habits. But if you curb your spending, all you've gained is an overall nasty relationship. If you scream at a child at the same time that you give the child the treat she wants, the child is still going to scream for the treat. It worked to scream, so she'll do it more often. And she'll try to make the screaming more painful for you the next time so you won't yell at her.

When you yell back at a disobedient child, but give him what he wants anyway, you are setting up a power struggle. The child is trying to train you not to scream at her as well as train you to give her the treat. So don't think that being nasty back is going to train your partner to do or not do anything. If your partner gets what he wants, for example if you spend less, he'll keep being nasty.

When your partner gets nasty, your first priority is to stay in control of yourself and your behavior. Don't reward the abuser by giving in. Remember that if you reward a behavior when he gets nasty, your partner is going to continue the behavior and continue to get nasty because that was successful. If he thinks that getting nasty causes you to give in, he'll get nasty more and more often. If you want your partner to treat you well, don't give him what he wants unless he does treat you well.

Show the abuser he is endangering the relationship when he punishes you.

It's not the case that all verbal abusers know consciously that they are being nasty on purpose just because it works. I don't mean that they aren't aware of your feelings, because most of them are. They don't connect their negative behavior toward you and your negative feelings about the *relationship*. Many verbal and emotional abusers have seen relationships in which one partner abused the other but both partners stayed together. These abusers don't believe that you will leave them because the abusive relationships that they grew up with didn't dissolve.

I once saw a woman for individual therapy who had married five times and her fifth marriage was ending. She came into therapy with me to deal with her hurt and frustration about the latest breakup.

As she described her life with her latest husband, it was clear that when they disagreed, she called him ugly names and demanded that he obey her. When I asked her why she did this, she said that she punished her husband because he deserved it since he was not meeting her needs. I told her that the man was probably leaving her because he didn't like the way she treated him.

She didn't agree with me at first. She said that her mother had treated her father the same way throughout her parents' sixty-three-year marriage. Therefore she was confident that her verbally abusive behavior hadn't caused her five husbands to leave. She felt that she was behaving acceptably when she was angry. She held the men responsible for her anger and she punished them when she was angry. She expected them to stay with her despite her constant abuse.

This same woman described her father to me as a womanizer and a workaholic who was hardly ever home. She was not describing a man who enjoyed his marriage, just a man who chose to remain in the marriage while doing exactly as he pleased. She didn't have a high opinion of men because of her father's behavior toward women, but she hadn't understood that her mother's abusive behavior didn't encourage her father to stay around to enjoy her mother's company.

This woman needed to realize that throughout five marriages she had been verbally abusive. She cannot count on a man hanging around and staying in a marriage if she behaves this way, no matter what her father did. If her husband had wanted to stay in the marriage and change her behavior, he would need to help her connect the dots between her behavior and his intention to leave her.

So your second goal is to help your partner connect his behavior and *your feelings* about the marriage. Give your partner insight into the *consequences* you will use when your partner behaves badly.

Many women believe that telling the abuser that he has made them feel bad should cause him to stop the abuse, but it doesn't usually work that way. An emotional or verbal abuser uses negative and abusive behavior *in order* to hurt you. His purpose is to make you feel badly, because your bad feelings make the abuse successful. If you were indifferent to his behavior, the abuse wouldn't work as a punishment. You wouldn't try harder to please him to avoid the punishment. So giving him insight into how you *feel* when he abuses you does not cause him to stop abusing you. He wants you to feel badly when he punishes you.

Therefore, your second goal is to help him connect his abuse to your attachment to the relationship. It may be hard for you to believe that your partner thinks that you will stay with him no matter how he behaves toward you, but he probably has a history of seeing relationships that were hostile, critical, abusive, but stable. The relationships he has seen may have lasted for long periods of time. He may well expect you to be willing to remain in a hostile, critical, abusive relationship. *For him to stop abusing you, he must believe that you will leave the relationship unless he changes.*

I told you that threatening the abuser with a bomb by threatening to end the relationship is not an effective procedure. He won't believe you if you threaten to end the relationship just because he won't take the garbage out now. And he'll be right. But there's a big difference between threatening to end the marriage because of an unresolved disagreement like who's going to take out the garbage, and promising to end the marriage unless he treats you better.

It sometimes helps to keep a tally of how often the other is doing the behaviors that you find abusive. Write the tally down on an index card so you don't have to depend on your memory.

First name the behaviors you don't like to the abuser, so he has no doubt how you are defining them, then mention the tally.

She: I don't like you calling me names, so I'm starting to keep track of how often you do it. I'll let you know when you do it so you can keep track too.

She: That's the third time you've called me a bitch today. It's really adding up!

Don't threaten consequences you won't go through with. If you aren't willing to leave him if he calls you "bitch" one more time, don't threaten it.

And don't start to leave and then change your mind when he apologizes. Your goal is not to have him apologize whenever he calls you a name. Your goal is for him not to call you names. You're using the tally to tell yourself, and him, just how often he gets abusive.

Stop rewarding him with your company and attention when he is verbally abusive

The abuser is in a time-out from you when he can no longer hear, see, or get attention from you. If the two of you are at home together, begin by turning your face away. Go out of the room and go about your business somewhere else in the house. If he tries to follow you, lock the door and turn on loud music or the TV so you can't hear him anymore. If you can't stop him from following you, put on earphones and tap into your iPod. Your goal is to take your attention somewhere else and to make him aware that you are not thinking about him or attending to his words. You have ended the abuse by ending your attention to the abuse.

If the abuser breaks down the door or snatches the earphones from your ears, then you are dealing with a batterer. He's not just a verbal abuser. Does he demand attention by physically inserting himself into your space when you don't want him to? Then you are dealing with someone prepared to use physical force to hold on to you as an audience, a target, and a victim. You are not safe with that person. Consider calling the police.

If you are on the phone with the abuser, warn him once that he is abusing you, then hang up. Here are some good examples:

"If you want to talk to me, lower your voice and don't call me names. Otherwise, I'm hanging up."

"I'm hanging up. Call back when you can talk without calling me names."

"We can talk again when you aren't drunk. Good-bye."

In other words, if the abuser will accept a time-out in the same space with you, by letting you go about your business without following you, then you have solved the problem for the moment. Prepare to exit all conversations when he gets abusive and you will train him not to call names and get obnoxious. If you treat your company and your attention as privileges, he will recognize that he has to earn them by good behavior.

If the abuser continues to shout at you through the door, no problem. Just don't respond.

If the abuser follows too closely to lock him out of your room, you need to take your time-out out of the house. Tell your partner where you're going and how long you'll be gone, then leave. Here are some examples of what you could say:

"I'm not listening to you anymore. I'm leaving. I'm going to Denny's and I'll be back in two hours. If you won't let me alone when I come back, I'll go to a motel overnight."

"I'm leaving. I'm going to my mother's overnight. I'm not going to answer you on my cell phone until tomorrow."

"I'm going to my meeting and I'm headed to the library afterward. If you haven't settled down four hours from now, then I'm going to Juliette's to stay on her couch."

You tell the other where you're going during the time-out because you're an adult and he needs to know how to get hold of you in an emergency. However, you aren't giving him leave to contact you during the time-out, so don't respond if he tries to contact you while you are away. Don't answer a phone call from him or respond to a text message. If he sits down next to you in the booth at Denny's, leave Denny's. If he interrupts your time-out, let him know that if you ever have to give him a time-out again, you won't tell him where you're going.

If you try to drive somewhere and he follows you in his car, drive to a police station and ask the police to speak to him while you drive out of sight.

You should tell him how long he'll be in time-out so he understands how long the negative reinforcement will last. Open-ended time-outs and open-ended punishments have bad side effects. They cause increased fear and anger from him. You are trying to give a specific duration of withdrawal related to the size of the offense.

If you're forced to leave a house for a time-out, two hours is a good time to stay away the first time. If he doesn't own the house and you do, or if his name is not on the lease, tell him to leave for at least that amount of time. Your company includes the use of your house, so you can forbid him the use of it while the time-out is occurring.

If the abuser promises to leave you alone in the house, you can believe him once. If he doesn't keep his promise one time, then don't offer him the opportunity to promise again. Just leave. Don't talk about what you're doing or why. Just leave. You don't need his permission or approval. Just leave.

Don't act like many ineffective parents do by threatening to give a time-out, then postponing and threatening some more. That gives the child ten times as much attention for misbehaving. Don't threaten to leave more than once. If you threaten once and the behavior you're objecting to doesn't stop, leave immediately.

Threatening a time-out isn't a punishment. Threatening a time-out gives the abuser attention and an audience for whatever he's doing you don't like. You are not trying to avoid giving him a time-out. You're trying to give him a time-out *consistently* and *rapidly* when he is emotionally and verbally abusing you. You're trying to let him have a taste of abandonment. You're trying to give him insight about the damage he is causing the relationship and what will happen if he doesn't stop.

While you are taking the time-out, sort through your thoughts and feelings. Prepare to promise (not threaten) what you will do in the future. Here are some examples:

She: I don't want to talk about the schedule. I didn't leave because we couldn't agree about the schedule. I left because of the way you were behaving when we talked about the schedule. I don't care how much you want your way. If you call me names and keep changing the subject, then I'm not going to talk to you anymore. Until we have an agreement about the schedule, I'm doing it the way I want it. If you want it different from that, you'll need to talk it over with me another time without behaving that way. But I'm not talking any more tonight. I'm going to bed.

She: I'm glad you're sorry, but I don't want an apology. I want you not to call me names again. Apologies don't make up for that. If you don't call your boss names to his face, you can stop yourself from calling me names no matter how you feel.

She: I don't care how angry you were. You don't treat your family that way, and you get just as mad at them. If you can keep from dumping on your father when he orders you around, you can keep from dumping on me when you don't agree with me. Your anger is no excuse for how you treated me.

The point of the time-out is to end your contact with the abuser. Choose to be distant without his permission or approval.

Don't keep talking to the abuser to get his permission or approval for the time-out. Don't keep postponing the time-out by giving the abuser more chances to behave. If you do, you lose any hope of getting distant. You are simply making the relationship closer and more negative which is exactly what he wants. You're trying to withdraw closeness from him, not positivity.

Above all, remember that taking an adult time-out is not a quick fix for long-term habits. You and the abuser have probably had these habits for a lifetime. I wish I could promise you that if you get up the nerve to leave the house once, you'll fix your partner forever, but that is unrealistic. To stop someone from verbally and emotionally abusing you, you have to change and you have to stay changed. You have to respond consistently and rapidly to the abuse. And you have to be persistent by refusing to tolerate abuse.

Even if you do decide to end the relationship with the person who is verbally and emotionally abusing you, you will still be glad you learned these skills. You can promise yourself that you won't get into any other relationship in the future, but you're likely to change your mind. And you may have children to raise who have learned negative habits from the abuser before you left him. And they've probably learned the habit of tolerating abuse by seeing you do it. Your refusal to tolerate abuse and your ability to leave an abuser are going to be important to you for your own health, now and in the future.

And if you do refuse abuse, are you guaranteed a happy relationship? Unfortunately, making the changes suggested in this book only removes some major negatives in the relationship. That may be all you need to live happily ever after, but ending the verbal abuse doesn't cause the abuser to be respectful, kind, considerate, or nurturing. Your improved control of yourself and your behavior won't remove his self-centered ways, or his need to put himself first all the time.

You can change, however, and I hope you're motivated to change. Your partner can change also, but he probably needs more motivation to change than just changing to please you. You won't regret making these changes in yourself because you are the number one beneficiary of the changes.

Your refusal to tolerate abuse is your best guarantee of happy relationships now and in the future. You can't have happy relationships unless you end the unhappiness in the relationship or end the unhappy relationship.

If a friend wants to yell at me, I can leave with an appropriate exit line, like one of these:

"I'm leaving. I don't like you calling me names."

"That's all, Ted. I'm going to the library for two hours. I hope you get over this."

"This conversation is over until you decide to stop talking to me that way. I'm going to watch TV, and I expect you to respect my privacy."

"I'm taking a walk around the block to consider everything that you've just said to me, and decide what I want to do about it."

Do tell the person where you are going and when you'll be back to continue the discussion, as in these examples:

"I'm going to the coffee shop. I'll be there two hours. Then I'll come back to see if you're ready to have a decent conversation with me."

"I'm going to Susan's house to spend the night. We can talk in the morning."

"I'm going to bed. I'm not talking to you about this again until you can stop yelling and interrupting."

Remember:

♦   Don't leave with an inflammatory exit line.
♦   Don't threaten that you won't come back.
♦   Don't call names as you leave.
♦   Don't try to get in a last word before you walk out.

What if the abuser doesn't want to let you go? What you do about this depends on what he does. Does he physically block your exit? Does he rip the phone out of your hand? Does he take your car keys? In all those cases you need to admit that you are a victim of battering and not just verbal abuse. Behaviors like those are illegal in most states.

If you discover your partner is willing to batter you to keep you there, it's time to consider your physical safety again. Would the abuser beat you up? Consult the bibliography at the end of this book. Get a book on escape from a batterer. Be cautious in your responses, thinking constantly of your physical safety. Most importantly, recognize that you are not *only* a victim of verbal abuse if the abuser is willing to use physical force to get his way.

Do you believe that someone has the right to force you physically to continue a conversation? Then why doesn't he have the right to beat you? The two acts are much the same. They both involve the abuser using violence to coerce and control you.

If you are confident the other won't resort to physical force to intimidate you, then proceed. If you are confident enough to risk finding out what will happen, then you need to confront the blocking behavior. Think of the following litany:

1. Name the violence.
2. Blame him (hold him accountable) for his behavior.
3. Explain your plan.

Name, blame, explain
Useful examples:

"Joe, you're standing between me and the door. You're using your physical size to intimidate me, and I won't tolerate it. It's also illegal. Step aside now, and let me walk out that door, or I'll do whatever I need to do to get rid of you."

"Susan, take your hand off my arm. I'm not going to continue with this argument. I'm leaving. It's not acceptable for you to hold me here physically. I don't let people do that to me."

"Dick, I'm going to take a time-out from you now, and I'm not giving you a vote about it. Breaking the phone to keep me from using it is illegal. I'm leaving by the door now. I don't tolerate someone getting physical with me."

"Jerry, I am going to leave, whether you like it or not. Calling me names won't change my mind. If you don't put my purse down, with the car keys in it, I will leave without it, and come back with the police."

If the abuser doesn't get physical to keep you with him, you can leave. But remember that you cannot control him. You should leave even though he isn't in your control. This means, you don't need the last word and shouldn't expect it and you don't need his approval for leaving and shouldn't expect it.

If you try to speak last, the abuser will keep talking to keep you there. If you try to get the abuser to say the equivalent of "It's OK for you to go. I'm sorry," you'll be trapped there.

Your goal is not control of the other. Your goal is not to get him to approve and be silent. Your goal is to remove yourself as an audience. You can only do this by going, not by trying to hurt him or make him suffer.

Wanting to leave, threatening to leave, or saying you are about to leave doesn't change the verbal abuser. Leaving changes him. Just as with children, threatening to give the abuser a time-out doesn't change his behavior, except temporarily. Giving the time-out makes a difference, but the threat does not.

Summary

Your major method to end the abuse is negative reinforcement, or withdrawal of rewards. The primary rewards you will withdraw are your company, your attention, and your approval.

Rewards work to increase behavior and you should use the rewards of praise and approval when the abuser does something you like. Punishment decreases behavior, and that's what the abuser is doing to you. It won't work to punish him back because he'll just step up the verbal abuse. You don't want a worse relationship than you have now. Withdrawing from the abuser works, both in the short-term and the long-term because the abuser mainly wants closeness to you. He doesn't care as much about your approval.

You have three primary goals when you are giving the abuser a time-out:

1. Stay in control of yourself. Don't give the abuser what he wants until he earns it with his behavior.
2. Show the abuser that he is endangering the relationship when he punishes you.
3. Stop rewarding the abuser with your company and approval when he is verbally abusive. When you withdraw yourself, you withdraw his major reward.

First leave the conversation, then the room, and finally the house if the abuser won't allow you to leave him when he is in the same space. Tell him where you're going and when you'll be back. Don't negotiate whether you're going to leave or not. Don't threaten to leave and change your mind when he hasn't changed his behavior. You're not trying to avoid leaving him. The goal is to leave him when he is abusive, not to find a way to stay. Leaving is not a punishment, it is a time-out. You aren't giving him a time-out if you stay and keep talking. The threat to leave won't change him. Only leaving will change him.

And most importantly, have no communication with him while you're gone. Don't answer your phone, respond to texts, or speak to him if he follows you. If he follows you, he's a stalker, so beware. If he tries to prevent you from leaving by physical means, he's a batterer and you should consider involving law enforcement to stay safe.

CHAPTER 10

Staying Realistic about Your Relationship

In this chapter we're going to look at several aspects of your current intimate relationship. The odds are that you're going to stay in your relationships with your family, both your family of origin and the family you made with your children. Are any of your relationships with family members abusive? Consider making those relationships more distant so they'll be more positive.

However, having relationships with friends and adult partners is optional. If your partner isn't meeting your needs, should you leave the relationship? In this chapter, we'll look at these questions:

1. Are you being realistic about the abuser?
2. How often does your current partner act in a positive way towards you?
3. Do you have to change?

Are you realistic about the abuser?

Lottery 1

The state has sold nine million tickets for this lottery, at one dollar each. The grand prizewinner gets nine million dollars. What are your chances of winning this lottery? How many tickets would you buy for this lottery?

Lottery 2

The state has sold nine million tickets for this lottery, at one dollar each. The grand prizewinner gets ten dollars. What are your chances of winning this lottery? How many tickets would you buy for this lottery?

You'd have the same chance of winning nine million dollars in the first lottery as you'd have of winning ten dollars in the second lottery. Your chances of winning each lottery if you bought a single ticket are at least nine million to one.

What if you bought four million, five hundred thousand tickets to either of those lotteries? You'd spend four million, five hundred thousand dollars. You'd have a one-in-two chance of winning the grand prize of nine million dollars in lottery 1, and a one-in-two chance of winning ten dollars in lottery 2.

Most people don't think of it this way. I doubt I could get you to buy any tickets for Lottery 2, but the reason nine million people would buy tickets for the first lottery is that they have fantasies of winning the big bucks. They are taking money they earned today, and betting (with nine million to one odds against them) that they will win the lottery. How smart is that?

Losing a dollar or even ten dollars on lottery tickets won't hurt as long as you can afford to waste the money. But would you bet your life instead?

Would you play Russian roulette for a grand prize of nine million dollars? Suppose one chamber of a six-chambered revolver had a bullet and you would win nine million dollars if you fired at your head five times and didn't kill yourself. Most adults would say that they wouldn't bet their life to get nine million dollars with five to one odds against them. They know that in five out of six cases they would die. In only one out of six tries would they win the money. They might gamble with a little of their money, but they wouldn't gamble their lives.

If you believe that the abuser will change even though you haven't made changes first, you're betting against the odds. If you believe that he'll treat you nicely today and continue to treat you nicely consistently in the future when you haven't changed, you are betting against the odds. You are entering a lottery similar to the two examples above. You know you may lose, but if you are willing to bet your *time* and your *happiness* against high odds, you are fantasizing about the future, not planning for it.

Betting that a verbal abuser will change in the future without you changing your behavior gives you odds that are somewhere between nine million to one and five to one. You're not betting spare cash, which you may waste a little of every day, and you're not betting your entire life. But you are betting *your time* and you won't get that back.

If you spend today being unhappy because you are living with a verbal abuser, you may figure that it's not a big deal because, after all, you're going to get another day tomorrow. And that's true. But your odds are not going to improve between today and tomorrow. In fact, your odds are going to get worse.

If you flip a normal coin, your odds of it coming up heads are one in two, or 50-50. If you flip a normal coin nine times, and get heads nine times in a row, how likely are you to get heads the next time you flip it? If there's nothing wrong with the coin, you have the same odds of one in two that you had on your first coin flip. Your odds don't improve because sometimes there's an unlikely run of coin flips that goes against the odds for a little while. If you decide to bet against the odds with your time and your happiness, what's going on with you?

You wouldn't bet the rent money on lottery tickets, counting on the prize money to pay your rent. The odds would be against you, and you'd know that and restrain yourself. The odds would also be against you if you believe your partner will change his behavior tomorrow without you making changes first. It is possible, but not probable that your partner will change for the better if you don't change.

It's not smart to predict against the odds. Believing that tomorrow your partner will give up a habitual behavior he hasn't been willing to change for the last ten years is predicting against the odds. You could be making a more realistic prediction. It would be smarter to predict that tomorrow your partner will continue to abuse you just as he has done for the last ten years.

Wishing ahead is betting or predicting against the odds. You are wishing ahead if you want something to happen and you put money on it because of your wishes. When you do that, you aren't preparing for the future that is more probable. You're only preparing for the future you want.

Do you believe that you are being realistic? Do you believe that your partner will become less abusive without you making changes first? Then how about putting your money where your mouth is? Commit your beliefs to paper, at least, so you will be aware of your previous predictions when you review them in the future.

Ask yourself these questions:

♦ What specific behaviors do you believe your partner is going to change?
♦ Why do you believe that your partner is going to change those behaviors?

Has your partner changed habits in his life by sheer willpower before? Has he stopped smoking without help? Kept up his exercise program? Lost weight and kept it off? What habits has your partner changed without outside help?

♦ What was his motivation for changing those habits?

Do you believe that if you asked your partner to change a habit, he would do it because you asked him to, even though he didn't want to change?

♦ Is he motivated to end the verbal abuse now? Why? What has changed?

What evidence do you have that your partner wants to change to stay with you? Does he believe you will leave him? Have you threatened to leave him before and not carried through with the threat? Have you hired an attorney, filed divorce papers with the court, moved somewhere else? Why would he believe that you are serious? Anybody can threaten, and you've probably done it before without following through. And he's probably pacified you before when you threatened, but he didn't stop abusing you.

And by the way, why do you believe that *you* are serious about leaving him if he doesn't stop the abuse? If all you have ever done is threaten, I'm sure he believes that if he doesn't stop the abuse you will *threaten* to leave him. He knows that's not the same as leaving him. It may have taken all your emotional energy to threaten to leave him, but you'll need a good deal more emotional energy to leave him and stay away from him forever.

Evidence about his motivation

Does your partner have help changing his verbal abuse so you believe that he will make changes now? What help does your partner have to change his verbally abusive behaviors toward you? Has your partner ever stopped or dropped out of a program of habit change before? For example, has he ever dropped out of therapy or marriage counseling?

Has a court ordered your partner to go to therapy? If so, good, but do you think he wants to change? Does he want to apply what he learns in counseling even though he goes to counseling against his will? If the court hasn't ordered him to go, why will he continue counseling if he doesn't want to go?

Has your partner agreed to go to marriage counseling with you? Has he agreed to go for three months, even if he doesn't like it and doesn't think it's helping? Does your partner always keep his agreements with you, even if he changes his mind about wanting the agreement?

Evidence about the changes themselves

What, specifically, are you saying your partner is going to change? Do you believe he will stop calling you names and cursing you? Then keep track of the times he calls you names or curses you. See if he is calling you names less often as time goes on.

Do you believe he will start asking you instead of ordering you? Then keep track of the times he orders you to see if he is ordering you less often in the future.

Do you believe he will stop insulting you and putting you down? Then keep track of the times he insults you to see if he does it less and less. Do you believe he will stop giving you the silent treatment or that he will stop withdrawing from you emotionally and physically? Then keep track of the times he withdraws from you. Record the times he is not enjoyable or positive to you. Are those times getting less frequent and less severe?

Do you believe he will nurture you and praise you in the future? Then keep track of the positive times in the relationship. Document the times he nurtures you, and the times he encourages you to have good feelings about yourself. Is he doing it more often?

Do you believe that he will take more responsibility for the work in the household? Or that he will contribute his share to the finances in the future if he has not in the past? Do you think he'll stop abusing you because you ask him? Then keep track of his contributions to the household and family and finances to see if there are improvements in his behavior in those ways.

If you've kept track of his behavior over time and answered all those questions so you can see that your predictions are correct so far, you've got the evidence to convince me as well as you. If you track the behavior of your partner, and he does make the changes you expect of him, then you were being realistic about him, and you were not just predicting what you wanted instead of what was realistic.

Did you decide not to commit to paper the reasons you thought he would change, and the changes you thought he would make? If so, was it because you didn't want to track or document what he was doing? Would that have made you depressed, or angry or anxious? Would it have ruined your day if you paid close attention to his behaviors toward you?

That's why I want *you* to make commitments. After all, nobody can make you pay attention when you don't want to. If you don't like what's going on in your relationship, were you hoping this book was going to tell you that he was a bad guy and you couldn't do anything about it but suffer? In that case you're reading the wrong book.

How often do I feel positive about my partner?

I don't think the positive moments in a relationship prevent negative moments and I don't think negative moments prevent positive moments. If there are more negative times, there will be fewer positive times. But if the negative moments decrease, will the positive ones increase? You hope they will, but it's not guaranteed.

Maybe you have many positive times with the abuser and you feel they outweigh the negative ones. Maybe you and your partner are both devoted to your children. If he abuses you less, you may enjoy his company more. You may join more activities together. You may find common interests that help you bond as a family.

Other partnerships that don't have children may bond as business partners, ski buddies, or sports fans. The partners enjoy being together more when there's less verbal abuse.

Other targets find that they still have few positive moments when the abuser stops verbally abusing her. The partners are like roommates with a joint history but no current intimacy. When the abuse level goes down, the partners lead separate lives. If he can't tell her what to do, he's not interested in her. Or she may still be too angry about the past to enjoy his company, even though he does treat her better now.

Other partnerships never had much in common. Each partner kept waiting for the other to make him happy. Even without the verbal abuse, neither one has a history of being happy or of encouraging others to be happy.

If you want to stay with your current partner, consider what would make you happy. Ask yourself these questions:

♦ *What are you doing to make yourself happy?* Do you enjoy your job? Do you have hobbies or passions that you look forward to working on?

Do you feel most complete when engaged with your children, or your church? What are your sources of satisfaction in life?

♦ *Is the abuser keeping you from being happy?* Be honest with yourself. The abuser may not be the only reason you're miserable. Were you happy before you began seeing the abuser? Why or why not?

♦ *If you were happy before seeing him, what were you doing then that you have given up now?* Couldn't you do those activities again without your partner's approval and consent? He probably isn't interfering with your actions. You're probably just refusing to do things without his approval.

Dr. Richard Stuart was a psychology professor of mine. He would draw two pie charts on a chalkboard, one showing where males got their satisfaction in life and one showing where women got their satisfaction. I don't know whether those percentages would hold up today, but there were some truths in those graphs that I have remembered ever since.

Dr. Stuart said that men got:

♦ Fifty percent of their satisfaction in life from their jobs,
♦ Twenty-five percent of their satisfaction from their wives,
♦ Fifteen percent of their satisfaction from their children, and
♦ Ten percent of their satisfaction from Moose Lodge (some all-male bonding activity.)

Dr. Stuart then drew a pie chart for the sources of women's satisfaction. He said that women without jobs got:

♦ Fifty percent of their satisfaction in life from their husbands,
♦ Twenty-five percent from their children,
♦ Fifteen percent from their mothers,
♦ And ten percent from the Parent-Teacher Organization.

If those figures are realistic, women are much more dependent on their marriages and husbands than their husbands are on them. Every moment a wife spends with her husband has to be twice as good for her to feel satisfied. Husbands are getting more of their satisfaction from work, so the marriage isn't as important for their happiness. Also, on average, children don't figure as largely in the male life as in the female life.

Of course many more women are working now than when I was in school. Do women need to go to work to be less dependent on the marriage as a source of satisfaction? That's not a one-size-fits-all fix for everything, but do give some thought to whether you have enough satisfaction outside your marriage to make your life happy.

What are your own sources of satisfaction in life? How satisfying would your relationship be if you could stop the verbal abuse, but nothing else changed? Would you have enough happiness?

It is no one's job to make you happy. Your adult partner shouldn't be your only, or even your main source of happiness.

A fine romance can make life exciting, and a dedicated partner can be a big help to you in achieving your goals if he shares them or even just supports you emotionally. If you obsess about your unhappy marriage, it's not surprising you don't enjoy the other parts of your life. But if your life is empty except for your partner, you're still going to be unhappy if he behaves better.

How much time do you spend with your partner?

Is that your choice or his choice? Do the two of you agree on how you should spend your time together? Does he want you to travel or camp more, while you want him to do more projects around the house, or more family activities with the children? Is your time full of activities that you see as fun and productive, or will you want your partner to give you more of his time if he is more pleasant to be around? And will that be OK with him?

If he's not pressuring you to be more what he wants you to be, will you take up pressuring him to be the husband you always wanted? In other words, will your use of time be something the two of you will have major disagreements about, even when you're getting along better?

Is he good at supporting you emotionally? Is he likely to be an asset to your emotional life if he isn't an abuser? People usually feel good because of what they say to *themselves* in their self-talk. If you tell yourself that you are valuable, wise, strong, nurturing, a good parent, and a good wife, you'll feel good about yourself.

If you tell yourself that you are fat, lazy, incompetent, stupid and worthless, you'll feel bad. The reason you need to end his verbal abuse is that he's been making lots of negative statements about you and you were starting to believe them.

But does he also criticize himself that way? Is he constantly saying that he's stupid, incompetent, and so on? If he's not good at supporting himself emotionally, he likely won't be good at supporting you. Is he negative to everybody around him as well as you? Or does he avoid everybody around him? If he doesn't support anybody, he'll need a lot of therapy to learn new ways to relate to himself and others.

Are you supposed to be the one supporting his ego by constantly telling him he's good and that you love him? If he's not returning the favor, then your role as ego support is going to wear on you anyway. If he doesn't nurture himself emotionally, he's not likely to take up nurturing you any time soon.

That is a case where sending him to therapy, if he will go, probably would be worth doing. Is he depressed? Has he had a traumatic childhood that he's never dealt with? Maybe he should get psychological treatment to meet his own needs. It will help the relationship indirectly. And you won't need to be his therapist or his mother.

Is your sex life meeting your needs?

I don't mean "Do you have an exciting and fulfilling sex life?" Not everyone wants more or better sex. If you aren't interested, feel free to write sex off.

But if your partner wants sex and you could care less, then you need to deal with the issue. Let me be clear about your behavior now, however. *Don't have sex unless you want it.* Saying yes just traumatizes you further and makes you hate it more. You can't enjoy sex when you say yes but don't want it. You are abusing yourself when you agree without desire.

Instead, you should seek out a counselor who knows something about sexual enrichment. But beware. Few counselors specialize in sexual matters. Most counselors aren't any more comfortable talking about sex than you are. When you've found the right therapist, you can usually learn to increase your sex drive and your sexual happiness.

The odds are good that you aren't frigid, and the odds are good that you don't have a naturally low sex drive. If you don't want sex often, it's probably because you haven't enjoyed it in the past and you don't look forward to it in the future. Sex is a conditioned reaction, like a knee-jerk, or an eye blink. If someone has sexually abused you, that's going to affect your reactions. If you've had lots of sex you didn't want, then your body isn't going to react positively to a sexual approach, even if there is nothing wrong with the specific sexual approach.

If it's your partner refusing to be intimate with you, try hard not to blame yourself. He may say that you don't turn him on any more, but that probably isn't the reason he's not having sex with you. Men are more easily aroused without love or beauty than women are. If you are a willing sex partner and he's saying no, most probably it's about him, not about you.

Is he aging and having trouble with erections but not willing to deal with it? Is he depressed and low on sex drive because his neurotransmitters are out of whack? Make sure he doesn't have a physical problem like diabetes or a heart condition. Then find a counselor who specializes in sexual enrichment. But if he won't go or won't accept his part in the issue, refuse to allow him to shift the blame to you.

On the other hand, if he's telling the truth and he's not attracted to you any more, then he may be sleeping around. Or he may be transitioning into leaving you anyway.

Maybe your partner likes sex with you and you like sex with him when you're not mad at him. Then you have a great future ahead of you when he has stopped abusing you. If he's cooperative, or trainable, or even motivated, you can probably teach him everything you want him to know and do to make your sex life happy. He can teach you what you need to know to make his sex life better also, but that's another book.

Is he a good parent or are you just pretending?

Most women feel that children are their territory and put themselves in charge of child-rearing in general. Does the verbal abuser in your life treat your children as badly as he treats you?

You would certainly intervene to protect your children from a stranger who abused them emotionally. Do you think that there's nothing you can do about it if your husband or partner is verbally and emotionally abusing the children? You can, but defending the children is more difficult and more draining than defending yourself. You aren't always there and he probably commits most of the abuse when you can't intervene. Also he may abuse the children when they genuinely need discipline. You may be confused because you know the kids need to learn to behave. But no one needs to abuse children to teach them good behavior.

Some mothers sabotage the abusive father by ignoring his harsh disciplinary commands behind his back and bad-mouthing him to the children. These mothers have poor boundaries and aren't behaving like parents. These mothers are pretending that both mother and children are all victims together, as though the mother could do nothing to protect the kids when he is around.

Of course the children know better than this. They know that you could leave the abuser and they know you are not successfully protecting them now. They will know your excuses for what they are, at least when they are older. Even if the children later forgive you for staying, the abuser is harming them now. You can protect them from contact with him. They won't have the positive feelings for you that they could have had if you had left the abuser. And they will have negative feelings about themselves caused by an emotionally abusive father or mother.

Sometimes mothers go to the other extreme by never disciplining the children and never teaching them to behave themselves. These mothers may be warm and nurturing and seek the children's approval as though training the children to behave well *required* abusive discipline. These mothers are pretending that if the children have one harsh disciplinarian for a parent and one permissive parent, it will average out into two just-right parents.

It's convenient to think that children reason that way, but it's not true. The children won't average their two bad parents. They won't learn healthy ways to control themselves or relate to others.

Many mothers, and especially those who come from divorced families, feel strongly that they should keep a father at home for the children. They may know that the father or stepfather is not all that attached to the children. They worry that if they leave the abusive man, he will pay no further attention to the children so the children will have no father at all. And those mothers may be right. Some fathers see children as part of a package with a white-picket fence and a wife. If the wife wants nothing more to do with him, the kids just don't rate on their own.

That's part of the reason that many abusive men threaten to take custody of the children after a separation. It's not that he wants to parent the children. He just recognizes that the mother is far more likely to stay with him if leaving him means losing her kids. Controlling men also tend to believe that they will still be able to control the mother after a divorce. Some abusers succeed in manipulating the attorneys, the mother, and a Guardian Ad Litem. Fortunately, most abusive men don't succeed in getting custody after a divorce.

If you're telling yourself the father basically loves the children and you shouldn't be denying the children access to their father, even if he treats you badly, think again. The man who verbally and emotionally abuses you is also verbally and emotionally abusing your children. That's how he acts toward people he sees as weaker than he is. He's not going to set good boundaries with the children. He sees them as possessions, not persons, just as he sees you.

Unlike adults, children lack the means to protect themselves from an adult verbal abuser. The children don't have enough experience of life to understand that if he calls them fat, it means that he's mad at them, not that they are fat. He will brainwash them into low self-esteem and they will see the world and themselves through his eyes. That's an unhealthy outcome for your children and you don't want to enable it.

Does the abuser want a stable, pleasant relationship?

Many targets of abuse think of their relationship as a roller coaster. The abuser is sometimes warm, charming, flattering, positive, and helpful. At other times, he is vicious, manipulative, and verbally violent. Most targets imagine the abuser is looking for a positive, steady path for the relationship because they know that's what they are looking for themselves. But that usually isn't true.

All relationships act like roller coasters at times. Even the worst relationships have many good moments. But abusers probably want it just the way it is. The abuser *chooses* to have an unstable, passionately involving relationship. The abuser chooses to make the other miserable. The abuser has a habit of sabotaging a relationship that is getting too positive and intimate by verbal assaults that send the relationship on a downward swing once again.

You may be the only partner in the relationship who wants a positive, supportive and close relationship. What kind of relationship did the abuser's parents have? Has the abuser had previous bad relationships with other girlfriends or wives? The abuser may want, and currently need, a close and negative relationship to feel normal.

Many people are not looking for happiness.
They're content feeling normal and for them,
that means feeling miserable.

Do I have to change?

We asked this question before, in *Chapter 7: Preparing Yourself to Change.* In that chapter I explained that if you want the abuser to change, then you have to change yourself. I haven't changed my mind about that conclusion. But let's admit that you may be making a third choice of how to handle your situation.

Some years ago I saw a couple for marriage counseling who had had a pretty good marriage. He was in the merchant marine and was gone from home for long periods of time. He made good money and his wife worked only part-time. The children were grown and gone and she enjoyed the perks that came with a hardworking and well-paid husband, even though she didn't see as much of him as she said she would like.

However, she had recently discovered that he was having an affair with a woman who worked for his company. She was devastated by the discovery and told him she was going to leave him unless he ended the affair. He told her he had ended the affair, but after several more months, she discovered evidence that he was continuing to meet with the woman at motels. That was the point where she demanded he go in for marriage counseling.

When I saw the couple together, he was frank about the situation. "I tried to end the affair, but then I found I didn't want to. I'm sorry my wife feels hurt, but I'm not going to stop seeing this woman. Maybe I'll feel differently after a while, but I'm still trying to make up my mind between them."

I met with the woman alone to help her decide what she wanted to do, but she already knew what she wanted to do. She wanted to threaten to leave her husband, and she wanted me, since I was her marriage counselor, to convince her husband to stay with her and leave the other woman.

I'm not in the business of telling people what decisions to make in their lives. I assured the wife that if he wouldn't give up the affair because it was hurting her feelings, he certainly wouldn't give up the affair because I told him he should. Besides, the husband was just as much my patient as she was. Why should I be trying to talk him into giving up the affair if he didn't want to? My job is to give people methods to get to their goals, not to set up the goals I think they should have.

So I suggested to the woman that she had two choices that she could make by herself. She could leave the marriage if she didn't want an actively unfaithful partner. Or she could decide that she wanted the marriage even if her husband was having an affair. But making the husband stop his affair was not one of her possible choices.

I also said that everybody has choices, but sometimes your choices aren't what you think they are. I pointed out to her that her husband didn't have only two choices in his own control at that moment. He had at least three possible choices:

- ◆ He could leave his wife, and take up more permanently with the woman with whom he was having the affair.
- ◆ He could leave his girlfriend, and recommit to his wife.
- ◆ He could continue to have intimate relations with both women.

The girlfriend knew he had a wife and the wife knew he had a girlfriend. Neither woman had broken off their relationship with him. He could go on having sex with both women if he chose. Neither woman had succeeded in forcing him to give up the other one.

For all the wife knew, her husband had always had affairs during the marriage. She had no idea what he had been up to in his time in other ports. He had likely been the source of her Herpes II and HPV infections. Once he had insisted that she go to her doctor for an antibiotic shot, which suggests that he might have given her a sexually transmitted disease at that time too.

In other words, his current affair might be the same infidelity she had been willing to deny throughout their marriage. His current girlfriend lived in the same port as his wife and the wife knew that the affair had been going on for some time. Still, the husband hadn't shown any evidence that he was going to leave his wife for the other women he had romanced.

So I asked her some hard questions. How has your life changed? True, you know now that you have an unfaithful husband. But if you aren't willing to leave him because he's unfaithful, why would he stop having affairs? He can continue to enjoy his affairs without cost, because it's clear you're not going to leave him, even when you know about his affairs.

So, if you're not going to leave him because of the affair, why are you making your life, and his, more unpleasant by constantly complaining to him about the affair? You could leave him right now, and everybody would say you were right. But if you don't intend to leave him, why would you make it more likely for him to leave you by making both of you miserable? Are you trying to get him to leave you? Why?

In other words, I tried to explain to this wife that she didn't know whether her husband would stay with her or not if she forced him to make a choice by leaving him. She did know that without leaving him, he didn't need to make a choice, and he wasn't going to.

Let's pretend that everybody wants an ideal relationship. Unfortunately, not everybody's idea of an ideal relationship is the same. You could be married to someone who is very happy with you, while you are miserable with him. In that situation, what are your choices? If you want something the other person doesn't want, because he wants to abuse and control you, then he has his first choice. But you don't have your first choice because you want him to be pleasant and positive and treat you as an equal.

So what's your second choice?

Choices he can make without her consent:

1. Sex with both women, marriage to one.
2. A relationship with only one of the women (but we don't know which one.)
3. Neither of these relationships.

Choices she can make without his consent:

1. Keep the status quo. Stay in the marriage while he continues the affair.
2. Leave him. (He might leave the other woman, or he might marry the other woman and move in with her.)

If the abuser wants relationships with both women, he currently has what he wants and he has no incentive to change. If the wife leaves him, maybe he would really ditch the other woman and recommit to being faithful (if he ever was.) But without leaving him, she will certainly end up with the status quo. If she wants a marriage to him without him continuing the affair, she has to risk losing the relationship with him altogether, by leaving him. Her first choice may be him without the affair, but she can't get that at all unless she's willing to leave him because he already has his first choice (both women) and has no incentive to change the situation.

Think about these choices in your own situation. In other words, if you don't make a verbal abuser choose between giving you what you want in the relationship and losing you, he's not going to change. Why should he? He already has his first choice. He already has the relationship he wants, verbal abuse and all.

So, even though he is verbally abusing you, you don't have to change. You can decide that it is a higher priority for you to keep the relationship and not risk losing him by changing your behavior.

Or you can decide it's a higher priority to leave him. You can keep away from him and anyone else who might abuse you in the future. If you can keep away from him now, you might be in a better emotional space to cope with abuse at some point in the future.

But saying you're *about* to leave him is not a solution. It's a third choice that is no choice at all. Nothing changes unless you change. Threatening to leave him doesn't change him.

Unfortunately, I have met and counseled far too many women (and men) who wouldn't leave the abuser *and* they wouldn't change their own behaviors. In those cases, the abuser's behaviors continued and the target continued to be miserable.

For many of them, the issue was money. They valued their partner mainly as a provider, not as a partner in a relationship, and they stayed for that reason. Who am I to judge? They each treated the other as an object, but they each had what they wanted most.

Many of the women who wouldn't leave and wouldn't change themselves wouldn't voluntarily give up their partners' approval. Their past relationships had been traumatic and their current adjustment was fragile. Consequently, they weren't willing to stop seeking approval from their partners.

Some of those women left therapy with me before making any other choice, which means they were making the choice to go on with their life as it was. Some of them returned to therapy years later, saying "You were right. Now I'm ready to change."

Summary

To predict the future accurately, you must look at the present realistically. You need to recognize exactly how the abuser is behaving and look for any specific evidence that he might change in the future, whether you change or not. If you aren't realistic about him, you're at risk for *wishing ahead,* or predicting the future based on what you want instead of based on the evidence you have.

If you predict that something will occur, document your predictions so you can see whether or not they are coming true. Write down what you think he's going to change and when. Then look back on your past predictions and see how accurate you were.

How often do you have positive times with him? How often do you think positively about him? Are you leaving your life empty and blaming him for your misery? It's your job to make yourself happy. He couldn't do it even if he wanted to. Arrange your life so you have many sources of happiness.

You will only change him by changing yourself. But you don't have to change. You could leave the relationship now, today. Or you could stay and accept his behavior, whatever it is. Many targets, though, take a third path. They decide that they're going to leave, so they don't bother to change themselves. Then they don't leave because it's too much trouble. They ignore the abusive behavior but they keep complaining about it to others. They aren't looking for happiness. They're looking for someone to blame for their unhappiness, and the abuser makes a great villain.

Let's say he has all the control, acts whatever way he pleases, and you are miserable. That may be exactly what he wants. And maybe you want to share control, get respect from him and be happy. But in that case, he has no incentive to change his behavior because he already has his first choice of a relationship.

You're the one who might want to change the relationship because you don't have your first choice. So what's your second choice? If your second choice is to stay in the relationship the way it is, you'll never get your first choice. If you accept what he most wants, no change will occur.

But if your second choice is to end the relationship, maybe he'll decide he wants you more than he wants control of you. You'll get your first choice and he'll get his second choice. Or, if he decides that he wants control more than he wants you, he'll accept the end of the relationship and go find somebody else to bully. Only if your second choice is to end the relationship does he have any incentive to change his behavior.

CHAPTER 11

Prediction in a Relationship

After getting out of an abusive relationship, many women are anxious about starting a new relationship. They ask,

"How could I have known? When we first started dating, he treated me like a queen. He never had a harsh word for me and he was so romantic and giving, he just bowled me over. He didn't start getting nasty until three years after the wedding and he didn't start hitting me until five years later. How am I supposed to predict whether a man will abuse me? Or could just anyone become an abuser?"

I don't know whether *anyone*, man or woman, could become an abuser. I do know that you can probably predict whether a particular person you're getting to know intimately will become an abuser. You can do so because the basic, underlying theme with a person who *is* or *will be* an abuser is that he wants to control you. So, before you make any lasting commitments to someone, you need to find out what happens when he discovers that you are not willing to be in his control.

How to predict that someone may be an abuser

Think about the early stages of a relationship. Both parties are on their best behavior. Both parties express positive thoughts and feelings toward the other. Both give in or give way readily when there is a disagreement. This is the honeymoon stage of a relationship, when each partner is trying to look like an ideal mate. If you're looking for a temporary good time, just continue to date and don't stay with anyone for long. But if you're looking for a long-term relationship, don't be fooled by the honeymoon. It's your job to watch for the red flags.

Sometimes a woman reports that her current partner tried hard to please her at the beginning of the relationship but later he became insulting and verbally abusive. How can you know whether the new man you're dating now will develop into a verbal abuser later?

You can and should watch a potential partner for signs of future verbal abuse and battering. Here are five red flags to help you predict the future behavior of a new partner.

- His history with other partners
- His sense of urgency about getting into the relationship
- How he treats you when you tell him no
- How he treats you when you disagree with him
- How he treats you when you behave independently

Red flag #1: History with other partners

This is the age of the Internet. You can probably find out if your boyfriend has previously been arrested for domestic violence. Some men will drop hints. He may say that his previous wife was crazy and had him arrested, even though he didn't lay a finger on her. Sometimes you'll know the previous wife or girlfriend and you can ask her for more information. When you're talking to a previous girlfriend or wife, you're dealing with someone who isn't very objective about the man, but that doesn't necessarily mean that she would lie about battering or verbal abuse.

No matter what the man says, you should always find out more about a man who has had previous arrests for domestic violence. He may tell you that his wife dropped the charges and recanted her lies. But the police report may say that he broke her collarbone and that he violated the restraining order three times before she moved out of town.

Don't expect a man to be candid with you if he was violent in a previous relationship. A man who isn't violent shouldn't object if you make discreet inquiries about how his previous relationships ended. If you've had bad experiences before, or worry about them, it's your right to do your homework.

Red flag #2: Urgency to get into a relationship

Someone who is likely to turn negative in a relationship may be urgent about getting into a relationship faster and deeper than you'd like. Although he is only one month post-separation from a wife of twenty years, he wants sex on the first date. After dating you for a month he wants to move in with you, or have you move in with him right away.

This really urgent guy may disguise the urgency by telling you how wonderful *you* are. He may tell you he has finally found true love and he's ready to settle down and get on with living happily ever after. Meanwhile you probably have a little voice in your head saying "But he doesn't even know me. And I don't know him. How can he be so sure?"

If he's an abuser, he can be so sure because he doesn't care what you're like. He plans to change anything about you that he doesn't like. After all, if he's an abuser, he plans to control you, not just date you. He doesn't like being between relationships and doesn't think of women as being different from one another. He figures that any woman willing to date him is probably as good as any other.

If a man is constantly pushing at your boundaries by demanding that you let him get closer to you than you feel comfortable with, push right back.

"No, thanks. I'm not ready to move in with anyone right now."

If he continues to demand that you move in, push back.

"I know what you want and you know what I want. It feels like you're trying to push me around to get your way. I don't want to have an unpleasant conversation with you about rushing the relationship."

Watch out here for manipulative ploys like *personal commercials*. If he says "You don't trust me!" or "You have a problem with commitment!" push back by agreeing with him.

"Of course I don't trust you. I've only known you for three months!"

Or

"I agree. I have a problem with commitment to men I've only known for three months."

Don't defend yourself by disagreeing with him when you're entitled to distrust him and entitled to postpone commitment.

Is he likely to leave the relationship because you won't move fast enough for him? Maybe he will. But if so, you found out what you wanted to know. He's not the man for you. He only wanted you when he thought he could push you around. Mourn the loss of what looked like a good prospect and try again.

Are you looking for a long-term boyfriend or just a good time now? A man who crowds you in the beginning will keep right on pushing for whatever he wants. By then you may have committed more to the relationship than you thought wise in the first place.

Red flag #3: Negative actions when you say no

Since an abuser wants to be in control of you, you're not going to see his true colors unless you stay outside his control. Therefore, you need to curb your natural desire to please him, at least some of the time. Be honest with him about what you want and don't want. Don't tell yourself that you want this relationship at any cost. If you do, it will cost you your ability to control yourself and to control half of the relationship.

He wants to go out to the movies tonight and you're tired and want to stay home. Curb the urge to give in just to please him. Offer him one alternative, then stick to your 'no.'

"No thanks. Feel free to go without me tonight or bring a movie to my house."

If he doesn't take no for an answer from you, what's going on? Everybody wants his or her own way. That goes for you as well as the new date you're evaluating for the long-term. You can get your way (stay home) without his permission. He can get his way (go to a movie) without your permission. What's at stake here is not whether he can have his way or whether you can have your way. You can each have your way without the other person giving permission or approval.

What's at stake is whether you can have your way, do what you want and *also* have the company or the approval of the other person. Have you offered to do without the other person's company for example by saying "Feel free to go without me tonight?" Is he refusing to go to the movies without you? Then the argument is about whether he can control you by luring you into accompanying him to the movies when you don't feel like it.

It's not unreasonable for your new date to want your company. It's flattering that he wants your company. He's not at fault for wanting you around, and if you punish him for inviting you places, the invitations probably won't continue. You don't have a right to expect him always to want what you want, or always to give in to you. But you do have a right to expect reasonable behavior from him when you tell him no.

What should someone do when you turn him down? Agreeing with you is not the only reasonable behavior. In the previous scenario, a man who says "OK, OK. I'll just go without you!" and slams the door on the way out is being childish— and feel free to tell him so the next time you see him. The slammed door was a punishment, but you did suggest he go without you as one of the alternatives. And he didn't need your permission to go without you.

A man who says "OK, I'll bring a movie over, but I get to pick the movie!" is offering a counterproposal. If you say, "So what do you propose?" and he proposes a movie you know you'll hate, make him another offer. For example, say "OK, but I plan to fall asleep as soon as it starts getting gory!" or "How about _____ instead? You know we'd both like that one." In both cases, the case where he decides to go alone and the case where he agrees to bring a movie over, the man has acted reasonably.

If the guy proposes *anything else* aloud as an alternative for the two of you or for himself alone, even if it is something that you might not like, it is probably a reasonable response. Of course if he says he's going to get drunk, or pick up his ex-girlfriend for the night, that's a punishment response as opposed to a reasonable one.

There are three kinds of negative responses he can make to you when you say no.

1. He may get negative and verbally abusive.

If he calls you names, comments on your character unfavorably, or curses, he is reacting in a controlling fashion. He is punishing you to cure your tendency to think for yourself.

If you dread saying no to a man, you likely have a good reason for those feelings. The man probably punishes you with negative behaviors whenever you do something he doesn't like. That's not a reasonable way to behave.

Many people who have been a target of verbal abuse in the past intend to trust no one in the future. They predict what the current boyfriend will do based on what their past boyfriend did. They aren't looking at the unfolding evidence of the new person's behavior. They become paranoid, viewing everyone negatively.

They effectively build walls around themselves that others cannot breach. Every approach from someone feels like an attack.

Building walls immobilizes targets, but it does not serve to protect them. Targets need to learn many different behaviors so they have a choice of defensive and aggressive tactics. They need to be mobile and flexible to enjoy life.

Learn to be vigilant and a good observer of others so you can choose the best responses to them. Get in touch with your own feelings so you notice whether this person is meeting your needs. Targets need skills in communication. They need to be able to thrust and parry in a conversation. People with good self-control need not resign themselves to domination by an abuser. They don't need to retreat behind fortified walls.

Those who refuse to enter new relationships are often refusing to trust themselves. They don't trust themselves to withdraw from a bad relationship.

Targets who don't trust themselves to leave may have stayed in abusive situations too long in the past. Your best choice in the long term is to learn to control yourself so you don't need to trust others not to attack. If you can trust yourself to leave a person or a relationship that isn't meeting your needs, you don't need to trust the other nearly as much.

Do you trust yourself to say no? Before you respond to a new person, think about rewards and punishments. Parents reward and punish children all the time and they'd be at fault if they didn't. It's the parent's job to teach children how to be healthy, well-socialized adults. That means the parent is often rewarding the child for doing what the parent wants and punishing the child for doing what the parent doesn't want.

Parents who use too many punishments and not enough rewards create angry, unsocialized, unpleasant children. Those children are far less functional as adults than the children of parents who reward them more often.

It's the same way in adult relationships. If you try to get what you want in an adult relationship by punishing the other when you don't get your way, you are (surprise!) an emotional and verbal abuser.

2. He may keep trying to coerce or manipulate you.

He may try to argue you into going out with him. Even if his words are sweet and loving, the fact that he isn't taking your no for an answer means that he is not being sweet and loving. It would be reasonable for him to believe that your 'no' meant 'no.' It is not reasonable for him to keep challenging your decisions and trying to change them.

If he tells you once that he disagrees with you and that he wishes you'd change your mind, he's given you a reasonable response. You needed the information that he disagreed with you because, overall, you need to please him enough to keep him around. But if he tells you ten times that he disagrees with you and that he still wants you to change your mind, he's not just expressing himself. He's harassing you and trying to punish you into giving him what he wants.

3.   He may withdraw and sulk.

A verbal abuser may stop communicating and stop participating in your life. For example, instead of saying he's going to the movies alone, he may simply walk out the door. You're left to wonder where he's going and what he's thinking. This is another punishment strategy. It is similar to the tactics of a man who curses you or calls you names.

The man who calls you names is approaching you and getting *close and negative*. The man who withdraws is getting *distant and negative*. That can seem more punishing. It may be harder to respond because you probably want a closer relationship.

The man who approaches you and calls you names to punish you is striking at your feelings about yourself. He wants to lower your self-esteem and your pride. The man who withdraws from you is striking at your safety and security in the relationship. He is activating your fear of abandonment. He wants you to be afraid he will leave you and to be afraid you will be alone. If abusing or withdrawing puts you in his control, he'll do it again.

You need to control your fear of abandonment to deal with someone who sulks or gives you the silent treatment. Use a brief time-out. Prepare to abandon him (temporarily) if he continues to behave that way. For example, if the man walks out the door, whether or not he goes to the movie, he probably expects you to be anxious and afraid when he comes back. He expects you to plead with him to talk to you about what's going on. Then he'll refuse to talk about it until you are desperate enough to give him what he wants.

The appropriate response to his withdrawal is a well-communicated withdrawal of your own. Does the man have a right to be in the house because he lives there? In that case, when he comes back, don't approach him or ask him to talk. Just ignore him. Don't do the things for him that you usually would. Act as if he doesn't exist and go about your business.

If he approaches you in any way, positively or negatively, give him the same verbal message:

"You didn't tell me where you were going or what you were going to do when you walked out. I'm ready to talk about the issue with you when you're ready. But I'm not going to continue doing things for you until we have an agreement about how we conduct disagreements."

If he comes back and ignores the whole issue, don't pretend that everything's fine between you. Don't let his withdrawal go unchallenged. Leaving the relationship in that way shouldn't be acceptable to you now or in the future. He was punishing you by his withdrawal and trying to train you to give him whatever he wants. He was trying to control you. Don't ignore the behavior.

Let's say he doesn't live with you. He walked out without a word and he stayed away for three days without contacting you. Then he calls you pretending nothing has happened. You don't have a right to demand he only do what you want. You don't have a right to demand that he tell you everywhere he goes ahead of time as though he were an eight-year-old. But if he has a right to leave you without a word and take up the relationship again on his own terms, you have the same right.

If your new guy is not willing to talk about his feelings and needs and agree about how the two of you will disagree, don't sit at home waiting for him. What you want is a relationship in which each of you pleases the other enough. You don't want a relationship where he is calling all the shots. Don't sit at home waiting for him to get around to you.

After he returns home, if he goes back to silence, you do the same. You only give him one message when he approaches you, but you do it over and over, without any variation.

The message you give him is this:

"You can leave me any time you want and I can't stop you, but I can also leave you and you can't make me take you back without my consent."

You want to let the abuser know that you don't intend to stay in a one-way relationship. You want to let the abuser know that you can't control him, but he can't control you. And you need to be prepared to end the relationship if he keeps withdrawing from you for long periods.

Don't tolerate a relationship in which the other holds his companionship hostage whenever you disagree with him or displease him. If he doesn't want you around unless he is in control of you, he's not worth having an intimate relationship with. You want a partner who is adult enough to stay in contact with you, even when he's mad.

Red flag #4: Negative actions when you disagree

If your new guy gets negative when you disagree with him, you may be tempted to play down your own opinions to appear more compatible with his. Don't do it.

Start and continue the relationship by being honest and open about the ways that you disagree with him. If you hold your peace when you may disagree with him, you won't be able to judge whether he becomes controlling when your opinions differ.

No two people hold the same opinions all the time, but why should they? If one of you is a Republican and the other a Democrat, it stands to reason that you will have areas in which you disagree, about candidates, philosophy, values, and issues. If you come from different backgrounds or different religions, of course there will be areas of disagreement. A disagreement isn't a problem. The problem is how he treats you (or how you treat him) when you disagree.

If you're a fan of rock and your partner is a devotee of classical music, there should be no problem. After all, when you're apart you probably each have plenty of time to listen to the music of your choice. You can listen to your choice of music with earphones on when you're in the same space. You don't need to force the other to listen to something he hates. In other words, there are plenty of ways to agree to disagree without either person having to give up what he wants.

Watch out for people who take it as a personal insult if you don't hold similar or identical views about the world. You shouldn't have to listen to negative comments about your music or your taste or the musicians you like. If you disagree about music, he shouldn't tell you that you are wrong. uninformed, immature, biased. or foolish.

Your boyfriend shouldn't try to change your opinion whenever he discovers that it is not the same as his. That's an enormous red flag about his wish to control you. You shouldn't have to agree with him in order for him to respect your thoughts and choices. You shouldn't have to defend your taste or your opinions against his attacks if it turns out that you have opinions he doesn't like. If you find yourself keeping quiet about your own opinions because you fear abuse or harassment, you know that you can expect more abuse like this in the future.

Red flag #5: Negative actions when you act independently

Abusers don't want you to be independent. That would diminish their control. If you're involved with someone who intends to keep you for himself, listen for his comments when you mention you're going to do something that doesn't include him.

If the new date shows that he's disappointed when you're planning to do something at a time he wanted your company, that's natural and reasonable. But if you get anger, threats, withdrawal, or frequent negative references to your independent activities, you should hear alarm bells.

It's natural at the beginning of a relationship to want to spend a great deal of time with the new partner, but beware if your new love tries to exclude others from your life. Some emotional abusers directly forbid or deny you their permission or approval to see someone else, even a family member or an old friend.

Sometimes abusers are more indirect, making critical and negative comments about someone with whom you already have a relationship. In the long run, an abuser will try to isolate you from anyone who might intervene on your side. He'd like you to give up contact with family or friends who would criticize his behavior or offer you emotional support or resources to leave him.

Your new love isn't going to like all of your friends and family, and it's unreasonable to expect that he will. It's not reasonable, however, for him to get upset when you stay in contact with your old friends.

In other words, if your new boyfriend doesn't want to join your bowling league, that's not unreasonable. It *is* unreasonable for him to badmouth the bowling league, your friends in the league, and your wish to continue. You are entitled to bowl since you enjoy it, even if he doesn't share your interest.

Shall I stay in my current relationship?

As I said, you don't have only two choices in response to that question. You have three choices about your current relationship.

1. You can stay with him and hope for the best, but be willing to accept whatever happens, or
2. You can leave the relationship.

As long as you think you have only two choices, you'll probably stay in the relationship, even if you don't much want to. That's why it's important to remember you have a third choice.

3. You can stay in the relationship, at least temporarily, but work to change your own behaviors. You can postpone deciding to leave him until you see whether or not your changes make such a big difference that you want to stay.

If you think you only have two choices, you probably think they are: (1) staying in the relationship the way it is and not changing yourself or (2) leaving the relationship in order to stop the verbal abuse. When you think of staying, you're actually thinking of putting up with the verbal abuse and not changing yourself.

Let's suppose you have a bad evening or a bad week or a bad month with your partner. You begin to think about leaving him. What will that mean for you?

To start with, if you're married to him, you're looking at a legal divorce, which will force major economic changes in your life. Even if you eventually come out better financially than you were during the marriage, which most women don't, you're liable to be broke in the short-term. Two people living separately can't live as cheaply as two people living together.

If you have children in common with him, you'll probably be forced to have sustained contact with him. You'll still be sharing parenting with him after you leave. He may tell you he'll get custody, but that's unlikely. He may tell you that you can't make it financially without him, but that's unlikely too. In the short run, however, you're looking at some hard times financially as well as emotionally.

If you're living with the person with whom you're breaking up, you have lots of issues to consider. You'll need to separate your property, separate your social lives, tell all your friends and relatives, and maybe even change jobs or move away. It's a lot of work to end a relationship, so you may decide that it's too overwhelming, and you can stand it a little longer. Let's look at the meaning of each of those choices.

I decide to stay with him just as he is

I adjust my self-esteem downward, and give up some of my goals in life. I pretend that my children aren't affected by his behavior, or I pretend that I can make up to the children for his behavior toward me and toward them, whatever that is.

I cope with life the way I always have. When he abuses me, I ignore it, or tell him how hurt I am. Maybe I escape into alcohol or drugs. Maybe I take up gambling or have an affair. Maybe I end up in a clinical depression and don't have the energy to do anything; that keeps me in the relationship. My partner won't approve of me treating my depression since I'm harder to control when I feel good, so maybe I put up with the depression also.

I decide to leave him permanently

I know it will be a long, difficult process, or I soon find out that it will be a long, difficult process. He doesn't want me to leave and he pulls out all the stops to get me back.

If I propose to leave him, he probably will alternate between treating me better and continuing the verbal abuse. Maybe I'll change my mind and decide to stay after he has treated me better for a short period of time. If so, I've just made the process of leaving him much more difficult. The next time I try to leave him, he won't believe I mean it. And he'll probably be right.

I decide to change myself and my behavior

This means I don't immediately decide to stay or to go. Instead I make a decision to change my own behaviors, even if it's hard. I decide to wait to see where the relationship ends up.

I work on the changes this book suggests, and maybe other changes that are unique to me and my situation. I try to find other resources that help me figure out what I'm doing that rewards his abusive behaviors. I stop giving him his way. I learn to control myself so he can't control me.

If I go with this choice, changing myself, there are many possible outcomes. Here are the most likely:

Possible outcome 1: He responds by grudgingly, and slowly, behaving in the ways I like. Since I'm spending more time now enjoying his company, and telling him so, he is enjoying the relationship more too. As I get better at responding rapidly and consistently to his abuse, he tries out on me the behaviors he already uses to get his way with his boss, his friends and his coworkers. Those non-abusive methods work with me also, so he continues to treat me in more responsible ways. Because I've been careful to give him plenty of positive feedback (when he deserves it) he's getting better at giving me positive feedback, even when he isn't trying to get something out of me. Gradually, I start to relax when he is around.

Sometimes we can laugh about how we used to behave with each other. However, I never totally forget to pay attention to his behavior. I've discovered that when I pay attention to how people treat me, all my relationships improve. I stay in this relationship because it's now non-abusive and meets my needs.

Possible outcome 2: He responds to the changes in my behavior by physically threatening me for the first time. I leave him, probably sooner rather than later. I may have to call the police first if he assaults me.

My refusal to accept the verbal abuse has uncovered the fact that he only wants a relationship with me, or any woman, if he remains in control and able to abuse me at will. He was a batterer in disguise all along, but he never had to get physical with me to get his way before.

However, I now have new skills in recognizing abusive behavior, in responding to abusive behavior, and in protecting myself from him and people like him. I feel confident about my decision to leave him, in part because he started to batter me physically. I will have many more demands of him during the divorce and I will have more ways to protect my children from him legally after we separate.

Possible outcome 3: His verbally abusive behavior becomes less frequent. Although things are better in that way, I discover that I don't enjoy his company very much. I have too many bad memories of the past. Our current relationship hasn't added more positive time together. I discover that even when he's not verbally abusing me, I don't like him anymore. Our lives increasingly go separate ways.

Maybe I decide I'm better off alone, and leave him. Or maybe he takes up with somebody at the office or the shop who is twenty years younger than he is. I find out about it and leave him, or he leaves me. I feel sorry for her and wish I'd left him first, but generally I'm content that the relationship is over.

And I have all the skills I've learned from the process. I notice abuse, respond to it rapidly and consistently, and don't take up with another abuser because I've gotten out of the habit.

So you see, unless you change, either leaving the relationship or staying in the relationship won't be a permanent or a safe choice. He doesn't want you to leave, so he makes it difficult for you to leave by promising to change, going into therapy with you, and bringing flowers. You don't really believe he's changed but you give it a try. Then you find out you were right, he hasn't changed permanently, and you didn't change either. So now you're back to thinking about leaving again but you're still there.

Deciding to leave him will take a very long time. He'll be showing you his worst behavior as well as his best. He begs your mother to intervene for him. He criticizes you to your boss hoping that you'll lose your job. He hides the assets so you won't get your fair share of money from the marriage.

Or maybe he takes up with another woman and you remember how much you used to love him and feel terribly jealous. Unless you're really working hard at your self-control, now you're ready to take him back.

If you believe that you have only two choices, you are likely to create your own roller-coaster. Your best bet is to learn to be consistent in your responses to him, so you can see him at his best. You may still decide to leave him, but leaving him will be a lot easier when he can't seduce you emotionally any longer.

Summary

In this chapter I've dusted off my crystal ball to look at what the future may bring you. If you're starting a new relationship, can you successfully predict whether the other will be an abuser in the future if he isn't one now? You probably can. Here are five red flags that predict someone could become an abuser.

1. He abused previous partners
2. He's urgent to get deeply involved with you immediately
3. He punishes you when he doesn't get his way
4. He punishes you when you disagree with him
5. He punishes you when you act independently

What is unreasonable behavior when you disagree or say no or act independently? Getting negative or verbally abusive is unreasonable. Working to get you to change your mind is unreasonable. And withdrawing or sulking is unreasonable. If he's punishing you, he's being unreasonable.

If you're trying to decide whether to leave your current relationship, notice that you have three choices, not just two. You can leave him. You can stay and accept the verbal abuse. Or you can stay and change your own behaviors. You're kidding yourself if you tell yourself that you don't have to change because you're going to leave him unless you are now actively working on leaving. If you aren't acting toward leaving, or working on changing your behaviors, then you're making the third choice, namely accepting the status quo.

So what's likely to happen if you do make these changes? I think there are three most likely results.

1. You may live happily ever after with him.
2. He may get physically abusive with you because he still intends to keep control of you. If so, I hope you'll leave him then, or
3. He may behave better, but you still won't find happiness with him.

No matter what the result with this partner, though, you won't lose your new confidence and your communication skills. What you've learned about stopping abuse will help you now with this abuser and with many others who have bad communication habits. You'll have a much better understanding of yourself and others, and you'll be able to protect yourself from verbal abusers.

CHAPTER 12

What Have You Learned?

You made it! You had many different thoughts, feelings and reactions as you read through this book, but you're still with me. Let's review what you've learned about verbal abuse and how to end it in your life.

If you control yourself, no one else can control you.

If you're a woman, you won't necessarily have inferior skills in fighting off verbal abuse. It's true that you are likely to be weaker physically. You probably have less training in combat sports than men do. But women can do just as much damage with verbal abuse as men can, and female verbal abusers have just as much to learn about stopping the abuse as male verbal abusers do.

Women may be more vulnerable to verbal abuse than men because:

♦ Mothers teach women to be peacemakers. Women often don't learn to fight back or even to stand their ground.

♦ Mothers raise their daughters to depend on the approval of others. The more abusive or harsh their upbringing, the more women may be willing to tolerate bad treatment from others.

♦ Women are more likely than men to tolerate a bad situation until they are ready to leave. However, women are more likely to leave a bad relationship than men are.

An appropriate name for someone who is on the receiving end of verbal abuse is target *because:*

♦ The abuser thinks of her as an object, not as a person.
♦ The abuser is directing the abuse to her, aiming and firing at her deliberately.
♦ The abuse has a goal. It isn't random behavior. The abuser's goal is control of the one he abuses.
♦ The abuser looks down on the object of the abuse. He sees her as inferior to him.

The abuser doesn't think of a relationship as a team of two people. He doesn't work to meet his partner's needs. The abuser thinks only about himself and the goods and services the target can provide him.

Not all abusers are willing to change their ways. The person you're in a relationship with may be one of the abusers who refuses to change. However, if you control yourself, you prevent the abuser from controlling you and the abuse is far less likely to occur. The abuser will change if you do because his old patterns of behavior don't work anymore. He has to find new patterns to use with you.

Changing your behavior is not easy, but you can do it. You'll need to change your beliefs as well as your actions. You'll need to understand the goals of the abuser as well as your own goals. After reading this book, you'll have the information and the opportunity to practice the skills necessary to end verbal abuse.

Make sure you're safe

Is the verbal abuser you're considering training a batterer in disguise? It's urgent that you consider that issue. If the abuser hasn't gotten physical with you yet, are you afraid of what he might do in the future? What gives you the impression that he might be willing to escalate and damage you physically? You should take your fears and his threats seriously.

Are you safe training the abuser to treat you better? If you are dealing with someone who is *only* a verbal abuser, it is worth trying. But don't provoke someone who is a batterer. If the abuser is someone who has been physically violent with you, with your children, or with previous partners or family members, it is not safe to defy him. You need to call on police and the courts to manage abusers who physically force you or physically punish you for going your own way. It is not safe to try to change his ways when you don't have witnesses and when he can retaliate in private.

It's not that abusers who only verbally and emotionally harass you are wonderful partners. They are scary and traumatic people, but you're much less likely to die at their hands. There are many violent people in this world who feel so strongly about owning the victim/target that they are willing to kill. Some of them are also willing to kill themselves if they don't feel in control of the target any more. You don't want to be one of those targets.

You need to evaluate whether the abuser is threatening you physically. You need to evaluate that over and over while you work to change him. Minimizing or denying the threat presented by an abuser could be the most dangerous, and possibly the most lethal, thing you ever do.

So, ask yourself, does the abuser have a history of violence against others? Has someone accused him of domestic violence before? Has he been arrested for assault? Has he been asked or forced to undergo domestic violence treatment? Do others think he has an anger problem? Has he had treatment for anger problems? Whether the abuser agrees that he has an anger problem or not, the fact that others around him have thought so is important evidence about his behavior.

If the one who is verbally abusing you has previously been violent in a relationship, you will not escape the same treatment. No matter what terrible things he says about his previous girlfriends or wives, it would be smart to consult them, or consult people who know them. You don't want this information to spy on the abuser and to pry into his past. You're asking because it is important for your safety and the safety of your children and friends.

Why should you dedicate your energy to retraining a batterer? If your partner is someone who is willing to hurt you and your family physically in order to get his way, what do you owe him? Leave him to the professionals. Even if you were a counselor or psychologist, he'd never be your patient. Even if he's wealthy, wouldn't you rather be alive to enjoy what money you have?

Of course a batterer can change, but if he doesn't want to, he won't. You can't change him against his will, although you can probably protect yourself against him whether he likes it or not. I doubt the relationship is offering you enough to risk your life, or the lives of your family members.

The longer you are around a batterer, the higher the risk. He is more likely to send you to the hospital or kill you the longer you stay with him. Look at the statistics. Domestic violence is the leading cause of injury to women—more than car accidents, muggings, and rapes combined. Every day in the United States, more than three women are murdered by their husbands or boyfriends. Don't let that be you.

Don't be fooled because the abuser has never laid a hand on you. If he punches a wall in front of you, he's a batterer. If he stops you physically from leaving a room when he wants to shout at you, he's a batterer. If he takes your purse, or the car keys, or the telephone when you are trying to leave him during an argument, he's a batterer. If he follows you to work, or doles money out to you dollar by dollar, he's a batterer. Batterers escalate from emotional and verbal abuse to physical and sexual abuse. Batterers don't strike their target one time and never do it again unless the target leaves him after that single episode. Four out of five battered women surveyed believe that the emotional abuse was worse than the physical abuse.

> *Remember that leaving a batterer*
> *is temporarily more dangerous*
> *than staying with him.*

The abuser is more likely to stalk you, threaten you, injure you or kill you *after* you separate from him than when you were still in the same household with him. Do not separate without doing your homework and learning how to keep yourself, and your children, safe.

But don't assume that someone *is* a batterer because you fear their anger or fear conflict. You may be afraid because of your experiences with previous men or previous partners or because of your experiences in childhood. If you don't have good evidence that your partner is a batterer, consider going to a therapist. Pick one who specializes in treating battered or abused women and share the incidents that concern you with the therapist. Let the professional help you understand whether he is genuinely threatening you or whether you are still feeling the fear from your past experiences.

Don't confuse the statements of the abuser with true statements. Just because the abuser says you will starve, that's probably not the reality. An abusive husband who says he won't pay alimony or child support won't continue to be in charge of your finances after a divorce. The judge will decide the financial matters, not your ex-husband. It's true that some men who are self-employed and criminal can pay you less by lying to you and to the court. But women are better able to collect support now than ever before. It won't be fun, but it will likely be possible.

Some husbands and boyfriends emotionally and physically abuse the children, and that makes the relationship a battering relationship. You are not doing the children a favor keeping them in a household with a verbal abuser, and you are definitely harming them if you keep them with a physical abuser. The state will consider you at fault as well as the abuser if you have not protected the children from harm. You can protect yourself and the children by reporting the abuser to child protection authorities.

Be particularly cautious about a man who stalks you. He may be the most dangerous abuser of all, even if he has not been physically violent with you in the past. More stalkers kill their victims than other sorts of batterers do.

Don't believe all the abuser's threats. The abuser is often bluffing. For example, the abuser may threaten to leave you but unless he moves out or serves you with legal papers, then he's not serious about ending the relationship. It's far more likely the threat is a ploy to make you more submissive. Don't believe the abuser will get custody of your children if he tells you he will. Don't even assume that he wants custody. Don't believe that you're crazy, or that anybody else will believe you're crazy just because he says you are.

If the abuser threatens to kill you or to kill your children, take the threat seriously and make a safety plan to escape. If the abuser threatens to kill himself, treat him as though he has threatened your life and be cautious. But you don't need to feel that you are responsible for keeping him alive. You couldn't do that even if you were a mental health professional. Someone who is willing to kill himself is often willing to kill you, your family, and your children as well. Take the threat seriously, but don't take it as a reason for staying. The threat may be a manipulation designed to keep you with him.

How does verbal abuse work?

Verbal abuse is any verbal behavior that is negative or punishing in intent or effect. Verbal abuse is a set of strategies designed to obtain or maintain control of the abuser's target. Verbal abuse is a method, not a goal in itself. It's bad for your health, your growth, your self-esteem, and your bonds to your family and your community. It can be devastating and it can effectively keep you in the abuser's control.

If a target isn't aware of the goals of the abuser, she may come to believe his negative statements and feel that she deserves punishment. You might think that the abuser will change the way he says something if you tell him it hurts your feelings. People who care about your feelings *would* change what they say. But abusers will rejoice if you tell them they have hurt your feelings. They *want* you to hurt because it helps them achieve their goals.

Abusers are 100 percent responsible for their behavior. They choose their strategies to reach their goals. The target is *not* responsible for the behavior of the abuser.

But targets do *affect* the behavior of the abuser because they give the abuser rewards and punishments for the way he behaves. If you *pay* someone to behave badly, he's likely to do it again. Your best choice will be to reward good behavior, when the abuser uses it, but take the rewards away when he verbally abuses you. Using that strategy, you will lower the frequency of his abusive behavior without setting up an aggressive fight with him.

Most people don't understand verbal abuse. They think that it's easy to train someone to treat you well. They may think that a target only stays with an abuser because she's weak or because she likes to be abused.

Abusers don't abuse in public often because they know it's not socially acceptable. Therefore, others don't realize what the abuser is doing because they don't know how often and how persistently the abuser behaves this way.

Most people can't believe that someone who loves them would abuse them. Targets keep trying to justify the abuse so they can still feel good about the abuser. Targets don't want to see the abuser as a bad person so they minimize and deny the abuse.

Targets of verbal abuse are often people who have been targeted before, in their childhood, by their parents and family. Those abusive parents have already told the targets cruel and demeaning things, so it's easier for those targets to believe that abusive statements are true.

Targets may also believe they are wrong because the abuser says so. Targets know they're not perfect, so they may think they deserve punishment. They still feel like a child approaching a parent. They don't recognize that an adult doesn't have the right to punish another adult to get his way.

But mostly targets don't know what to do about verbal abuse. They may try many different tactics to stop the abuser, and give up when nothing works. They believe that abuse is a normal part of relationships. They decide that if they want the relationship, they have to put up with the abuse.

Preparing to change

Verbal abuse works well on targets who are dependent on the approval of their partners. Many targets keep working for approval, no matter how little approval they are getting. They think they can earn approval from him. But the abuser withholds approval to keep targets submissive and to stay in control of them. Because targets want approval, they continue to try to get close to the abuser to *solve* the disagreements. They try to be nicer to the abuser. The energy and effort the target offers serves the abuser far more than it does her.

Relationships can be described as positive or negative, close or distant. Abusers want a different sort of relationship than their targets want. The abuser most wants *closeness* to the target while she wants more positive times. He wants to punish the target into giving him love and affection, goods and services. He is willing to keep the relationship negative, because he thinks the negativity keeps her close. If targets respond by staying close to the abuser and accepting the negative tone in the relationship, then the abuser has the relationship he wants: close and negative.

To extricate yourself from a close and negative relationship, you are best off getting more *distant* from the abuser by denying him an audience, and by not giving him your companionship and attention. The abuser wants the target's services as an audience and companion. He expects to get them even though he is abusing you. To change this, you will need to accept a more distant relationship than the abuser wants, and maybe more distant than you want.

A verbal abuser can't abuse you if you aren't listening. A verbal abuser can't punish you if you aren't around to take punishment. You can stop the abuse from succeeding simply by avoiding the abuser when he abuses, and letting the abuser know that your company is a privilege that he has to earn with good behavior.

Recognizing verbal abuse

Let's define abuse as wrong or improper use or misuse. Verbal abuse involves bad or improper treatment, harsh or coarsely insulting language, or corrupt or improper behaviors. Not everyone recognizes abuse when she hears it, probably because some abuse involves constant repetition of the negative actions or words.

The abuser won't see his actions as abusive. He thinks he's telling the truth or expressing himself or letting it all hang out. He believes the target deserved it or earned it or made him do it. He isn't looking for other ways to talk because these actions and words work, and he knows it. He believes that it is more important for him to get his way than for the target to be happy. He recognizes that his target won't like his actions but he believes that he can, and should, force her to be present and to continue to associate with him anyway. He believes that he can force her to love him.

But a statement isn't abusive just because you don't like it. If someone *tells* you he is angry, as opposed to *showing* you that he is angry, that is appropriate. You need to learn to cope with disapproval and to disagree without fear. Adults learn to give and take in relationships. If someone can control you by disapproving of you, your life will have much more conflict and much more disapproval.

Statements like these are not necessarily abusive:

"I'm mad at you for what you just did, because...."
"I don't agree with you and I think you're wrong."
"No, I'm not going to do that. I'm going to keep on doing it my way."
"I'm right about this and I don't think you should be mad at me."
"We don't agree on this and I don't think more conversation about it will help."

Here are some kinds of verbal abuse to recognize and watch for:

- ♦ *Name-calling*
- ♦ *Repetition* of something negative already said or already expressed
- ♦ *Harsh and unjust criticism*
- ♦ *Mind-reading,* or telling the target what the abuser thinks she feels or means
- ♦ *Stereotyping* the target, or groups the target may belong to
- ♦ *Commanding and demanding* instead of asking or trying to agree
- ♦ *Judging,* deciding what is right and wrong for the target
- ♦ *Accusing the target of something true* so it sounds terrible
- ♦ *Minimizing and denying* the target's feelings
- ♦ *Blaming the target* for her bad feelings

- *Hostile humor*
- *Public criticism*
- *Constant arguing,* by bringing up the same problem over and over.

Changing your beliefs to create change in your relationship

The abuser is responsible for his words and actions. He has a choice of ways to respond and behave. But the target is also responsible for her actions and words. Since she is in control of her words, unless she is in physical danger, she needs to hold herself accountable for resisting his abuse.

Suppose there is an interaction in which the target prepares dinner later than the abuser wants. The abuser calls the target names, so she apologizes and tries hard never to be late again. The abuser is 100 percent responsible for calling her names. She couldn't have made him call her names so she is not responsible for his behavior. However, the way she behaves after the abuse is *her* responsibility. If she apologizes and tries harder to please him, she is paying him for behaving that way. You can't change the abuser by trying to please him before the abuse happens. You change the abuser by the way you respond to him after the abuse.

For starters, don't give the abuser his way after he has treated you badly. Acting sad or fearful, whimpering, crying, and continuing to try to please the abuser after the abuse doesn't help. It tells him that he was right to abuse you and his tactics were successful. He'll do it again in similar circumstances.

Trying to punish the abuser by screaming, raging, and attacking isn't the answer either. There will be no winners in that situation. Targets shouldn't try to be *better* at verbal abuse than the abuser.

Is the abuser an all-around nasty guy? Does he have few friends because he treats them badly? Does his family avoid him, or act just like him? Are you the only one who has been willing to tolerate the abuser long-term? Is the abuser self-employed, or employed in an industry that doesn't call for him to work with people, only with things? Then you've got a hard row to hoe. If an abuser treats everyone badly, he probably doesn't know how to treat anyone well and may not want to. He may want a negative and close relationship because that's the only kind of relationship he knows and he may not be willing to change because he doesn't see anything better for himself coming out of the change.

But if the abuser gets along on the job and has a few friends, he knows how to get his way without abuse. He may be willing to get along with you without abuse in the future.

You cannot delegate the responsibility to train the abuser to someone else. If the abuser doesn't want to change, seeing a counselor or a marriage counselor for an hour a week isn't likely to help. You have to change yourself.

Anger management training won't hurt the abuser. It's likely to train the abuser to count to ten before he speaks. But it doesn't usually train the abuser how to get his way without abuse. It also doesn't usually address control issues.

Group treatment for domestic violence abusers *is* likely to help the abuser. But if he's never physically battered you, he isn't likely to be motivated when he attends batterers' treatment and he isn't likely to feel that he belongs there. Domestic violence treatment *will* deal with the power and control issues that abusers have. But that still won't save you if you keep rewarding the abuser for treating you badly.

Self-help books and speakers sometimes tell you that change is easy, but that's not true. Change is hard. You behave automatically now. Your old scripts seem to take over your brain before you think of doing something different. You have to recognize the triggers for your old behavior *before* you have responded to abuse. And you'll be anxious and uncomfortable for a long time. You'll need to act deliberately in new ways that won't have the approval of the abuser.

Dr. Prochaska and Dr. DiClemente proposed the theory that people who make major behavioral changes go through certain stages of change:

Precontemplation: In this stage, you don't see the need to change the behavior.

Contemplation: You may wish to change, but you're still not ready to take any steps to change yourself. .

Preparation: In this stage, you want to change and you begin to prepare yourself.

Action: You use the plan you have prepared and you try to fix the behaviors that don't work.

Relapse: You find that your efforts aren't perfect. Rather than giving up, you must adjust your plan based on new information about what works and what doesn't.

Maintenance: In this stage, your changes have matured. You do them automatically, without conscious thought.

Those are the *stages* of changes. What follows are the *steps* to change. Think of your behaviors as being an ARROW aimed toward a target:

AFFIRM your new beliefs about verbal abuse. Hold yourself ACCOUNTABLE for your actions that contribute to the problem.

RESOLVE to change. Make a clear decision that you are going to make changes and choose the new behaviors that you are going to try.

REHEARSE the new behaviors. Write your proposed words down ahead of time. Practice doing the new behaviors in front of a mirror or in front of a friend.

OPERATE with the new behaviors. Put them into action at the right place and time.

WITNESS the changes you've made. Tell yourself and others how well you've done. Remind yourself how hard you've worked and what's still ahead. WOW! You did it! You're on your way!

Here are the most important new beliefs to adopt:

Those negative hurtful statements are abuse

I'm the target of the abuse, not the cause of it.

I don't deserve the abuse. I deserve good treatment because I treat people well.

I don't have to submit to abuse.

I can control myself.

Angry people still have a choice of behaviors. Anger doesn't cause verbal abuse.

The abuser isn't telling the truth when he abuses me.

The abuser doesn't believe everything he's saying. He says it to hurt me.

The abuser isn't abusing me for attention. Ignoring the abuse won't make it go away.

I can change if I want to. If I believe in myself and I persist toward my goal, I will change in the way I want.

My feelings of anger and hurt are normal and acceptable. They are warning signals telling me to change something.

I don't need to be perfect to be acceptable. I don't need to be perfect to deserve love.

Nobody is perfect and I don't need to be either.

I need to be realistic about the abuser. He is treating me badly and he will continue to do so unless I change.

My wishes won't change the abuser. If he isn't changing now, I don't have good evidence that he will change at all.

I'm responsible to keep myself safe. I can count on myself when I need to. I'm not going to tolerate bad behavior in the future in the way I have in the past.

The abuser is trying to control and dominate me. He isn't acting that way because he has an anger problem.

The abuser is purposely hurting me. It isn't just an emotional reaction. His abuse is goal-directed behavior.

The abuser doesn't lose control of himself when he abuses me. He is saying what he allows himself to say and nothing else. He can stop himself from abusing others so he can stop himself from abusing me.

I need to be realistic about myself. Doing nothing isn't the same as planning to leave the abuser.

If I'm not making active plans to leave, then I'm really planning to stay. If I'm planning to stay, I'm better off changing myself to end the abuse.

He's not going to leave me just because he says he will. Unless he serves me with papers, or moves out of the house, he has no plans to leave.

When I ignore his abusive behaviors, I'm increasing the conflict and stress in my life.

Self-defense that doesn't work

There are many effective strategies that will reduce the frequency of verbal abuse in your life. But there are many tactics that just don't work. They are ineffective because they don't address the strategies and needs of the abuser. Here are some of those ineffective defense strategies.

Ignoring an attack rewards the abuser by giving him your attention and company without giving him any unpleasant consequences.

Begging or pleading with the abuser rewards him by showing him that he is more powerful. It tells him you still want to please him, and that you will continue to submit to his control.

Attacking the abuser puts you in competition with him. You don't want to become a better abuser.

Depending on others to defend you means you don't increase your skills at self-defense. Only you are there to defend yourself all the time.

Ignoring attacks he makes in public pays him for embarrassing you publicly. If he chooses to attack you in public, defending yourself in public is the best option.

Don't defend yourself by staying on the abuser's subject and protesting his words. That sets up an attack-defense loop. Do comment on the abuser's behavior and the consequences you can give him.

Don't speak to someone who is drunk or high. He won't remember it and he isn't in his right mind so he can't learn anything new.

If the abuser says something that's true, feel free to agree with him.

Do not act positively to the abuser or reassure him that you love him when he attacks you. Save your positive words for times when he is treating you well.

Don't keep threatening to leave him. The abuser won't believe you, and you won't believe yourself either.

Don't abuse the abuser. Give him rewards or withdraw rewards but don't punish him.

Don't give the abuser attention and time if he is giving you the silent treatment. Be ready to withdraw from him after he's done withdrawing from you.

Don't try to delegate your problems to a therapist by sending the abuser into therapy alone. You have to change too or your relationship won't improve.

Self-defense that works

Some strategies work to cut down the frequency and severity of verbal abuse. Here's a summary of those strategies:

Think about the future and about the way you plan to respond to his comments. Rehearse and get ready to put it into practice

Comment on his behavior, his manners, and his inappropriate words, not what he said about you. Don't respond to his attacks with defense or defend others like your family or friends.

Tell the abuser what he said that was abusive. Hold him accountable, and tell him what the long-range consequences of the behavior will be.

Name, blame, explain.

Remind the abuser that you control some of his rewards because you control yourself.

Get more distant from the abuser, in word and deed. Don't get emotional or personal with him.

After you've made your response, change the subject. Make your response and move on. Don't stay on the abuser's topic. Change the subject to something you do agree to talk about.

Be ready to respond rapidly, but slow the conversation down, or leave it, if he's trying to push you to go faster than you feel comfortable.

Pay attention to what the abuser does. If you react and deflect all of his abusive comments rather than just trying to respond to the worst attacks, you'll be more successful. He'll learn faster if you repeat the lesson over and over.

Reward the abuser often for trying to change or for making small changes. Don't wait until he is perfect before you comment. He'll learn better and faster if he knows what pleases you.

Be consistent. Respond rapidly and try to give similar responses to his behaviors. Consistent feedback helps people learn.

Expect the learning process to take time. You're not going to get one revelation that changes all your behavior immediately and neither is the abuser.

Include an adult time-out in your list of strategies. Do short time-outs for small problems, longer time-outs that may mean leaving the house for periods of time when his behavior gets more extreme.

When an attack occurs, keep control of yourself, no matter how the abuser behaves.

Staying realistic about the relationship

I haven't told you to leave the abuser, or to stay with him for that matter. But I do think there are some important questions that you should answer for yourself about the relationship.

It's important to be realistic about the future and to make realistic predictions about what's going to happen in your relationship. Without better evidence, you should predict the abuser is going to behave the same way tomorrow that he did today. There's no sense believing that he *may* change or he *could* change when the odds are against it, especially when you know he doesn't want to change. Don't buy lottery tickets with the rent money.

Your happiness today is worth something, and you aren't going to get today back to do over. Saying that it's worth waiting around to see if he changes is saying that it's worth being unhappy for a long time when there's no guarantee that he is ever going to change. If you don't change, there's no reason to believe that he will change. If you do change and he doesn't, what are you waiting for?

Don't tell yourself the abuser *could* change or the situation *could* change without going further. Put your specific predictions on paper now so you can tell in the future whether your predictions turn out to be accurate. Commit to being realistic by observing what is happening and adjusting to it, rather than pretending that your wishes are reality.

Give thought to the balance of happiness in the relationship. How much time do you spend with your partner being happy or being content in his company? How much time do you spend being fearful, angry, or sad? When you aren't with your partner, are you thinking about positive times with him? Do the times when he praised you or acted in thoughtful and caring ways come first to mind? Or are you reviewing the bad times when he isn't there?

Relationships don't always break up because of the bad times. Many relationships break up because there aren't enough good times. If the bad times with your partner ended, would the good times be sufficient to keep you there? Do you spend positive time together now? Do you share interests, including interests in children? Would you want your partner for a friend if you met him for the first time now?

The issue isn't only how positive your partner is to you. It's also how positive you are toward yourself. You are the only one in charge of your happiness whether or not you're married or living with someone. If you sit home alone thinking about the bad times, you're not going to live a happy life even if you leave him. To lead a happy life you need to know what you value and enjoy, and you need to act on your values.

Prince Charming isn't going to sweep you off your feet and offer you a full, rich life by meeting your needs. You need to know what your needs are and you need to meet them. The odds are good that your abusive partner is not preventing you from doing many things you would enjoy. Getting rid of him isn't going to make you do those things in the future. It's your job to make yourself happy!

Frankly, your partner may not be looking for the same relationship you are. You may be looking for a positive, stable, happy relationship. He may be looking for the same kind of relationship that his father had with his mother. He may want to dominate his wife and then ignore her while he watches sports. He may want a stable and unhappy relationship because that's what's normal for him and that's what he's used to. He may want a relationship that's full of chaos and anger so he can feel justified in seeking out other sexual partners on the side. He may live with you only because he wants an unpaid housekeeper and sex partner. He may want your income in his account and not want you to ask him for anything. Just because you want a stable positive relationship doesn't mean that he does too.

But I hope you're looking for happiness. If you're looking for a way to blame someone else for all of your misery, I don't think this book has given you much help.

I can show you how to end verbal abuse but I can't make it pain-free to change yourself. I can't make changing yourself easy, and I can't guarantee your changes will change your current partner. I've given you some information and encouragement to grow but you're still in charge of your life.

Suppose you do decide to leave the abuser. How can you avoid starting a new relationship with an abuser in the future? If you've learned to end verbal and emotional abuse, the new man won't abuse you because you won't let him. If you're willing to end an abusive relationship, you'll be open for a healthy one.

Plus, abusive men show red flags even at the beginning of a relationship. For example:

♦ He has battered or abused other partners in the past. He has a history of violence.
♦ He wants the relationship to move too fast so he can get on with living together.
♦ He punishes you when you tell him no.
♦ He punishes you when you disagree.
♦ He punishes you when you act independently.

Prediction in a relationship

I can't answer all of your questions, but I do have some recommendations:

Don't spend years trying to make up your mind. Set a deadline for deciding to stay or go, maybe three months or six months from now. During the interim, make pro and con lists and find out what your options are. Do research both on staying with him and on leaving him. Find out what you need to do to get the best outcome in each of those scenarios.

If you decide to stay, spend your time actively making the best of it. Work on changing your behavior and ending the verbal abuse. Work on increasing your happiness in other ways so you lead a happier life. Don't let the abuser run your life as much as he does now. Become your own person.

If you've decided to stay, stop thinking about leaving and start thinking about how to respond right now when he abuses you. Don't rethink the decision to stay or go. If you've decided to stay, then make it better while you're there.

If you decide to go, make a plan and carry it out. Talk to a lawyer. Talk to your local woman's shelter. Get a job or get a better job or go back to school. Fill out a checklist on planning for divorce. Get the local real estate ads. See a therapist or join a women's divorce group. Make plans for your life after this relationship and act on them. Make your life the best it can be without the abuser.

Think less about the abuser and more about other parts of your life. Read some books on the subject. Go forward with the legal, the logistical and the emotional aspects of leaving the relationship.

This isn't the end of the journey for me or for you. You have a new day ahead of you. Make it the happiest possible. You can improve your emotional health in many ways. That work may include changing your beliefs. Some of it may call for changing your actions or your words. You may find better ways to go forward than this book suggests. Or you may find that this book plus everything else you know is enough to work on just now.

Thank you for considering my thoughts and words. I hope they have been helpful. I hope they aroused your protective instincts and your positive feelings about yourself. I hope you feel more competent, more responsible and more hopeful about the future.

I wish you great happiness in the journey ahead of you.

Appendix I: Forms

A. Checklist of Abusive Behaviors

Look through this checklist. Copy it if you'd like. Check off the items that apply.

___ He made unwanted physical contact although he didn't hurt or injure you.
___ He pushed you.
___ He shoved you.
___ He slapped you.
___ He punched you.
___ He hit you.
___ He stabbed you.
___ He burned you.
___ He choked you.
___ He spit at you.
___ He pulled your hair.
___ He pinched you.
___ He bit you.
___ He tied you up.
___ He pulled your hair.
___ He cut you.
___ He threw you down on the floor or ground.
___ He held you down to keep you from leaving.
___ He kept you from leaving by using force
___ He threw objects at you.
___ He used force to have sex with you.

___ He forced you to have sex after beating you or threatening to beat you.

___ He forced you to have sex with others.

___ He pressured you to do something sexual that made you uncomfortable or hurt you.

___ He physically injured sexual areas of your body.

___ He refused to use birth control, or let you use it.

___ He forced you to end (or not end) a pregnancy.

___ He locked you in a room.

___ He locked you out of the house.

___ He physically forced you to go somewhere against your will.

___ He left you somewhere dangerous.

___ He sent nasty messages to you through your children.

___ He threatened to kidnap or kill the children.

___ He punished or deprived the children when he was mad at you.

___ He abused your children.

___ He threatened to sexually abuse the children if you didn't have sex with him.

___ He punched holes in the walls.

___ He smashed or broke your property.

___ He threatened to hurt or kill a family pet.

___ He was cruel to household pets or other animals.

___ He injured or killed pets to frighten you.

___ He displayed weapons in a threatening way.

___ He cleaned his weapons immediately after or during a threatening argument.

___ He threatened to hurt you with a weapon.

___ He hurt you with a weapon.

___ He tried to hit you with a car or force you off the road with a car.

___ He drove unsafely on purpose while you were in the car.

___ He denied you medical care when you needed it.

___ He refused to help when you were sick, injured or pregnant.

___ He threatened to leave you.

___ He told you to leave.

___ He threatened to commit suicide.

___ He made you drop the charges against him.

___ He threatened to report you for illegal acts.

___ He threatened to report you to welfare or child abuse investigators.

__ He threatened to leave town with the children.
__ He forced you to take drugs or drink alcohol.
__ He deliberately prevented you from sleeping.
__ He stopped you from calling for help by taking or disabling your phone.
__ He demanded that you dress a particular way.
__ He made you commit illegal acts.
__ He told you that you had a mental illness
__ He told others that you had a mental illness.
__ He interfered with your work or school.
__ He kept track of where you were all the time.
__ He phoned or unexpectedly showed up somewhere to check on you.
__ He drove you to and from places so you couldn't go places alone.
__ He purposely and repeatedly followed or stalked you.
__ He came to your home uninvited, or after you told him not to.
__ He broke into your home to assault you or steal from you.
__ He harassed you by purposely and repeatedly making hang-up calls.
__ He repeatedly called your home or place of employment to make contact when you didn't want contact with him.
__ He used alcohol or drugs abusively, and acted unsafely while toxic.
__ His alcohol use made him negative, irritable, violent, and unpredictable.
__ His prescription drug use (whether legal or not) made him negative, irritable, violent, and unpredictable.
__ His recreational drug use made him negative, irritable, violent, and unpredictable.
__ He tried to kill himself.
__ He threatened to hurt your family or friends.
__ He threatened to hurt or kill someone you love.
__ He threatened to kill you.
__ He threatened to kill a member of your family.
__ He said he'd never let you leave him.

Now write down a detailed account of each incident of negative physical and emotional contact you experienced and each act that frightened you. Ask yourself:

__ Does the verbal abuser have a mental health disorder like depression, bipolar disorder (manic-depressive illness) or schizophrenia?

___ Has the verbal abuser refused treatment for a mental health disorder?

___ Was the abuser drunk or high when the incidents occurred?

___ Has his substance abuse gotten worse or more frequent in the past year?

___ Has his physical violence gotten worse or more frequent in the past year?

___ Have his threats gotten worse or more frequent in the past year?

When you have checked off all the things the abuser has done, and written a detailed account of them, what have you learned? Is he abusing you more frequently? Is he abusing you more severely? Have you previously thought he was physically dangerous to you? Do you think so now?

B. Analyzing an Abuse Encounter

If you're trying to understand what is going on during a verbal abuse encounter, and you don't know what to do, try asking yourself these questions.

What do I want?
Is it in my control?

If it's in your control, you can do it. You don't need approval or permission. If you want someone else to do something, rethink your goal in terms of what you can do.

What's my second choice?
Is it in my control?

If it's in your control, you can do it. You don't need approval or permission. If you want someone else to do something, rethink your goal in terms of what you can do.

What price will I pay?

Will there be any price to pay besides disapproval? If so, what is it?

Is the price too high?

If the only price is disapproval, what are you waiting for?

What actions shall I take?

What should I do with my hands and feet? Shall I stand or sit or move?

What words shall I use?

Formulate your thoughts into statements about yourself like, "I will..." "I'm going to..." "My plan is..." "I'm giving you the choice to..." "You may..."

What nonverbal behaviors shall I use?

Speak softly. Make eye contact...

C. Affirmations After an Incident

Today, I'm proud of myself because:

_____

Today, I learned:

_____

Next time, I'd like to:

_____

Today, I'm proud of myself because:

_____

Today, I learned:

_____

Next time, I'd like to:

_____

Today, I'm proud of myself because:

_____

Today, I learned:

_____

Next time, I'd like to:

_____

D. Abuse Log

Date:

What did the abuser do/say?

What did I do/say?

My feelings afterward?

What did I learn?

Date:

What did the abuser do/say?

What did I do/say?

My feelings afterward?

What did I learn?

Make log entries in your abuse log daily or as often as possible. Make them in many different settings. Pay attention to the ways you are responding now and your feelings afterward. Ask yourself if the abuser is still getting what he wants because of the abuse. Ask yourself if you are still giving him approval without meaning to.

E. Plan Your Responses to Verbal Abuse

"I'm leaving this discussion."

"I hate it when you _____ (name the abusive behavior), so I'm not going to keep talking to you."

"I'm going _____ (where)"

"I'll be home by _____ (time)".

"But I still won't talk about this. I'm done talking to you for _____ (period of time)."

"We can talk about this again _____ (when) but only if you agree not to (make abusive comments)."

"If we can't agree, I'll decide what to do by myself and I'll do that, whatever it is, whether you agree or not."

"I'm leaving this discussion."

"I hate it when you _____ (name the abusive behavior), so I'm not going to keep talking to you."

"I'm going _____ (where)."

"I'll be home by _____ (time)".

"But I still won't talk about this. I'm done talking to you for _____ (period of time)".

"We can talk about this again _____ (when) but only if you agree not to (make abusive comments)".

"If we can't agree, I'll decide what to do by myself and I'll do that, whatever it is, whether you agree or not."

F. Tracking the Negatives

Date	Time spent with partner	Negative time spent with partner	Time spent in negative thoughts about partner

Appendix II: Resources

Readers may use these resources to increase their safety, to work on recovery after leaving an abusive relationship, and to learn more about emotional and verbal abuse.

If you are in physical danger as well as emotional danger, don't try to train the abuser to stop his verbal abuse. That's likely to result in violence against you. Batterers are abusers who are not willing to stop at verbal violence. They will use physical violence to keep you in control. Consider using some of these resources to make yourself safe:

Books

Copeland, Mary Ellen, and Maxine Harris. *Healing the Trauma of Abuse: A Women's Workbook*. Oakland: New Harbinger Publications, 2000.

This book offers step-by-step exercises to work through and reduce the effects of a traumatic event.

De Becker, Gavin. *The Gift of Fear and Other Survival Signals that Protect Us from Violence*. New York: Dell, 1999.

Gavin de Becker ran celebrity security systems and is an expert on the psychology of violence. He describes the signals of the *universal code of violence* and helps readers recognize and act on the warning signals of a potential attacker. He shows that becoming violent can be a predictable process.

Dugan, Meg Kennedy, and Roger Hock. *It's My Life Now: Starting Over After an Abusive Relationship or Domestic Violence*, 2nd Edition. Florence, KY: Routledge; 2006.

Survivors of an abusive relationship learn that leaving is not the end of the nightmare. It is the beginning of a difficult and challenging journey of recovery. This book offers readers practical guidance, emotional reassurance, and psychological awareness to heal and reclaim their lives after leaving their abusers.

Durve, Anisha. *The Power to Break Free Workbook: For Victims and Survivors of Domestic Violence*. Malibu: Power Press, 2012.

This workbook is for victims and survivors of domestic violence to facilitate healing, process the deep-seated trauma of abuse, and find the necessary steps to recovery. Exercises will help survivors evaluate the relationship, the effect of the abuse, and the level of safety. Healing exercises will increase your confidence in your ability to move forward and embrace a new, abuse-free future.

Ellis, Albert, Robert A. Harper, and Melvin Powers. *A Guide to Rational Living*. Chatsworth, CA: Wilshire Book Company, 2007.

Dr. Ellis is the founder of *Rational Emotional Therapy*. This classic book teaches readers that thoughts are irrational when they are untrue and have unwanted outcomes. Readers learn to dispute the irrational thoughts that lower self-esteem and personal effectiveness by lowering needs for approval, reducing fears of failure, and lowering anxiety.

Ellis, Albert, and Marcia Grad Powers. *The Secret of Overcoming Verbal Abuse: Getting Off the Emotional Roller Coaster and Regaining Control of Your Life*. Chatsworth, CA: Wilshire Book Company, 2000.

Anger, not love, is the basis of abusive relationships. Survivors must first love themselves to appreciate any romantic relationship. This book focuses on holding the target responsible for her feelings, but shades into blaming the target for the abuser's behavior. It is true that you cannot control or fix the abuser, but that does not give the abuser the right to abuse. Ellis believes that teaching the target to demand love and respect will be helpful, yet this is a tactic that is largely a waste of time. This book is helpful for targets to deal with their own feelings and rights, but not necessarily helpful to stop the abuse.

Evans, Patricia. *Teen Torment: Overcoming Verbal Abuse at Home and at School.* Avon, MA: Adams Media Corporation, 2003.

This book aims at parents, teachers, and teens. Evans defines verbal abuse, shows how teens are vulnerable to it and discusses the role of verbal abuse in violent behavior. Evans surveys verbal abuse in the media, in sports, at home, and in school. Her closing section uses checklists, charts, and a section of additional resources to show practical ways to stop abuse.

Evans, Patricia. *The Verbally Abusive Relationship: How to Recognize It and How to Respond* (Third Edition). Avon, MA: Adams Media, 2010

This is the third edition of this bestselling classic that inspires readers to consider whether they are victims of verbal abuse and suggests ways to deal with it. Evans teaches how to recognize abuse, respond to abusers, and lead a happier life. In this update she outlines levels of abuse and offers strategies, sample scripts and action plans.

Evans, Patricia. *Verbal Abuse Survivors Speak Out: On Relationship and Recovery.* Avon, MA: Adams Media, 2003.

Patricia Evans has worked in counseling and recovery settings with battered women. She received hundreds of letters from verbal abuse survivors around the world after she published her first book, *The Verbally Abusive Relationship*. Those letters form the basis of this book.

Evans, Patricia. *Victory Over Verbal Abuse: A Healing Guide to Renewing Your Spirit and Reclaiming Your Life.* Avon (MA): Adams Media, 2011.

Verbal abuse permeates the culture, homes, schools, workplaces, and other institutions. This book is a companion to her best-selling book, *The Verbally Abusive Relationship*. It contains tools to guide the reader through a healing process. She reviews therapy options and strategies for dealing with abusers. She inspires readers with messages of support, encouragement, and affirmation.

Farmer, Steven. *Adult Children of Abusive Parents: A Healing Program for Those Who Have Been Physically, Sexually, or Emotionally Abused*. New York: Ballantine Books, 1990.

Therapist Steven Farmer teaches how to grieve for your lost childhood, how to become your own parent, and how to heal yourself spiritually, physically, and emotionally. Children crippled by mixed messages, family secrets, and reversed parent-child roles can benefit from this step-by-step self-help program that includes exercises and journal work for recovery.

Goetting, Ann. *Getting Out: Life Stories of Women Who Left Abusive Men*. New York: Columbia University Press, 2000.

This author tells how sixteen women finally got away for good. *Getting Out* recounts the women's life histories leading up to the battering and the resources they drew on to escape. Leaving is a process rather than an event, often marked by reconciliations and resumption of abuse.

Goldstein, Barry. *Scared to Leave, Afraid to Stay: Paths From Domestic Violence to Safety*. Bandon, OR: Robert Reed Publishers, 2010.

This book, by an attorney who practices family law, presents stories of ten women as they fought the courts and their abusers to gain safety for themselves and their children. The author shows how courts handle issues like divorce, custody, visitation, orders of protection, and crimes when domestic violence erupts. He discusses legal tactics abusers commonly use to control their partners.

Greek, Janet. *The Divorce Planner: Self-defense for Women When They Need It Most*. Phoenix, OR: Interactive Media Publishing, 2006.

This book is like a day planner with confidentiality. It provides a step-by-step guide through the process of divorce and keeps the details of meetings and plans in one organized location. It includes worksheets and calendars for finance and child custody issues.

Holly, Kellie Jo. *Domestic Violence Safety Plan: A Comprehensive Plan That Will Help Keep You Safer Whether You Stay or Leave.* Charleston (SC): CreateSpace, 2013.

This brief book by a survivor of domestic violence provides a well-organized safety plan.

McCaig, Mari, and Edward S. Kubany. *Healing the Trauma of Domestic Violence: A Workbook for Women,* Oakland: New Harbinger Press, 2004.

Here are step-by-step exercises for recovering from abuse and taking back your life. The book includes a treatment approach to posttraumatic stress disorder for abused women.

Meloy, Michelle, and Susan L. Miller. *The Victimization of Women: Law, Policies, and Politics.* New York: Oxford University Press, 2010.

This book includes a balanced and comprehensive summary of research on the victimizations, violence, and victim politics that disproportionately affect women. The authors examine the history of violence against women, the surrounding debates, the legal reforms, the related media and social service responses, and the current science on intimate-partner violence, stalking, sexual harassment, sexual assault, and rape.

Miles, Al. *Domestic Violence: What Every Pastor Needs to Know.* Minneapolis: Fortress Press, 2011.

Pastoral caregivers often share the misconceptions about domestic violence of the general public. This book explores the dynamics of abusive relationships and the role that clergy members can take to heal painful interactions. Miles focuses on helping clergy and other pastoral ministers develop a more compassionate response to victim-survivors who are gay, lesbian, bisexual, and transgender.

Potter, Hillary. *Battle Cries: Black Women and Intimate Partner Abuse*. New York: NYU Press, 2008.

African American women endure more domestic violence than any other racial group in the United States. Yet, Potter argues, black women are more likely to fight back than accept the label of victim. The book is based on intensive interviews with forty African-American women abused by their male partners. The analysis considers variations in their experiences based on their socioeconomic class, education level, and age, and discusses the abuses they endured and some views that they share.

Prochaska, James O., John Norcross, and Carlo DiClemente. *Changing for Good: A Revolutionary Six-Stage Program for Overcoming Bad Habits and Moving Your Life Positively Forward*. New York: William Morrow, 2007

These three psychologists discovered that change is a six-stage process. Knowing how it works lets you manage it successfully. This book offers simple self-assessments, informative case histories, and concrete examples to help clarify each stage in the process.

Ristock, Janice. *No More Secrets: Violence in Lesbian Relationships*. Florence, KY: Routledge, 2002.

Ristock interviewed victims and social workers to discover how and why lesbian relationships become violent. She comments on the ways the medical and criminal justice systems react when they do. Domestic violence affects one in four gay and lesbian couples but the problem has remained hidden. This book seeks to break the silence, share the secrets, and name the forms of abuse.

Roberts, Albert R. *Battered Women and Their Families: Intervention Strategies and Treatment Programs*, Third Edition. New York: Springer Publishing Company; 2007.

Roberts updated this classic text to include new case studies, cultural perspectives, and assessment protocols. This is a treatment tool for clinical social workers, nurses, physicians, and graduate students who work with battered women daily. There are new chapters on same-sex violence, working with children in shelters, immigrant women affected by domestic violence, and elder mistreatment.

Roberts, Barbara. *Not Under Bondage: Biblical Divorce for Abuse, Adultery and Desertion*. Elk Park, NC: Maschil Press, 2008.

This work reports that women married to spouses who have already broken their faith and vows can have hope and freedom without losing their faith. Roberts refers to the scriptures in their original languages to show how many translations are incorrect and misleading. Churches that insist that a woman is in sin if she doesn't submit to the offending spouse after abandonment and/or abuse are unfaithful to true Christianity.

Van Wormer, Katherine and Albert R. Roberts. *Death by Domestic Violence: Preventing the Murders and Murder-Suicides*. Santa Barbara: Praeger, 2009.

Each year, spouses, partners, or lovers murder about 33 percent of all women and 3 percent of all men who die from homicide in the United States. Nationwide, murder by an intimate is the number one cause of death for pregnant women. This text examines the psychology of the batterer and the psychology of domestic murder, and domestic murder-suicide. These two widely known social workers include a safety plan for those at risk and a chapter providing narratives of women in prison for killing their abusive husband or partner.

Websites about Domestic Violence and Safety

Thehotline.org The National Domestic Violence Hotline.

This website provides a wide variety of resources in addition to the telephone hotline. The blog covers areas such as safety planning with children.

Womenshealth.gov/violence-against-women. The Office on Women's Health.

This government website from the Office on Women's Health, US Department of Health and Human Services, provides a safety-planning list of things to do and take to be safe. Womenslaw.org

This website provides tips and plans on getting ready to leave, ending the abusive relationship, safety in rural areas, tips for stalking victims, safety with social media, and safety in court. This site has state-by-state legal information and advice on how to leave an abusive situation, how to gather evidence of abuse, and how to prepare for court.

NCALL.us/content/physical-disability-safety-planning. National Clearinghouse on Abuse in Later Life.

This website provides a detailed handout on safety planning for those with physical disabilities who may be subject to violence from intimate partners, other family members, personal assistants, or caregivers.

NNEDV.org/resources/safetynetdocs/technology-safety-plan. National Network to End Domestic Violence

This website provides detailed information for technology safety planning for survivors of domestic abuse. Learn how to be safe online. Education and Job Training Assistance Fund (nnedv.org/projects):

NCDSV.org/publications_safetyplans. National Center on Domestic and Sexual Violence.

There are a variety of publications here on safety plans for teens, holidays, stalking, lethality assessment, and technology safety planning.

National Domestic Violence Hotline (800-799-7233): Open 24 hours a day, 365 days a year, this line is a resource for safety information and can connect any caller with shelters and protection advocates in her area. For support and more information please call the National Domestic Violence Hotline at 1-800-799-SAFE (7233) or at TTY 1-800-787-3224.

VineLink.com

VineLink.com is active in forty-seven states and allows women to search for an offender in custody by name or identification number. You can register to receive alerts if the offender has been released or transferred, or has escaped.

Domesticviolence.org

This website gives a detailed personalized safety plan for staying safe from violent partners.

Author Biography

D r. Nyblade has practiced as a clinical, school, and forensic psychologist in the state of Washington for more than thirty-five years, specializing in working with relationships.

She graduated with a bachelor's degree from Oberlin College in Oberlin, Ohio. She earned her PhD in clinical psychology from the University of Washington in Seattle. Her doctoral dissertation was a study of the ways couples agree (and don't agree) to share housework. While in graduate school, she studied neuropsychological testing and brain-behavior relationships.

Dr. Nyblade earned her license to practice psychology in Washington in 1977. She obtained her initial certification as a school psychologist in Washington in 1981 and the continuing certificate in 1984. She offers forensic evaluations and forensic consultation to attorneys and the courts. The state of Washington certified her as a provider and supervisor of a domestic abuse program to treat domestic violence offenders in 1994. She continues to offer individual treatment of abusers, anger management treatment, and relationship counseling.

Dr. Nyblade began the practice of assessment and therapy at a small community mental health center on San Juan Island, Washington. She moved to Bellingham, Washington, and has continued in clinical practice since then. She has provided assessments for children and adults for agencies and the courts. She specializes in diagnosing learning difficulties, attention problems, brain dysfunction, affective and anxiety disorders, and post traumatic stress disorder. She has offered preemployment evaluations for law enforcement agencies, vocational and disability assessments, and evaluations of parents at risk for abuse and neglect of children. She consults for school districts in her role as a school psychologist.

Dr. Nyblade has taught undergraduate and graduate students at Western Washington University, including classes in adolescent psychology, psychology of sex roles, family counseling, and assessment for counseling. She has supervised clinical students during their practicums, internships, and residencies, and she has supervised academic projects for students working on their master's degrees.

Dr. Nyblade has a general clinical practice of adult psychotherapy. As a psychotherapist, she works with couples, individuals, and groups. She sees people for a variety of problems, especially relationship difficulties, depression, anxiety, domestic violence, and verbal abuse issues. She has special training and interest in trauma treatment, improving sexual functioning, and gender concerns. She also works with families about parenting issues, discipline of children, and improving family functioning.

As a health psychologist, she has helped patients take charge of their own medical symptoms and medical care by working with the mind-body interface. This has included working with headaches, irritable bowel syndrome, insomnia, and other medical conditions that are affected by stress.

She places great emphasis on trying out and using new points of view to understand painful past events or to cope with current stressors. She likes to help people question old beliefs and habits, and learn new ones that will prove more satisfying. She has great respect for the physical aspects of problems such as depression or learning disorders, and she encourages additional medical treatment where it may be helpful. When working with relationship difficulties, she helps couples reach agreements on their differences, and she works well in situations of high conflict. Overall, she takes a very active role in the process of psychotherapy.

She believes that people can heal and change if given information, opportunity, and support. She finds it a great joy to work with people as they grow. It is an honor to participate in that healing process

Dr. Nyblade's website is mindingyourspirittogether.com. At that location, you'll find many articles on topics related to relationships and abuse. She also writes a weekly blog: Minding Your Spirit.